Drew University Studies in Liturgy Series

General Editors: Kenneth E. Rowe and Robin A. Leaver

PULPIT, TABLE, AND SONG
Essays in Celebration
of Howard G. Hageman

edited by
Heather Murray Elkins
Edward C. Zaragoza

Drew Studies in Liturgy, No. 1

The Scarecrow Press, Inc.
Lanham, Md., & London

SCARECROW PRESS, INC.

Published in the United States of America
by Scarecrow Press, Inc.
4720 Boston Way
Lanham, Maryland 20706

4 Pleydell Gardens, Folkestone
Kent CT20 2DN, England

British Cataloguing-in-Publication Information Available

Library of Congress Cataloging-in-Publication Data

Pulpit, table, and song : essays in celebration of Howard G. Hageman / edited
by Heather Murray Elkins and Edward C. Zaragoza.
p. cm. — (Drew Studies in Liturgy ; no. 1)
"A chronological bibliography of the works of Howard G. Hageman /
complied by Rochelle Stackhouse"
1. Liturgics. I. Hageman, Howard G., 1921–   . II. Elkins, Heather Murray.
III. Zaragoza, Edward C. IV. Series
BV176.P85   1996   264—dc20   95-35830   CIP

ISBN 0-8108-3068-X (cloth : alk. paper)

Printed in the United States of America

♾™ The paper used in this publication meets the minimum requirements of
American National Standard for Information Sciences—Permanence of
Paper for Printed Library Materials, ANSI Z39.48–1984.

CONTENTS

PART ONE: REFORMATION TO EVANGELICAL REVIVAL

PART TWO: 19TH-CENTURY REVIVALS/20TH-CENTURY RENEWALS

PART THREE: PROFESSOR HAGEMAN AND HIS CONTRIBUTIONS

SERIES EDITORS' FOREWORD

One of the fruits of the liturgical renewal movement in the late twentieth century has been renewed attention to study of the liturgy in all of the churches. This monograph series aims to publish some of the best of this new scholarship. Fresh studies of Episcopal, Roman Catholic, and Orthodox liturgy will be included, along with studies of the full range of Protestant liturgies.

Much liturgical writing to date has concentrated on liturgy as text. This series will not ignore such studies, but will seek to reflect more recent thinking that understands liturgy not only against the background of theological principle, liturgical tradition and ritual text, but also in terms of liturgical practice and setting.

Clarity of focus, relative brevity, and freshness of scholarly contribution will be the principal criteria for publication. Revised dissertations will be considered. Edited collections of essays and texts may be included when they have a unified topical focus which may significantly advance scholarship in the field.

As the inaugural number in the series we are pleased to publish a rich collection of essays honoring Howard Hageman, one of the founding members of Drew University's Graduate Program in Liturgy. The essays have been prepared for publication by Heather Murray Elkins of Drew University and Ted Zaragoza of Phillips Theological Seminary.

Robin A. Leaver, Westminster Choir College of Rider University and Drew University

Kenneth E. Rowe, Drew University

EDITORS' PREFACE

Liturgy constitutes that vital inner rhythm of Word and Sacrament which from the beginning has been the very pulse of the Church. In liturgy faithful hearing occurs, doctrine takes on life, and God's presence is made known.

The study of liturgics involves examination of the ordering, rites, and ceremonies of the Christian traditions from theological, historical, and aesthetic perspectives. Throughout the program we encourage students to design their course work and research to ensure the required breadth without sacrificing depth of inquiry.

These opening words have served as the archway into Drew University's program in Liturgical Studies since its founding in 1977. **Howard G. Hageman**, one of the cornerstones and founding members of the program, mentored students and colleagues in liturgics, whose **raison d'etre** is the work of the people of God. This "vital inner rhythm of Word and Sacrament" marked his life of scholarship and ministry, and its echoes can be clearly discerned in this volume of essays, *Pulpit, Table, and Song: Essays in Celebration of Howard G. Hageman.*

The ecumenical stretch of this volume could have been predicted by a simple listing of the areas of Dr. Hageman's scholarly expertise: Catholic Apostolic Church liturgy, history of Christian Worship, Mercersburg movement, and reformed liturgiology with particular reference to the Dutch and German Church. Pennsylvania Germans and their beloved Palatinate Liturgy are sketched into the context of American eucharistic theology by **Kenneth E. Rowe**, while **Gregg A. Mast** details the rich liturgical texture of the Catholic Apostolic Church in an American landscape dominated by pulpits and mourners' benches. The language of worship in the accents of present-day United Methodists, Dutch reformers, early American colonists and mid-Victorian Anglo-Catholics can be heard in these collected essays, whose authors seek to ensure required breadth without sacrificing depth of inquiry.

Daniel James Meeter traces the worshiping identity of the contemporary Reformed Church by reviewing the textual roots of its family tree. The evangelical zeal of Anglo-Catholic sacramental life is articulated in **Martin L. Cox Jr.'s** "Storming the Forts of Darkness," and even nineteenth-century Methodists, targets of liturgical scorn, find a voice for their hymn texts and tunes in **Fred Kimball Graham's** essay, "Singing Lustily: Hymn Tune Favorites in the Methodist Episcopal Church of the Nineteenth Century."

"Lection, Sermon, and Congregational Song" by **Robin A. Leaver** keeps up the lively pulse for scholarly reflections on practice of liturgy in its historic and contemporary settings. **Norman J. Kansfield** documents Hageman's unique contribution as a pastoral hymnologist to the worship life of the Reformed Church in North America as **A. Casper Honders** scans the musical contributions made by the sixteenth-century Reformers.

Traditionally, liturgics examined the orders, rites, and ceremonies of Judeo-Christian traditions from theological, historical, and aesthetic perspectives. Contemporary contributions from sociology, anthropology, and ritual studies stretch the boundaries of the field into the context of the worshiping community. In **Edward C. Zaragoza's** study, structural analysis of sacred space leads to a realignment of sacramental assumptions. Indeed, even the work of historians undergoes re-formation as evidenced in **Randall Balmer's** essay, "The Historiographical Neglect of Religion in the Middle Colonies."

"People are the primary liturgical documents," according to James F. White, and, therefore, many of these essays direct attention to the reformers themselves. John à Lasco emerges from the sidelines of reformation history in **Dirk W. Rodger's** essay. **Horton Davies** focuses a corrective lens on Zwingli's eucharistic theology so often distorted in the myopic vision of scholars of the liturgical movement. John Nevin's double vision of Word and Sacrament is the recurring protestant dream beginning to be a waking reality through the work of twentieth-century reformers in **Heather Murray Elkins'** essay.

No collection of essays entitled *Pulpit, Table and Song: Essays in Celebration of Howard G. Hageman* would be complete without a hymn. "And as this Grain has been Gathered" is a eucharistic hymn by Hageman, set to music by **David M. Tripold**. **Rochelle Ann Stackhouse** provides the final note to this festschrift with a chronological bibliography of Howard G. Hageman's published work.

Just as no rite emerges *ex nihilo*, no single historical perspective captures the delicate balance between individual and community. A community of liturgical scholars is necessary for the ongoing work and worship of God. The authors of these essays belong to the community created by

the lifework of Howard Hageman. It is fitting, therefore,
that the inaugural volume of Drew University Studies in
Liturgy be the work of many hands, lifted up in memory of
one who was a *berakah,* blessing to the Lord.

JOHN À LASCO'S LITURGY OF PUBLIC REPENTANCE: A CONTRIBUTION TO THE REFORMED, PRESBYTERIAN, AND PURITAN TRADITIONS

Dirk W. Rodgers
Drew University

In 1626, elders of the English church at Middelburg bristled when asked about their practice of public confession:

> Why then doe we not rather follow the generall example of all reformed Churches in all Countries...Why not of the English churches comonly throughout all these dominions here...—all which generally, I say every where doe (as they ought) require this publique presence of the offendour.[1]

Though exaggerated, their claim points to a propensity within Puritan and other Reformed churches toward public confession of sin, primarily when transgressions were openly offensive or when they endangered the entire membership. Nevertheless, despite general acknowledgement of this practice, its particular ritualistic forms remain essentially undocumented. One remarkable example survives, however, in a church order composed by John à Lasco, a little-known, Polish-born reformer who worked among religious refugees in London during the reign of King Edward VI.[2]

When à Lasco first arrived in England in 1548, he had already achieved a certain notoriety. Nephew to the Archbishop of Gnesen, former dignitary of the Polish Catholic Church, diplomat, friend of Erasmus, Superintendent of the churches in East Frisia—all these credentials commended him both to Cranmer and the crown. Thus, in 1550 he was named by Royal Charter as Superintendent of the Strangers' Church of London—a *corpus corporatum* comprised of three congregations; i.e., Dutch, French and Italian.[3]   These assemblies were conjointly given the privileges of selecting their own ministers and employing their own rites, a grant which essentially contradicted the 1549 Act of Uniformity.[4]   Accordingly, the London Strangers' Church constitutes an early example of legalized nonconformity within Protestant England.

Primarily for the Dutch congregation, à Lasco compiled a series of liturgies and institutions which were immediately translated into the common tongue by John Utenhove.[5] Later, however, the Superintendent expounded and defended these practices for a more general readership in his *Forma ac Ratio tota ecclesiastici ministerii* (Frankfurt, 1555).[6] Although published after he departed England, the *Forma ac Ratio* by and large represents accurately the use of the London strangers. As such, it stands among the earliest and most complete church orders within the Reformed tradition.

A distinguishing feature of this treatise is its emphasis upon ecclesiastical discipline, marked by three disciplinary liturgies.[7] Each rite in this trilogy addresses a separate phase in the process of public correction: 1) public repentance, 2) excommunication, and 3) public restoration. Of these services, the first holds special significance since trajectories of influence can be clearly traced to later liturgies.[8] Moreover, the rites of repentance and restoration are quite similar, with the same exhortations and prayers often used in each liturgy. Given this perspective, à Lasco's rite of public repentance can be treated individually. The liturgy will first be described in a manner highlighting its characteristic features, and then an attempt will be made to outline its influence upon later formulations.

The Liturgy of Public Repentance[9]

Like many reformers, à Lasco viewed excommunication as a last resort, implemented only when members stubbornly scorned the ministry's admonitions. Several opportunities, therefore, were given wayward souls to repent from their errors before at last they were banned from the Lord's Supper. Most often this repentance could be conducted privately, between members of the church or before the coetus (synod) of pastors and elders.[10] Public repentance was required, however, in cases of open sin; i.e., when an individual consistently despised the admonitions of the coetus, or when, in the judgment of the ministry, the deed itself was either known by many or else presented a danger to many.[11] Once any of these conditions had been fulfilled, and fallen members wished to acknowledge their error, they first had to address the coetus. If the leadership accepted their sincerity, they were admonished to admit their sin to the entire church, and a day was appointed to meet this obligation. Specifically, the service was scheduled at the conclusion of regular Sunday morning worship, just prior to the final Psalm.[12] In this way, penitents were assured a good hearing!

The rite begins with a short sermon that sets forth the nature of public repentance, citing foundational proofs from Scripture.[13] Particular reference is made to Matthew

5:23f. and James 5:16, in which believers are taught to acknowledge guilt and to reconcile themselves with those offended. Thus, by implication, "If we offend the entire Church, or at least a good part of it, then we must also reconcile ourselves to the entire Church."[14] Likewise, upon the basis of Matthew 18:17, in which the Church receives authority to bind and loose sins, and Luke 17:1f., in which Christ pronounces woe upon those through whom offense comes, it is argued that only public reconciliation can overcome such deliberate disobedience.[15]

After establishing the biblical moorings for public repentance, the exhortation describes "its three marks" (*de tribus notis illius*).[16] These include: 1) "a true denunciation and accusation of ourselves in our sin"; 2) publicly declared faith (*fiducia*) in the forgiveness of sin, and 3) "a public edification of the entire Church..., so that everyone in the Church might understand that the sin repented of by the brother does not so much belong to him alone, but also to the entire Church."[17] In God's eyes, argues the minister, everyone must equally be reconciled in Christ.[18] With this assertion, the exhortation concludes.

The repentant member then advances to the front of the assembly, faces the congregation and is surrounded by the pastors and elders. When the procession is completed, the officiating minister publicly presents the individual as one who desires to confess guilt, "to his own shame, but also to the glory of our Lord God and to the edification of our Church."[19] Consequently, the people are reminded that they all "were trapped in sin," and therefore cannot justly accuse or condemn the one who stands before them. "Indeed," says the minister, "we must confess that this deed, which we see elsewhere practiced by others, could equally be done by us, were we not preserved by the singular kindness of God."[20] Everyone thus receives the charge:

"Let us join our prayers with his prayers and our tears with his tears, and together address our prayers to God, as our brother truly and from the heart acknowledges and condemns the guilt of his sin, to the glory of the divine name, to his own salvation, and to the edification of our entire Church."[21]

With this invitation, the entire congregation is led in prayer by the minister. God is addressed as one who "desires not the death of sinners," but rather that "[they] should turn and live...."[22] Accordingly, the prayer contains two central petitions. First, through the agency of the Holy Spirit, God is asked to stir "all our hearts to a true and salvific acknowledgement of our sins."[23] Again there is an emphasis upon communal guilt in an effort to protect the repentant member from excessive accusation. Nevertheless, the minister does pray "especially for the heart of this our fallen brother," who then is directly named.[24] Having thus admitted guilt, the second petition seeks God's forgiveness, "both for him and for us," and asks that, through the Holy Spirit, they might all be protected from falling into sins of this sort.[25]

At the conclusion of the prayer, the minister turns to the repentant one and offers yet another admonition. The person is charged to confess publicly the guilt of his or her sin, with the added caution that God "looks into the inner recesses (*penetralia*) of our hearts."[26] The confession itself takes no prescribed form. The offender simply expresses sorrow for sin and a desire for forgiveness and reconciliation. If the individual cannot speak for him or herself, "either out of a lack of ability or else out of shame," the minister may speak for the penitent, who then simply renders his or her assent.[27] When the confession is completed, in whatever form, the presiding pastor addresses the other ministers and elders, who are standing around the repentant member. They are collectively asked whether anything else is required in order for this public repentance to be accepted. If there is such a request, it is dealt with accordingly.[28] If there are no objections, however, the minister proceeds to admonish the confessed offender.

This oration focuses first upon the joy bought about by the individual's repentance. The entire congregation rejoices with the member, for by this act, "you have brought shame not so much upon yourself and your weakness, but rather upon Satan himself."[29] For this reason, the believer is warned against "indulging in your sins," since the enemy "will stop at nothing to entrap you once again."[30] On the contrary, he or she is to rest solely upon Christ, who through the agency of the Spirit protects the Christian from Satan's attacks.[31]

So much for the one restored; the minister must now, once again, address the church as a whole. The congregation is exhorted to imitate the example of this brother or sister, by accusing themselves as sinners and by earnestly imploring the mercy of God. Furthermore, if any of them should fall into public sin, they should quickly follow in the penitent's footsteps, making preparations for public confession. Lastly, everyone is charged to forgive the fallen member and to embrace him or her with Christ's love.[32]

From this final exhortation, the minister moves into a prayer of thanksgiving, so that the person might have "a sure indication and testimony of his reconciliation."[33] On behalf of the congregation, the pastor expresses gratitude for the fact that, though they all deserve eternal death, God has called them to repentance and received them into grace because of Christ and his salvific merit. Indeed, they are especially thankful for the "testimony" (*testimonium*) of this kindness manifested in the public repentance of their fellow member. Yet, they all beseech God for a repentant heart, by which they accuse themselves in their sin—and all this "to the glory of your worshipful name, to the salvation of all of us here and to the edification of your catholic Church, through your Son, our Lord Jesus Christ."[34]

At the conclusion of this prayer, the minister asks the repentant individual whether he or she will submit thereafter to the church's discipline, to which the person responds, "I will" (*Etiam*).   With this affirmation, the minister pronounces, "full and complete forgiveness of his sin before God and his Church...."[35] All the pastors and elders then extend the right hand of fellowship in the sight of the whole congregation, attesting the member's full reconciliation. Then everyone sings Psalm 103, "Bless the Lord, O my soul," or else some other psalm, and the service concludes with the commendation of the poor and benediction.[36]

In analyzing this liturgy, three central themes emerge. First, it carries a strong didactic tone. A total of five exhortations are packed into this relatively brief rite, and the prayers are likewise intended to reinforce proper notions of guilt, confession and forgiveness. Even the penitent is something of an object lesson, leading observers to regard themselves as sinners, to seek divine grace and to refrain from public offenses. This emphasis is so marked that one wonders who was primarily to benefit from the service. The need to exhort the people often seems to overshadow the *prima facie* objectives of hearing the member's confession and granting both forgiveness and reconciliation. In other words, the ritualistic and potentially sacramental value of the liturgy has been downplayed, so that it essentially becomes another means of preaching, another service of the Word.

This is not to say, however, that à Lasco overlooks the plight of the fallen individual. A second theme in the liturgy stresses the corporate bond between the one confessing and the rest of the membership. Because all have sinned, all require divine forgiveness. Accusations, therefore, cannot be directed at the penitent without also condemning the accuser. Moreover, since everyone remains equally susceptible to Satan's attacks, every person must take heed lest he or she fall. For a reformer who elsewhere champions the cause of ecclesiastical discipline, this openly compassionate stance may seem anomalous. Nevertheless, this corporate emphasis had its practical value. The promise of a warm reception might lessen the sting of a humiliating public repentance—enough perhaps to encourage offenders to come forth. Even if this were not the case, however, the service clearly intends to build church unity through mandating mutual forgiveness and reconciliation. For an alien congregation being watched by suspicious hosts, the preservation of such unity became especially important.

A third theme in the liturgy concerns its treatment of ecclesiastical authority. On the one hand, the very fact that the rite is conducted publicly indicates a certain regard for the role of the people. The coetus cannot act independently to bind or loose sins but must bring the matter before the entire assembly. This assumption emanates from à Lasco's basic objection to clerical dominance, as he found it expressed in the Roman Church.[37] At the same time, however, the place of the coetus is firmly maintained. It is the ministers and elders, not the people, who decide when doctrinal or moral infractions necessitate public repentance. Within the service itself, the coetus is given a prominent position at the front of the assembly, symbolizing its authority to govern the disciplinary process. Accordingly, the leadership, rather than the congregation, is ceremonially asked whether the person's confession is acceptable.[38] Still, it is significant that this authority is granted to the entire coetus, as opposed to a single priest or bishop. The Superintendent thereby illustrates his intention to navigate the difficult strait between clerical domination, on the one hand, and complete membership rule, on the other.

Influence upon Subsequent Practice

The origins of à Lasco's liturgy of public repentance probably go back to his days as Superintendent in East Frisia. Soon after resigning this charge in 1549, one of his colleagues, Gellius Faber, compiled a vindication of Emden ecclesiastical practice in response to anabaptist criticism.[39] In the context of this defense, the author reports that within his church individuals who sin publicly are required to repent publicly, "im aventmal."[40] Unfortunately, however, no further liturgical details are provided.

Nevertheless, the first positive evidence of à Lasco's rite appears shortly thereafter. In 1550, while the Strangers' Church organized itself in London, Vallerand Poullain established a Walloon congregation in Glastonbury, under the auspices of Duke Somerset.[41] In 1552, he prepared a version of the Strasbourg rite for use in this church: *L'Ordre des Prières et Ministere Ecclesiastique, avec La forme de penitence pub. & certaines Prières de l'Église de Londres, Et La confession de Foy de l'Église de Glastonbury en Somerset.*[42] The order also appears in various Latin editions, with the title, *Liturgia Sacra.*[43] The French version, however, is unique in its inclusion of the following section: *De la Penitence Publique des*

pecheurs repentans avant qu ilz ayent esté excommunié.
Par monsieur Ian à Lasco Superintendent des Eglises
estrangiers à Londres.[44]   A comparison with the
penitential rite found in the *Forma ac Ratio* indeed
demonstrates substantial agreement between the two
liturgies, with only a few exceptions.[45]

A slight modification, for example, has been made
to the beginning of the service, where, according to
Poullain's rite, the penitent is brought to the front of the
church *prior* to the opening exhortation.[46] Moreover, the
translation does not provide an *argumentum* for this
admonition.   Instead, à Lasco's sermon has been
substantially condensed and placed at the front of Poullain's
liturgy, as a general introduction to the rite.[47] Finally, in
place of à Lasco's request directed to ministers and elders
as to whether anything else is required of the penitent's
confession, Poullain simply has the officiating pastor
proceed with the service, "si ceste confession est
suffisante."[48]   These variations could be a result of
Poullain's editing activity, who might have sought to reduce
the length of à Lasco's rite.   It is also possible, however,
that they reflect an earlier version of the liturgy, which was
then later modified for inclusion in the *Forma ac Ratio.*[49]
Nevertheless, apart from these minor exceptions, the two
rites are largely identical, both in order and in substance.

The appearance of this translation is important for at
least three reasons. First, it explicitly attributes authorship
to à Lasco. This corroborates other evidence suggesting
that he was primarily responsible for the rites of the
Strangers' Church.[50]   Second, it confirms the fact that the
liturgy was in existence by 1552, some three years before
it appears in the *Forma ac Ratio.* Moreover, since it was
composed within the first two years of à Lasco's arrival in
England, it quite possibly could have been brought from

Frisia, thus supporting the testimony of Gellius Faber, cited above.[51] Finally, by selecting à Lasco's liturgy, Poullain indicates that no comparable rite was available from Bucer or Calvin. The absence of such a service in either Strasbourg or Geneva left him with little alternative but to adopt the liturgy of his London counterpart.[52]

Poullain's translation, therefore, provided à Lasco's liturgy with exposure beyond the limits of London and introduced it to the readers of Calvin's tongue. Indeed, it is interesting to note that public repentance continued to play a role in the French Reformed Churches, as attested by various parish records.[53] While no detailed liturgy for this practice has been found, it remains possible that Poullain's rite, borrowed from à Lasco, may have exerted some influence in this regard. Such postulations at this point, however, must remain largely speculative.

Nevertheless, this was not the only French edition of à Lasco's service to appear. While the Superintendent's liturgical compositions were primarily intended for his Dutch congregation, they also helped to shape the practice of the French church in London, likewise placed under his authority.[54] The rites employed by this community are contained in a tripartite volume housed by the Bodleian library.[55] The first section, *La forme des prières ecclesiastique* (1552), reproduces the main Strasbourg rites, interpreted along the lines of Poullain.[56] It represents an initial attempt of the French congregation to compile its own service book. Accordingly, the third portion contains an edition of Calvin's Genevan catechism, produced in London specifically for the French strangers.[57] More to the point, however, is the second document, bearing the title: *Doctrine de la Penitence Pvblique. Et La Forme d'icelle ainsi comme elle se practique en l'Eglise des estrangiers a Londres, deuaut qu'on vienne a l'excommunication. Ensemble aussi la forme d'administrer la saincte Cene* [London, 1552].[58] The inclusion of this section reveals a probable shift in the use of the French congregation. Whether by choice or compulsion, certain adjustments were quickly made to its initial effort, *La forme des prières.*

As indicated by the last sentence in this title, a new form for celebrating the Supper has been introduced. Calvin's Strasbourg rite has been set aside and in its place stands à Lasco's liturgy, rendered into French. The cause for this substitution is not entirely clear. Whether the Superintendent's personal eucharistic views played a part, or whether it was merely a decision stipulated by the Privy Council—these are questions better left to other studies.[59]

The inclusion of a service for public repentance, however, is perhaps more easily explained. As the tide of xenophobia rose amidst fears of sectarian insurgency, the English authorities required constant assurance that the aliens were under control.[60] À Lasco's predilection for a rigid ecclesiastical discipline meshed naturally with this concern. His public service of repentance would therefore serve the dual purpose of maintaining discipline within the church as well as presenting concrete evidence of the ministry's commitment to orthodoxy and Christian morality. From this point of view, the French probably had little choice in accepting à Lasco's penitential rite. A translation was therefore quickly prepared, thus providing another "corrective" to the earlier, *La forme des prières.*[61]

By these two French translations, then, the existence of à Lasco's service is attested as early as 1552, three years prior to its publication in the *Forma ac Ratio.* Another translation, however, shares a similar distinction. Upon the accession of Queen Mary, the majority of the Dutch congregation in London took to sea in search of another refuge.[62] This allowed Marten Micron, one of the pastors of this community, to reestablish himself in Norden in 1554.[63] For the church there, he completed his own account of the London rites, which he published in Emden with the title, *De Christlicke Ordinancien* (1554).[64] Micron complied the order in Dutch and kept it considerably shorter than the *Forma ac Ratio*. It was therefore more easily adapted for church use. Nevertheless, à Lasco's contributions to this practical enterprise cannot be overlooked. The two authors worked conjointly upon their respective projects as their residence in England hastened to a close.[65] Indeed, Micron later acknowledges having been greatly helped by à Lasco's "book."[66]

Within the *Ordinancien*, therefore, are the same disciplinary liturgies found in the *Forma ac Ratio*.[67] With regard to public repentance, the two rites retain precisely the same order of service. Occasionally, however, the exhortations in Micron's liturgy are shorter than those penned by à Lasco.[68] Since the Dutch version was intended for use by the Norden congregation, this brevity is understandable. In fact, Micron probably reproduces the rite in a fashion which more closely resembles its original use in London, since à Lasco freely admits that he expanded some of the admonitions prior to publishing his treatise.[69]

In any case, the introduction of Micron's liturgy into East Frisia in a sense completes the circle. It was in Emden, after all, that à Lasco was first inspired to produce a rite of public repentance.[70] The emergence of this service within the Low Countries, however, is also significant for another reason. The region eventually played host to a number of English Puritans, whose practice embraced a strong commitment to church discipline.[71] Their insistence upon the use of public repentance has already been suggested, with specific reference to the elders at Middelburg.[72] The Middelburg Puritans provide a unique example, for they elsewhere exhibit a marked dependence upon the à Lasco/Micron order. The so-called Middelburg Order of 1602, for example, borrows freely from the London ordination rite.[73] In this light, their mutual concern for public repentance might not be coincidental. Indeed, during the Marian exile English predecessors had settled in the Low Countries, specifically in Emden, just as Micron published his *Ordinancien* and à Lasco put finishing touches upon the *Forma ac Ratio*.[74] The connection between Dutch Puritans and the London church order therefore possesses some historical basis. The result is a very intriguing suggestion. English immigrants, settled in the Low Countries, were apparently influenced by the rites of Dutch refugees, previously exiled in England!

À Lasco's liturgy of public repentance, then, had already received considerable exposure prior to its publication in the *Forma ac Ratio*, through its use in the Strangers' Church and by virtue of both French and Dutch translations. This attention was enhanced, however, when the treatise itself finally appeared in Frankfurt in 1555. With its publication in Latin, the text was made available to the ecclesiastical leadership of various nations. Likewise, the following year, a complete French translation added to its circulation.[75] À Lasco had come to Frankfurt in April, ostensibly to aid a Dutch congregation which had formed there, but also to find a publisher.[76] He came barely a month after John Knox had left the English refugee church in the midst of their famous "troubles."[77] Although the two reformers did not meet on this occasion, it is apparent that Knox was favorably impressed with the *Forma ac Ratio*, which his allies in Frankfurt no doubt forwarded to him. In at least two particulars, he borrowed from it extensively. In 1560, superintendents were appointed to aid in organizing the blossoming Scottish Presbyterian Church.[78] Whether à Lasco's example as Superintendent of the Strangers' Church in any way contributed to this strategy must remain a matter of speculation. Nevertheless, the rite used for installing these leaders clearly depends upon the *Forma ac Ratio*. In "The Form and Order of the Election of Superintendents, Elders, and Deacons" (1560/1561), there exists several passages remarkably similar to those in à Lasco's service.[79] For example, in the examination of candidates, the following question is proposed in both liturgies:[80]

1560/61 Scottish Order

> Believe ye not that the doctrine of the Prophets and Apostles, contained in the books of the Old and New Testaments, is the only true and most absolute foundation of the universal Kirk of Christ Jesus, insamekill [i.e., inasmuch] that in the same Scriptures are contained all things necessary to be believed for the salvation of mankind?

Forma ac Ratio

> Do you believe that the doctrine of the Prophets and Apostles, contained in the Biblical writings of the old and new testaments, is the one true and most absolute foundation of the universal Church of God in Christ, such that in those scriptures is fully contained everything necessary for salvation?

The two questions are essentially identical.

Another example, from later in Knox's career, pertains specifically to the issue of public repentance. In 1587, *The Scottish Book of Common Order* appended to its section on discipline, "The Order of Excommvnication and of Pvblike Repentance vsed in the Church of Scotlande, and commaunded to be printed by the generall assemblie of the same, in the month of Iune, 1571."[81] The service of repentance contained in this order undoubtedly makes use of the *Forma ac Ratio*, employing both its structure and its language. Thus, the Scottish service proceeds as follows:

> Presentation of the individual
> Opening statement regarding the biblical mandate for
>   and nature of public repentance
> Prayer
> Charge to the offender
> Confession (in a non-prescribed form)
> Congregation is asked if anything further is
>   required for reconciliation
> Admonition to the one being restored
> Admonition to the Church
> Prayer of thanksgiving upon bended knee
> Penitent promises to submit to discipline
> Absolution
> Ministry extends right hand of fellowship
> Psalm 103, Dismissal with benediction.[82]

Only two deviations from the *Forma ac Ratio* are evident in this order. As in Poullain's rite, the opening exhortation has been placed after the presentation of the penitent.[83] Furthermore, the entire congregation, rather than merely the coetus, is asked for objections to the person's reconciliation.[84] The confession itself, however, is modeled after à Lasco's liturgy. It takes no set form, and the minister can speak for those who, out of shame or inability, cannot speak for themselves.[85]

By introducing this service of public repentance in 1571, Knox attests his acquaintance with à Lasco's work, published sixteen years prior to this date. More importantly, however, he provides yet another translation/edition of this liturgy. While it was previously available in French, Dutch, and Latin, now it also appeared in English. In this form, it could impact an even broader sphere and, in particular, the growing tide of English Puritanism.

À Lasco's works were known at least by some of the early Puritans. His treatise against vestments, for example, was rendered into English and appeared in the anonymous Puritan anthology, *The Fortress of Fathers.*[86] Likewise, Matthew Parker, chief agent of the crown in suppressing the anti-vestment party, diligently consulted the comparison earlier composed by Cranmer between à Lasco's views, on the one hand, and Bucer's ideas, on the other.[87] Not surprisingly, the *Forma ac Ratio* also received attention. Within a collection of Puritan tracts, housed by the Bodleian Library, a contemporary English translation of the work has been found which was being prepared for publication.[88]

This common ground between à Lasco and the Elizabethan Puritans did not go unnoticed. Even in Strype's time, his reputation lingered:

> There is one thing that is wont to be urged against him, and which makes him to this day to be some-what ill thought of: which was, that he opposed himself so openly, by writing against the habits prescribed the clergy, and the posture of kneeling at the reception of the holy sacrament; whereby he incurred the censure of a meddling temper, and of ingratitude to that nation that so kindly had entertained him.[89]

On a broader basis, the very existence of nonconforming, alien communities provided fuel for the Puritan fire. Shortly before his death, Thomas Earl, who in 1565 was suspended from the ministry for refusing to wear vestments, wrote:

> Yt semethe ryghtfull that subiects naturall receve soe much favoure as the churches of natyonall straungers have here with us. But we can not once be harde soe to obtayne. Thys with them: they an eldershippe; we none. They frely electe the doctor and pastor; we maye not. They their deacons and churche servauntes with dyscyplyn; and wee notte.[90]

Likewise, in May, 1572, a "Bill Concerning Rites and Ceremonies," was introduced by nonconformists into the House of Commons.[91] In part, it proposed that bishops should be allowed to use in their churches:

> ...[S]uch forme of prayer and mynistracion of the woorde and sacraments, and other godlie exercises of religion as the righte godlie reformed Churches now do use in the ffrenche and Douche congregation, within the City of London or elswheare in the Quenes maiesties dominions and is extante in printe.[92]

This controversial reference to the rights of foreigners apparently was not well received, for it disappears from the second reading of the bill.[93]

Taken together, these examples show that the Elizabethan Puritans felt slighted when rights of nonconformity were granted to foreigners yet denied to themselves. At the same time, they suggest a common approach to worship in general and church discipline in particular. Earl's previously cited sentiment, that "They [have] their deacons and church servaunts with dyscyplyn;

and wee notte," is indicative of this agreement. While no disciplinary rites survive from the early Puritans, the possibility of influence still exists on a broader plane. By virtue of the institutions established by à Lasco, the English had ready access to a detailed system of ecclesiastical discipline, enforced through a coetus of ministers and elders. Unfortunately, however, without a more detailed investigation of the discipline used by Elizabethan Puritans, the extent of this influence cannot be conclusively measured.

Nevertheless, in the final analysis, à Lasco's liturgy of public repentance clearly received considerable attention. Several possible trajectories of influence have been suggested in this study. First, various French translations of the rite at least raise the question of a potential impact upon the use of public repentance among the French Reformed Churches. Second, Micron's Dutch edition, together with the publication of the *Forma ac Ratio*, brought the liturgy on to the Continent, where it could be perused by the Marian exiles in Emden, Frankfurt and elsewhere. Particular signs of influence are detected in Middelburg among the Dutch Puritans. Third, it is clear that John Knox made use of the service by translating it into English and introducing it to the Scottish Presbyterian churches. Finally, at least some Elizabethan Puritans were well aware of à Lasco and were thus positioned to glean assistance from his disciplinary institutions.

Apart from questions of its influence, however, à Lasco's service of public repentance deserves consideration in and of itself. On the one hand, it attempts to validate the gospel by affirming the possibility of forgiveness in Christ. The fallen one is constantly held up as an example and an impetus toward repentance, confession and reconciliation. At the same time, however, it confirms the authority of the ministry. The coetus retained the right to require public repentance and thus reinforced its role as God's ordained institution for the preservation of both moral and doctrinal standards. As such, the rite illustrates a fundamental Reformation struggle to affirm both Christian freedom and ecclesiastical responsibility. It, therefore, constitutes one practical experiment within the complex history of Reformed/Puritan ecclesiologies.

Endnotes

1. Consistory Register, I, 34-36 (June 13, 1626), cited in Keith L. Sprunger, *Dutch Puritanism: A History of English and Scottish Churches of the Netherlands in the Sixteenth and Seventeenth Centuries* (Leiden, Netherlands: E. J. Brill, 1982), 192.

2. Standard biographies include Oskar Bartel, *Jan Laski: Czech I, 1499-1556* (Warsaw, 1955); German translation, *Jan Laski*, trans. Arnold Starke (Berlin, 1964; repr., 1981); 1981 edition includes translation of Halina Kowalska, *Dzialnosc Reformatorska Jana Laskiego, Polsce, 1556-1560* (Warsaw, 1969); Hermann Dalton, *Johannes à Lasco* (Gotha, 1881); partial ET, *John à Lasco: His Earlier Life and Labours*, trans. Maurice J. Evans (London: Hodder and Stoughton, 1886); Basil Hall, *John à Lasco 1499-1560: A Pole in Reformation England*, a published address delivered to the Friends of Dr. Williams Library, October 19, 1971 (London: Dr. Williams's Trust, 1971); George Pascal, *Jean de Lasco, Baron de Pologne, eveque catholique, reformatevor protestant, 1499-1560: son temps, sa vie, ses ouvres...* (Paris, 1894). See also Harold Ogden Joseph Brown, "John Laski: A Theological Biography. A Polish Contribution to the Protestant Reformation" (Ph.D. dissertation, Harvard University, 1967); and Dirk W. Rodgers, "John à Lasco in England" (Ph.D. dissertation, Drew University, 1991).

3. The charter may be found in Johannes Lindeboom, *Austin Friars: History of the Dutch Reformed Church in London 1550-1950*, trans. D. de Inough (The Hague: M. Nijhoff, 1950), 198-203. Though the document mentions only French and "german" (i.e., Low German, or Dutch) congregations, an Italian assembly was likewise included within the privileged body. At some point, a Spanish congregation was also formed, though concrete evidence of its existence does not appear until the Elizabethan era. G.B. Beeman, "The Early History of the Strangers' Church, 1550-1561," Huguenot Society of London, *Proceedings* 15 (1933-1937), 261-282; J.S. Burn, *History of the French, Walloon, Dutch, and Other Foreign Protestant Refugees Settled in England...*(London, 1846); Lindeboom, *Austin Friars*; Frederick A. Norwood, *The Reformation Refugees as an Economic Force* (Chicago: American Society of Church History, 1942); *idem*, "The Strangers' 'Model Churches' in Sixteenth-Century England," in his *Strangers and Exiles: A History of Religious Refugees* (Nashville and New York: Abingdon Press, 1969), 1:289-308, also in *Reformation Studies*, ed. F.H. Littell (Richmond: John Knox Press, 1962), 181-196; Andrew Pettegree, *Foreign Protestant Communities in Sixteenth-Century London* (Oxford: Clarendon Press; Oxford University Press, 1986); Symeon Ruytinck and Caesar Calandrinus, *Geschiedenissen ende Handelingen die voornemlick aengaen de Nederduytsche Natie ende Gemeynten wonende in Engelant ende int bysonder tot Londen*, ed. J.J van Toorenenbergen, Marnix Society, series 3, part 1 (Utrecht, Netherlands, 1873); A.A. van Schelven, *De Nederduitsche Vluchtelingenkerken der XVIe Eeuw in Engeland en Duitschland in hunne Beteekenis voor de Reformatie in de Nederlanden* (The Hague, 1909); Fernand de Schickler, *Les Églises du Refuge en Angleterre*, 3 vols. (Paris: Fischbacher, 1892); Marten Woudstra, *De Hollandsche Vreemdelingen-Gemeente te Londen gedurende de eerste Jaren van haar Bestaan* (Groningen, 1908).

4. This act required ministers to use the newly compiled *Book of Common Prayer*, "and none other or otherwise." *Documents Illustrative of English History*, ed. H. Gee and W.T. Hardy (London: Macmillan, 1896), 360.

5. "Waer onder gheweest is Jan Wtenhoue, die dese onse teghenwordeghe ordinantien in onse Nederlandtsche sprake wten latyne ouergheset heest." Marten Micron, *De Christlicke Ordinancien der*

Nederlantscher Ghemeiinten te Londen, ed. W.F. Dankbaar (The Hague, 1956), 37. Regarding Micron's order and its relation to à Lasco, see below, pp. 10f.

6. John à Lasco, *Opera tam Edita quam Inedita Recensuit, Vitam Auctoris Enarravit...*, ed. Abraham Kuyper (Amsterdam, 1866), 2:1-283.

7. *Ibid.*, 184-226. À Lasco regarded ecclesiastical discipline to be the third "notam" of the Church, along with faithful preaching of the Word and proper administration of the Sacraments. *Ibid.*, 132, 436.

8. See Section B., below.

9. À Lasco, *Opera*, 2:184-194.

10. The ministry of the Strangers' Church was cast in a quasi-presbyterian mold. Technically, there were two orders, pastor/elder and deacon. Within the former order, however, some distinction was maintained; elders shared in the supervision of the church but did not preach or administer the Sacraments. A Superintendent was appointed to oversee these three refugee communities, though à Lasco took pains to distinguish his position from the Papal office of bishop. *Ibid.*, 51-81, 228-334.

11. "Publicae disciplinae usus in plebe Ecclesiae non alias locum habet, nisi aut post contemptas privatas admonitiones omnes, aut si facinus ita sit publicum, ut caelari non amplius possit, aut ita alioqui grave, ut propter graviora multorum totiusve Ecclesiae pericula publicari omnino oporteat." *Ibid.*, 179, cf. 181.

12. *Ibid.*, 182-185.

13. "...Ecclesiastes orditur tractatiunculam de publica poenitentia in Ecclesia Christi atque illius fontes in scripturis sanctis paucis commonstrat." *Ibid.*, 185.

14. "...[S]i totam forte Ecclesiam aut bonam alioqui illius partem offenderimus, toti nos etiam Ecclesiae reconciliari oportere." *Ibid.*

15. *Ibid.*, 185f.

16. *Ibid.*, 186.

17. "Postremo de publica totius Ecclesiae in publica istiusmodi lapsorum fratrum poenitentia aedificatione, nempe ut quisque in Ecclesia cogitet peccatum fratris ita poenitentis non tam ipsius solius, quam suum etiam totiusque adeo Ecclesiae esse...." *Ibid.*

18. "...[S]eque pari apud Deum reconciliatione in Christo opus habere." *Ibid.*

19. "...[N]on recusat peccati sui culpam, quo Dominum Deum euisque Ecclesiam offendit, publice agnoscere, ad suam quidem, ut videtis, erubescentiam, sed ad Domini Dei nostri gloriam et Ecclesiae huius nostrae aedificationem." *Ibid.*, 187.

20. "...[Q]uin eadem quoque opera fateamur, nihil a nobis alienum esse, quod ab aliis quoquo etiam modo patrari videmus, nisi singulari Dei beneficio praeservemur." *Ibid.*, 187f.

21. "Coniungamus preces nostras cum ipsius precibus, coniungamus et lachrymas nostras cum lachrymis ipsius Deumque supplices pariter omnes invocemus, ut frater hic noster culpam peccati sui vere et ex animo agnoscat et deprecetur, ad nominis divini gloriam suamque ipsius salutem et totius nostrae huius Ecclesiae aedificationem." *Ibid.*, 189.

22. "...[T]e nolle mortem peccatoris, sed potius ut resipiscat et vivat." *Ibid.* For similarities with the penitential rite in the 1552 *Book of Common Prayer*, cf. F.E. Brightman, *The English Rite: Being a Synopsis of the Sources and Revisions of the Book of Common Prayer* (London: Rivingtons, 1915), 1:131ff., 155ff., 2:898f.; *The Two Liturgies, A.D. 1549, and A.D. 1552: With other Documents set forth by authority in the Reign of King Edward VI*, ed. Joseph Ketly, for the Parker Society (Cambridge: University Press, 1844), 383; *The Two Books of Common Prayer Set Forth by Authority of Parliament in the Reign of King Edward the Sixth*, 3rd ed., ed. Edward Cardwell (Oxford: University Press, 1852), xxx-xxxi; C.G. Cuming, *A History of the*

Anglican Liturgy, 2nd ed. (London: Macmillan, 1982.), 104f.; and Rodgers, "John à Lasco in England," 217f.

23. "...[U]t corda omnium nostrum excites per Spiritum sanctum tuum ad veram ac salutarem peccatorum nostrorum agnitionem." *Ibid.*

24. *Ibid.*

25. *Ibid.*, 189f.

26. *Ibid.*, 190.

27. *Ibid.*, 191.

28. *Ibid.*. Since the coetus was intimately involved in the whole disciplinary process, it would seem that this question was largely formal. It was probably intended to demonstrate to the congregation that no one minister had determined the necessity of public repentance; rather, the decision was established by the common consent of the entire church leadership.

29. "...[T]u non tam sane te ipsum tuamque infirmitatem, quam potius Satanam ipsum...pudefecisti." *Ibid.*

30. "...[N]ihil non esse tentaturum proculdubio, ut te quoquo rursum modo illaqueat." *Ibid.*, 192.

31. *Ibid.*

32. *Ibid.*, 192f.

33. "Atque, ut ipse certum iam suae vobiscum [i.e., Ecclesiam] reconciliationis indicium ac testimonium habere possit...." *Ibid.*, 193.

34. "...[A]d nominis tui adorandi gloriam, salutem nostrum hic omnium et catholicae tuae Ecclesiae aedificationem, per filium tuum Dominu m nostrum Iesum Christum." *Ibid.*

35. "Tum Minister annunciat at contestatur veram ac plenam peccati ipsius coram Deo et eius Ecclesia remissionem." *Ibid.*, 193f.

36. *Ibid.*, 194.

37. See Philippe Denis, "Jean Laski et le Retour au Papism," *Les Églises et leurs Institutions au XVIeme Siécle*, Actes du Veme Colloque du Centre d'Histoire de la Réforme et du Protestantissme, ed. Michel Péronnet (Montpellier, 1978), 3-17.

38. When John Knox adapted à Lasco's liturgy in 1571 for use in the Scottish Presbyterian Church, he changed this rubric to allow the entire assembly to express objections. See below, p. 13.

39. Gellius Faber, *Eine antwert Gellii Fabri dener des hilligen wortes binnen Embden up einen bitterhönischen breef der Wedderdöper darynne se etlike orsaken menen tho qeuen worumme se in unse Kercken umme Gades wordt tho hören unde mit der Gemene de hilligen Sacramente tho bruken nicht kamen willen unde de Kercke Gades sampt eren denernschentliken lasteren unde schelden* [n.p., n.d.], significant portions of which are contained in *Niedersachsen: Die ausserwelfischen Lande*, ed. Anneliese Sprengler-Ruppenthal, vol. 7/1 of *Die evangelischen Kirchenordnungen des XVI. Jahrhunderts*, ed. Emil Sehling (Tübingen, Germany: O. R. Reisland, 1963), 323n., cf. 644n.

40. *Ibid.*, 323n.

41. Karl Bauer, *Valérand Poullain: ein kirchengeschichtliches zeitbild aus der mitte des sechzehntrn jahrhunderts* (Elberfeld, 1927), 148-158; Henry J. Cowell, "The French-Walloon Church at Glastonbury, 1550-1553," Huguenot Society of London, *Proceedings*, 13 (1923-1929), 483-515; Schickler, *Les Églises*, 1:59-67.

42. Text in Valerand Poullain, *Liturgia Sacra (1551-1555)*, ed. A.C. Honders (Leiden, Netherlands: E. J. Brill, 1970), printed in parallel columns with the Latin edition (cf. the following note). A copy of this document is listed in *A Short-Title Catalogue of Books Printed in England, Scotland, & Ireland and of Books Printed Abroad 1475-1640*, 2nd ed., ed. F.S. Ferguson and Katherine F. Panzer (London:

Bibliographical Society, 1986), no. 16573. The title, however, has been incorrectly entered as: *L'ordre des prières et ministere ecclesiastique de l'eglise de Londres, et la confession de foy de l'eglise de Glastonbury en Somerset* (London, 1552). The parablepsis which occurs between the phrase, "l'eglise de," and the term,"Londres," omits specific reference to the penitential rite and "certaines Prières," thus leaving the erroneous impression that the treatise contains the entire London (rather than the Glastonbury) order.

43. *Liturgia Sacra, seu Ritus Ministerii in Ecclesia peregrinorum profugorum propter Evangelium Christi Argentinae* (1551, *et seq.*).

44. Poullain, *Liturgia Sacra*, 241, see *ibid.*, 241-263.

45. Sprengler-Ruppenthal compares these services in some detail. *Die evangelischen Kirchenordnungen*, 7/1:572-575n.

46. Poullain, *Liturgia Sacra*, 247. In à Lasco's rite, the exhortation is delivered prior to the repentant member coming forward. See above, pp. 3f.

47. Poullain, *Liturgia Sacra*, 241ff.

48. *Ibid.*, 257.

49. À Lasco admits that the text of the *Forma ac Ratio* was expanded before its publication, enough to cause a few irregularities in pagination: "Sed in itineribus demum meis, ubi Angliam reliquissemus, multis locis recognitus est atque in concionum praeterea argumentis admonitionibus Ecclesiasticis magna ex parte auctus, quae res paginarum quoque ordinem in ipsa libri aeditione nonnihil interturbavit." À Lasco, *Opera*, 2:35.

50. À Lasco, *Opera*, 2:12; À Lasco to Martin Bucer, London, 12 October 1550, in Constantin Hopf, *Martin Bucer and the English Reformation* (Oxford: B. Blackwell, 1946), 149; also in J. V. Pollet, *Martin Bucer: Études sur la Correspondance* (Paris: Presses universitaires de France, 1958), 1:277; Micron, *De Christlicke Ordinancien*, 39.

51. See p. 7.

52. Cf. René Bornert, *La Réforme Protestante du Culte a Strasbourg au XVIe Siècle (1523-1598)* (Leiden, Netherlands: E. J. Brill, 1981), 408-417. Poullain may also have adopted à Lasco's liturgy in response to concerns of the English crown. Cf. the discussion below with regard to the French church in London, which also introduced this service.

53. Raymond Mentzer, Montana State University, is currently investigating these parish records and has offered a preliminary report of his findings in "Excommunication in the French Reformed Churches," a paper presented to the Society for Sixteenth Century Studies, Philadelphia, October 19, 1991.

54. See above, note 3.

55. Bodleian Library, Oxford, Th. Seld. 8vo. 7. 12.

56. *La forme des prières ecclesiastique. Avec la maniere d'administrer les Sacret mens, & celebrer le Mariage, & la visitation des malades, Et aussi la maniere de confirmer & imposer las mains aux Ministres, Anciens, & Diacres...* ([London], 1552). *A Short-Title Catalogue*, no. 16572.3.

57. *Le Catechisme de Geneue...A Londres 1552. A Short-Title Catalogue*, no. 4391.

58. *A Short-Title Catalogue*, no. 16572.7.

59. À Lasco's liturgy of the Lord's Supper is overwhelmingly didactic, ever fearful that Calvin's language admitted confusion of sign and mystery. Karl Hein, *Die Sakramentslehre des Johannes a Lasco* (Berlin: C. A. Schwetschke und Sohn, 1904); Karl A. R. Kruske, *Johannes a Lasco und der Sakramentsstreit* (Leipzig, 1901); Bryan Spinks, *From the Lord and "The Best Reformed Churches"* (Rome: C. L. V. - Edizioni liturgiche, 1985), 109ff.; Anneleise Sprengler-Ruppenthal, *Mysterium und Riten nach der Londoner Kirchenordnung der Niederländer* (Köln, 1967), 90ff.; Rodgers, "John à Lasco in England," 119-136, 162-212. For the tensions which existed between

the Dutch and French congregations, caused chiefly by a difference in rites, see Calvin's letter to the Ministers of the Strangers' Church, Geneva, September 27, 1552, in *Corpus Reformatorum*, 42:362-365; and partial ET in George C. Gorham, *Gleanings of a Few Scattered Ears during the Period of the Reformation in England* (London, 1857), 284ff.

60. Thus, according to King Edward's journal, on June 29, 1550, "It was appointed that the Germans [i.e., Dutch] should have Austin Friars to have their services in, for [the] avoiding of all sects of Anabaptists and suchlike." *The Chronicle and Political Papers of King Edward VI*, ed. W. K. Jordan, for the Folger Shakespeare Library (Ithaca: Cornell University Press, 1966), 37.

61. A comparison of this French translation with that produced by Poullain leaves little doubt that they were compiled independently.

62. John Utenhove, *Simplex ac Fidelis narratio de instituta ac demum dissipata Belgarum, aliorumque peregrinorum in Anglia ecclesia* (Basil, 1560); repr. in *Bibliotheca Reformatoria Neerlandica*, ed. Samuel Cramer and F. Pijper (The Hague: M. Nijhoff, 1912), 9:29-186; cf. À Lasco, *Opera*, 2:680-693, 697f., 701f., 703-708; *Lasciana nebst den altesten evang. Synodalprotokollen Polens 1555-61*, ed. Hermann Dalton, vol. 3 of his *Beitrage zur Geschichte der Evangelischen Kirche in Russland* (Berlin, 1898), 335-338. Modern treatments of this exilic journey include Rudolf Kayser, "Johannes a Lasco und die Londoner Flüchtlingsgemeinde in Hamburg," *Zeitschrift des Vereins für Hamburgische Geschichte*, 37 (1938), 6-13; Karl Mönckeberg "Johannes a Lasco und seiner Fremdengemeinde Aufnahme in Danemark und Norddeutschland," *Zeitschrift für kirchliche Wissenschaft und kirchliches Leben*, 4 (1883), 588-604; Fredrick A. Norwood, "The London Dutch Refugees in Search of a Home, 1553-4," *American Historical Review*, 58 (1952-1953), 64-72; and Andrew Pettegree, "The London Exile Community and the Second Sacramentarian Controversy, 1553-1560," *Archiv für Reformationsgeschichte*, 78 (1987), 223-251.

63. The older bibliography by Jan H. Gerretsen, *Micronius, zijn leven, zijn geschriften, zijn geesterichting* (Nijmwegen, 1895), has not been superseded.

64. Marten Micron, *De Christlicke Ordinancien der Nederlantscher Ghemeiinten te Londen*, ed. W. F. Dankbaar (The Hague, 1956); also in *Die evangelischen Kirchenordnungen*, 7/1:579-667.

65. À Lasco, *Opera*, 2:35, 677; Gorham, *Gleanings*, 296f.; and Micron, *De Christlicke Ordinancien*, 39.

66. "...[I]ck grootelick beholpen hebbe gheweist, wt den boeck die de voornoemde Jan a Lasco, onse Superintendent, vander ordinancien onser Ghemeinte op het lankst bescreuen heest...." *Ibid.* À Lasco had substantially completed the *Forma ac Ratio* by the time that he departed England in 1553, though he edited and expanded the treatise before it was finally published in 1555. À Lasco, *Opera*, 2:35.

67. Micron, *De Christlicke Ordinancien*, 105-140.

68. This difference is most notable in the first admonition to the one repenting. The Latin and Dutch versions of this exhortation, together with Poullain's French translation, are compared in parallel columns by Sprengler-Ruppenthal, *Die evangelischen Kirchenordnungen*, 7/1:573f fn.

69. See above, note 49.

70. See above, p. 7.

71. Sprunger, *Dutch Puritanism*, 58f., 98f., 192f., *et passim*; Alastair Duke, *Reformation and Revolt in the Low Countries* (London and Ronceverte: Hambledon Press, 1990), 283-287.

72. Above, p. 1.

73. The questions presented to the ordinands are adapted from à Lasco's liturgy, and the final blessing is translated almost verbatim. Paul Bradshaw, *The Anglican Ordinal* (London: SPCK for the Alcuin Club, 1971), 51-56; William D. Maxwell, *The Liturgical Portions of the Genevan Service Book* (Edinburgh and London: Oliver and Boyd, 1931; repr., Westminster: Faith Press, 1965), 172.

74. C.H. Garrett, *The Marian Exiles. A Study of the Origins of Elizabethan Puritanism* (Cambridge: University Press, 1938), 285f. Among the refugees at Emden was Sir John Checke, former tutor of Edward VI and personal friend of à Lasco. *Ibid.,* 114-117.

75. *Toute la forme & maniere du ministere ecclesiastique, en l'eglise des esträgers, dressée a Londres. Par J. a Lasco. Tr. de Latin,* [Emden:] G. Ctematius [i.e., G. van der Erve], 1556. *A Short-Title Catalogue,* no. 16574.

76. À Lasco, *Opera,* 1:243-269, 2:35, 714-720; Bartel, *Jan Laski,* 171-190; Dalton, *Johannes à Lasco,* 454-486; Pettegree, "The London Exile Community," 238ff.

77. *A Brieff discours off the troubles begonne at Franckford in Germany Anno Domini 1554* (London, 1575); modern ed., *A Brief Discourse of the Troubles at Frankfort. 1554-1558 A.D. Attributed to William Whittingham, Dean of Durham. 1575 A.D.* (London: Elliot Stock, 1908); Jasper Ridley, *John Knox* (New York and Oxford: Oxford University Press, 1968), 189-214.

78. *John Knox's History of the Reformation in Scotland,* ed. William Croft Dickinson (New York: Philosophical Library, 1950), 1:334, 355.

79. For Knox's order, see *Ibid.,* 2:273-277, also 1:355n., 2:293ff. The work is broken into two parts, dealing, on the one hand, with superintendents, and, on the other, with elders and deacons. The former section is entitled, "The Form and Order of the Election of the Superintendents, which may serve also in election of all other ministers. At Edinburgh the 9th of March 1560, John Knox being minister." *Ibid.,* 273.

80. *John Knox's History,* 2:274. À Lasco's Latin text reads: "Creditisne, Propheticam atque Apolisticam doctrinam veteris et novi testamenti, in Biblicis scripturis comprehensam, esse unicum verum atque absolutissmum fundatmentum catholicae Dei Ecclesiae in Christo, sic ut in scripturis illis ad plenum contineantur omnia, quaecunque ullo modo sunt necessaria ad salutem...." À Lasco, *Opera,* 2:70. While à Lasco's rite includes only three questions in his examination, Knox's

service has a total of nine. Nevertheless, the content of each examination covers the same ground.

81. *The Scottish Book of Common Order* (1587), 35-58. *A Short-Title Catalogue*, no. 16852.

82. *Ibid.*

83. Cf. above, p. 8. This similarity raises the issue of whether Knox took the rite of repentance directly from the *Forma ac Ratio* or from its rendering in Poullain. The verbal agreement between Knox and à Lasco, however, seems to argue against this possibility. Unlike Poullain, for example, they both explicitly call for Psalm 103 to be sung at the conclusion of the service. Cf. À Lasco, *Opera*, 2:194; *The Scottish Book of Common Order* (1587), 58; Poullain, *Liturgia Sacra*, 263.

84. *The Scottish Book of Common Order* (1587), 54.

85. *Ibid.*; cf. À Lasco, *Opera*, 2:191.

86. *The Fortress of Fathers* (c. 1566); modern ed. in *Elizabethan Puritanism*, ed. Leonard J. Trinterud (New York: Oxford University Press, 1971), 83-127. À Lasco's address bears the title, "The Judgement of Master John à Lasco of removing the use of singular apparel in the church ministry, written the 20th day of September, in the fifth year of the reign of King Edward VI." *Ibid.*, 110-117. Scholars have generally overlooked the recently-discovered Latin text of this address, *De tollendo vestium peculiarum usu in ministerio Ecclesiae*, 20 September [1551], Bodleian Library, Oxford, ms. Nov. Coll. 343, f° 2, cited in *Les Lettres a Jean Calvin de la Collection Sarrau*, ed. Rodolphe Peter and Jean Rott (Paris: Presses universitaires de France, 1972), 42n.

87. *Summa controvesiae de re vestiaria inter Bucerum et Lascum*, À Lasco, *Opera*, 1:lv-lvi.

88. Bodleian Library, Oxford, Ms. Barlow 19. See Robin Leaver, *'Goostly Psalmes and Spirituall Songs': English and Dutch Metrical*

Psalms from Coverdale to Utenhove, 1535-1566 (Oxford: Clarendon Press, 1991), 161; Pettegree, *Foreign Protestant Communities*, 273.

89. John Strype, *Memorials of the Most Reverend Father in God Thomas Cranmer, Sometime Lord Archbishop of Canturbury*, ed. Philip Edward Barnes (London: Oxford University Press, 1853), 2:279f.

90. Thomas Earl's notebook, Cambridge University Library, MS. Mm.1.29, f. 2, cited in Patrick Collinson, "The Elizabethan Puritans and the Foreign Reformed Churches in London," Huguenot Society of London, *Proceedings* 20 (1964), 539.

91. Text in *State Papers, Domestic, Elizabeth* (London, Public Records Office), lxxxvi, 45, 46, 48. The two versions of the bill have been combined in *Puritan Manifestoes: A Study of the Origin of the Puritan Revolt*, ed. W.H. Frere and C.E. Douglas (London, 1907; repr.: SPCK for the Church Historical Society, 1954), 149ff. Cf. J.E. Neale, *Elizabeth I and her Parliaments, 1559-1581* (New York: St. Martin's Press, 1958), 297-304.

92. *Puritan Manifestoes*, 151. Cf. Collinson, "The Elizabethan Puritans," 543f. Whether this means that the bishops would be free to use the strangers' rites *per se*, as opposed to forms modeled after these rites, remains unclear. Speaker of the House, Robert Bell, believed that it would allow such variations from the *Book of Common Prayer* that did not differ substantially from the alien order. Bell to Burghley, 20 May 1572, in *Puritan Manifestoes*, 152.

93. Thus, the reference is included in brackets in *Ibid.*, 151.

THE ZWINGLIAN RITES RECONSIDERED[1]

Horton Davies
Princeton and Drew Universities

Introduction

The shadow of present-day disapproval lies upon Zwingli's contribution to the understanding of the Eucharist. Luther's contemporary is remembered as a memorialist, an iconoclast, and a Humanist. While he might have regarded these descriptions as honorable, they are the measure of the opprobrium of today. When Lutherans complain of Zwingli's insensitiveness to the numinous element in worship, and Calvinists deplore his predominantly retrospective view of the Lord's Supper, it might be doubted whether he deserved even honorable mention in a history of the reformed rites. A truer judgment would, however, recognize his importance both as critic and reformer.

His importance as a critic can be established by a consideration of his eucharistic theology.[2] This strictly determined the form and content of his two rites. The first of them was little more than a radical revision of the later medieval Mass. Its importance is, therefore, critical rather than constructive. For the full fruit of his constructive liturgical work it is necessary to turn to the second rite, which was an entirely new vernacular order. In both rites his characteristic "memorialism" is evident. As an

33

explanation of the importance he attached to the contemplation of the original supper and the cross which immediately succeeded it, it ought to be remembered that Zwingli believed that through the obedience of the worshippers to the Dominical command[3] the Lord would reveal himself to them. His "memorialism" was the recovery of a precious element in the eucharist, although he minimized the complementary sense of the eternal priesthood of the Son of God.

De Canone Missae Epicheiresis[4]

This exhaustive attack upon the Canon of the Mass appeared in 1523, the year in which Luther's *Formula Missae* was published. It is noteworthy as an independent and more thorough criticism, not only of the Canon in particular, but of the Mass as a whole. The reformer's primary intention was to prune the Canon of its inconsistencies and incoherences, as well as to eliminate all unbiblical doctrines. So many and so radical, however, were his alterations and excisions, that he felt compelled to provide a substitute for the "weaker brethren."[5]

The Liturgy of the Word required, in his view, less severe treatment than the Liturgy of the Upper Room. Hence most of it is retained with the repeated proviso that the various items should be selected exclusively from the sacred scriptures, excepting, of course, such collects as were agreeable to the Word of God. Lections, sequences, and collects for saints' days are omitted. Sequences are condemned forthwith as "old wives' tales" sung to "country tunes"[6] and the setting of the gradual is derided as cacophony.[7] On the other hand, the lectionary has been simplified for the building up of the faith of the worshippers, and, for the same reason, both lections and sermons are to be delivered in the vernacular.

The Liturgy of the Upper Room is subjected to a more radical simplification. The offertory and the *Sursum Corda* are omitted, but the Preface and *Sanctus* are retained. In place of the Canon, Zwingli supplies four eucharistic prayers. These are succeeded by the Institution narrative (I Cor. 11. 23-26) and the comfortable words of our Lord (Matt. 11. 28). Then follows the communion, which is concluded by a brief general prayer of thanksgiving and the *Nunc dimittis*. The four eucharistic prayers are of considerable importance, since they are the basis of the new "Canon" in the reformed rite celebrated in Zurich. The first is a thanksgiving for our creation, for our redemption from the fall through the incarnation and sacrifice of our Lord Jesus Christ, who also gave himself to be our food and drink, beseeching that the unworthy worshippers may never cease to give thanks to God for his grace. This was concluded with the Lord's Prayer. The second eucharistic prayer is a petition that the faithful may be fed by the celestial Bread, the Word, by a spiritual manducation. The latter is precisely defined.[8] The third prayer is an affirmation of obedience to God's Word, and of faith that "as we believe that the offering of thy Son once made has reconciled us to the Father, so may we steadfastly believe that He offered himself as the food for our souls under the forms of bread and wine that the memory of his gracious deed might never pass away."[9] A petition ensues that our faith may be increased that as He conquered the bitterness and shame of the cross to lead us to grace, so may we under his guidance and protection overcome the cares and afflictions of the world, while we partake of our Lord's body and blood, and that the members of his Body may be united, as He is with the Father. The fourth prayer is a petition for forgiveness in the name of the Lamb of God, ending with the plea that God may enable them to approach in faith the most sacred banquet of His Son, who is both host and feast.

Compared with the Mass which it was intended to supersede in Zurich, this rite has three distinguishing characteristics. It was more biblical in bases: edifying to the worshipper; and provided a more intense, if restricted, sense of the fellowship among the believers. In the first place, this rite was reformed according to the Word of God. Zwingli's fidelity to the Scriptures is seen in the use of unaltered words of institution, with the extra verse (not found in the Canon) taken from the Pauline tradition of the Lord's Supper. This dependence upon the Bible is clearly manifested in the phraseology of the Eucharistic prayers, as also in the omission of the rite. Two doctrines underlying the Canon, and perverted out of all recognition in later medieval Masses, came in for Zwingli's forthright criticism. Because they seemed to him to be unscriptural, they would have necessitated an entire reorientation of the Canon, even if Zwingli had not felt compelled to provide a substitute for the Canon. The first was the conception of sacrifice underlying the rite. The intention to represent to God the sacrifice offered by anticipation at the Last Supper seemed a flat contradiction of the teaching of the Scriptures that the sacrifice of the Cross was made "once for all," and was therefore unrepeatable. On this account Zwingli had no scruples in omitting the offertory, and in objecting to certain parts of the Canon, notably the *Quam oblationem* and the *Unde et memores*. The second doctrine was that of the "merits" of the saints. He took particular exception to the conclusion of the *Communicantes* which seemed not only contrary to the teaching of the Scriptures, but also inconsistent in pleading the merits of the saints and the name of the sole mediator Jesus Christ. It is not surprising, therefore, that his excisions were severe, nor that he was overzealous. His overmastering aim was to reform the Mass by the Word of God.

The second mark of his liturgical reconstruction was edification. The rite was to build up the faith of the worshippers in Zurich. It was, therefore, a prime necessity that the service should be understood by the people. This accounts for the simplification of the lectionary, and explains, if it does not condone, the didacticism of the prayers, which occasionally read like excerpts from a Catechism, so meticulous are their theological definitions. It is for this reason, also, that lections and sermons were to be delivered in the vernacular. This also accounts for the cavalier treatment of the musical settings.

The third emphasis, although a narrowed one, is the new sense of fellowship expressed through the delivery in both kinds, and it is expressly stated in the conclusion of the fourth eucharistic prayer.[10] It might be expected that the characteristic "memorialist" doctrine would loom large in the rite, but this emphasis is not unduly prominent. The sense of commemoration is there, necessarily, but with it there is a recognition that at this banquet Christ is present as host and feast.[11]

Action oder Bruch des Nachtmals[12]

This rite of 1525 is the full fruit of Zwingli's constructive liturgical endeavors. It was the first German rite to be used in Zurich. In the preface to it Zwingli states that it is his high aim to reform, under God's guidance, the abuses of the Lord's Supper, as Hezekiah and Josiah had purified the celebration of the Passover. He is not presumptuous, however, since he claims that this rite is intended only for the use of the church in Zurich; other churches are entitled to worship God according to their own liturgies.

The preface consists largely of rubrics. Divine service is to be conducted by a pastor assisted, if convenient, by two deacons. The communicants are instructed to place themselves in the chancel between the choir and the aisle, the men on the right and the women on the left. The bread is to be carried to the communicants by the deacons on flat wooden patens, and the wine in a wooden cup. The elements are to be received in a sitting posture, and each communicant is allowed to break off a morsel of the unleavened bread for himself and to raise the wooden chalice to his own lips. The communicants are to say "Amen" at reception. Communion is to be celebrated four time during the year: at Easter (when there are several celebrations), Autumn, Whitsun and Christmas.

Two of these rubrics are of historic importance. The first is the recognition of the practice of infrequent Communion. Zwingli was alone among the Reformers in permitting this. If the Genevan tradition perpetuated Zwingli's precedent, it was most certainly against the judgment of Calvin. The second innovation was the sitting posture for the reception of the elements. Unusual as this is, it follows logically from Zwingli's eucharistic doctrine. If the rite was to be a commemoration of the Lord's Supper and not a sacrifice, then clearly a holy table had to take the place of a holy altar. If kneeling is the appropriate gesture at the altar, then sitting is the appropriate gesture at a table. It was, moreover, fitting that communicants should be seated to mark their status as privileged guests at the divine feast.

The extreme simplicity of the rite can be gauged from the following outline of its structure.

The Liturgy of the Word

The Morning Service (concluding with a Sermon and Confession).
The preparation of the elements.
Invocation in the Triune Name.
Collect (for a true celebration of the Lord's Supper).
Epistle: *I Cor.* 11. 20ff.
Gloria in excelsis.
Gospel: *John* 6. 47ff.
The Apostles' Creed.

The Liturgy of the Upper Room

Exhortation (concluding with the Fencing of the Table).
The Lord's Prayer.
A Prayer of Humble Access.
The Institution Narrative.
Fraction and Communion of the Ministers.
Delivery and Communion of the people.
Psalm 103 (recited antiphonally).
Brief prayer of Thanksgiving.
Dismissal.

It will be seen from the above outline that the second Zwinglian rite is even simpler than the reform envisaged in the first. In the earlier rite four prayers took the place of the Canon of the Mass. These have now disappeared. In their place is a brief prayer of humble access. This, it is true, contains a more explicit *anamnesis* than was to be found in any of the eucharistic prayers of the first rite. The omissions are significant. The complete excision of the Preface and *Sanctus* is a grievous mutilation, particularly as there is no substitute by which to express the conception of the Church Catholic, militant and triumphant, uniting with the worshippers in their celebration. There is no prayer of consecration nor is there a prayer of

intercession. Further, all use of music is proscribed. Both
the *Gloria* and the 103th Psalm were to be recited, not
sung. Another remarkable feature is the simplicity of the
ceremonial.[13]

There is little doubt that the rite was intelligible to
the faithful at Zurich, for it was simple and written in the
vernacular tongue. It was, indeed, so completely intelligible
as to be little more than an object-lesson on the Atonement,
rather than a vehicle of devotion. This rite had sacrificed
mystery in the interests of edification. The simple wooden
patens and the wooden chalice, as also the sitting posture
for reception, were intended to reproduce the historical
circumstances of the Lord's Supper in their original
simplicity. The effect was to produce a rite that had more
affinity with the primitive *agape* than with the apostolic
eucharist. It is also true that this rite expressed the
fellowship of believers participating at the Lord's Table and
that the people were given their vernacular responses at
various parts of the service. But this conception of
fellowship was limited and local. The worshippers were
not reminded that they were a part of the Universal Church
in heaven and on earth; they were simply God's table-
fellowship in Zurich. These serious criticisms must,
however, be mitigated by the remembrance that Zwingli
was a liturgical pioneer, that his rites avoided what he was
convinced were the corruptions of the Roman rite, and that
he made a sincere attempt to recover the apostolic Lord's
Supper.

A Final Estimate

There are four serious charges to be brought against
Zwingli's eucharistic doctrine and practice. In the first
place, in his desire to recover the commemorative aspect of

the Lord's Supper, Zwingli overstressed it to the detriment of the aspect of communion with Christ. Occasionally, as in the four eucharistic prayers of the first rite, his language speaks of the *unio mystica*, but this is overshadowed by the historical reference. The Zwinglian rites are more a memorial than a communion with the crucified and risen Lord. Secondly, the prayers are didactic rather than devotional; they are precise theological definitions rather than ascriptions of praise or passionate petitions. They preach or teach, when they ought to beseech. The whole rite is intended to be an acted sermon, a rehearsal of the benefits of the cross, instead of being a communication of them. If Luther's liturgical reforms are the products of a man liberated from the cloister, Zwingli's seem to be the products of a man still incarcerated in his study. In the third place, the iconoclasm of Zwingli was responsible for a mutilated rite. There is not prayer of consecration, nor of intercession, while the Preface and *Sanctus* are also jettisoned to the great impoverishment of the rite. Moreover, even music is abandoned in favor of antiphonal recitation. This mistake, however, was righted in Zurich before the end of the sixteenth century. Finally, the infrequency of communion resulted in a divorce of the Lord's Supper from the Lord's day. Hence communion became occasional, and ceased to be the norm of Christian worship.

On the other hand, the Zwinglian rites cannot be dismissed as mere skeletons. Chief among their merits was a return to the spirit and circumstances of the Lord's Supper. Defective as Zwingli's rite was, its simplicity was a more faithful copy of the original than the late medieval Mass. It was essentially a biblical reconstruction made, as he believed, in fidelity to the apostolic account of the Lord's Supper. Moreover, he was also faithful in obeying the Apostle's demand for edifying worship. Translation into the vernacular and communion in both kinds made it more of a holy meal than a holy and mysterious spectacle which the faithful watched, but in which they did not participate. Then, again, these rites express a rich conception of faith. In this connection it is wise to heed the warning of Dr. Alexander Barclay, who writes of Zwingli "...if one reproaches him, that from the point of view of the Lutheran doctrine his teaching is poor and insignificant, it is because one forgets that what one does not find in his eucharistic teaching is already present in the riches and depth of his notion of faith...."[14] Finally the rite did not omit a proper ethical emphasis. The eucharistic prayers and the fencing of the table were vivid reminders that the Christian must bring forth fruits worthy of repentance. If Justification by faith was the dominant doctrinal emphasis in the Lutheran rites, then Sanctification was stressed in the Zwinglian rites.

The merits of these rites would perhaps have been esteemed more highly if Zwingli's work had not been corrected, implemented and incorporated in the Genevan tradition. It was to the advantage of the Reformed tradition in Christian worship as it was to the disadvantage of Zwingli's reputation, that the best in him, mediated through Bucer, is remembered as the work of John Calvin. The reputation of the pioneer is ephemeral; it is the destiny of a morning star to be drowned in the clear light of noon-day.

Endnotes

1. There is probably a special relevance in an essay on Zwingli in a volume dedicated to honor the liturgical expertise of my friend and colleague, Howard Hageman, since it demonstrates the weakness to which Reformed liturgies can descend if they do not take the high ground of Calvinism and drop into memorialism, though there are qualities in Zwingli which should not be forgotten. Often the consolidator (as in Calvin's sense) benefits from the daring of the innovator (in this case Zwingli).

2. See Schmidt-Klausing's *Zwingli als Liturgiker* (Göttingen: Vandenhoeck & Ruprecht, 1952), the best book on its theme. Other useful secondary sources are August Baur, *Zwinglis Theologie. Ihr Weden und ihr System*, 2 vols., (Halle: M. Niemeyer, 1885-1889); Frédérick Bresch, *Strasbourg et la querelle sacramentaire* (Montauban: J. Granié, 1902); C.J. Cadoux, Chapter X of *Christian Worship. Studies in its History and Meaning*, Nathaniel Micklem, ed., (Oxford: Clarendon Press, 1936); Charles Garside, *Zwingli and the Arts* (New Haven: Yale University Press, 1966); Marcus Jenny, *Zwinglis Stellung zur Musik* (Zurich: Zwingli Verlag, 1966); and G.R. Potter, *Zwingli* (Cambridge: Cambridge University Press, 1976).

3. Luke 22:19.

4. This will be found in the *Corpus Reformatorum*, Vol. LXXXX, Leipzig, 1908, and also in the Schuler and Schultess edition of the *Opera*, Zurich, 1828-1861. For a slightly abridged version, see *Quellenbuch zur praktischen Theologie*, Vol. I (*Liturgik*), edited by Carl Clemen (Giessen, Germany, 1910).

5. *Et quamvis haec omnia difficilia sint as observandum, commodious tamen paulo habituros spero infirmos, quam si omni consilio destitueremur.* Carl Clemen, *Quellenbuch zur praktischen Theologie*, Vol. I. (*Liturgik*) (Giessen, Germany, 1910), 44-45.

6. *Prosae, quas sequentiae vocant, plerumque sunt aniles fabulae et rithmi imurbanissimi. Ab eis abstinendum censemus. Ibid.*

7. *Quid enim fastidiosus audiri potest, quam tot voces sub una vocali boare? Ibid.*

8. *Oramus igitur, o domine, ut verbi tui cibo nos nunquan destituas, sed continua bonitate pascas. Ipsum enim panis est, qui dat vitam mundo; frustra enim carnem filii tui et sanguinem edemus et bioemus, nisi per fidem verbi tui hoc ante omnia firmiter credamus. Nam ipse dixit carnem nihil prodesse, spiritum esse, qui vivificet. Ibid.*

9. *..ut sicut filium tuum pro nobis semel oblatum patri reconciliasse credimus, ita quoque firmiter credamus eundem sese nobi animae cibum sub speciebus panis et vini praebuisse, ut liberalis facti memoria numquam aboletur. Ibid., 46-47.*

10. *...Da ut quotquot ex huius filii corporis sanguinisque cibo participaturi sunt, unum solumque spirent et exprimart, ac in eo qui tecum unus est. Ibid., 47.*

11. *Trahe, domine, pectus nostrum tui liminis gratia, ut digne, hoc est: ea fide, qua oportet, ad hoc sacrosanctum filii tui convivium accedamus, cuius ipse et hospes est et epulum. Ibid.*

12. This will be found in the Schuler and Schultess edition of the *Opera*, Vol. II, Part II. An abridged edition can be found in the more accessible *Quellenbuch zur praktischen Theologie*, Vol. I (*Liturgik*), edited by Carl Clemen (Giessen, Germany, 1910).

13. Zwingli prescribes "as little ceremonial and ecclesiastical ritual as we can for our people in the use of the Lord's Supper...(which nevertheless, is a ceremony, although one ordained by Christ); so that there shall be no future renewal of the old error. We have ordained such ceremonies as serve the occasion, namely such as promote a spiritual commemoration of Christ's death, an increase in faith and brotherly love, and an improvement in behavior...." *Ibid.*, 48.

14. Alexander Barclay, *The Protestant Doctrine of the Lord's Supper* (Glasgow, 1927), 47.

THE REFORMERS ON CHURCH MUSIC

A. Casper Honders
Groningen University, The Netherlands

Whoever investigates the now "canonical" literature[1] that deals with the reputations of the sixteenth-century reformers—Luther, Zwingli and Calvin—on the matter of church music soon encounters questions and problems. There are the obvious and coarsely drawn popular images: the Luther-on-church-music, after which can be placed a very appreciative plus sign; the Zwingli-on-church-music, after which comes an intriguing minus sign; and the Calvin-on-church-music, after which both minus and plus signs appear together. Lutheran scholars are particularly pleased with this representation and do not fail, after attesting their great admiration for Luther, to address their critical and negative remarks to Zwingli and Calvin. How could a Swiss like Zwingli and also a Frenchman like Calvin be so backward when compared to the pervasive and happy opinions of the great reformer Luther?

It seems to me that this all-pervasive *communis opinio* concerning the attitudes of the reformers to church music needs to be reinvestigated, since the issue itself has built-in questions, incomprehensibilities, uncertainties, and arguments that are not entirely convincing. The primary question, as I see it, is to decide whether the problems lie with Zwingli and Calvin or with some debatable points that might be discovered in our imperfect analyses. Anyone who sets out to traverse the terrain of historical investigation always does well to pay attention to the fact that our analyses are never final, but can be added to and improved. Opinions should always be open to second thoughts.

When we direct our attention to the decisions that were made regarding church music during the Reformation era, we must make the distinction—more than has been customarily done thus far—between music *within* worship and music *outside* of worship. Christian worship throughout the centuries has been a completely distinct phenomenon, especially with regard to the nature of music that might be heard within it.

If we take note of how the reformers viewed the practice of music *outside* the church service, that is, in general social life, then we have enough statements from them that makes it clear that they valued music, and that all of them, with a warm heart, esteemed the general practice of music (which, at that time, can be generally characterized as "church music"). Confining our discussion to Zwingli: according to his clear conviction, music belonged to that general sphere of life. Music was practiced in the family, in the school, and among friends. For Zwingli, music was a thoroughly free human expression which gave sound, color, composure, comfort, inspiration, and depth to human society. Zwingli had a broad and open outlook, and in his view of music was far from narrow-minded. On the contrary, the open field that he saw before him was spacious and allowed for all kinds of possibility. For Zwingli, I maintain, music was not confined to ecclesiastical-liturgical events but was rather a general humanistic opportunity and expression. It was autonomous, independent, and, in terms of the traditional ecclesiastical context—completely emancipated.   For Zwingli, music really stood on its own two feet.

If music, as treated by Zwingli (and Calvin), moves away from the liturgy towards the extra-liturgical of secular society and culture, then the much-repeated inquiry into the nature of the reformers' personal understanding of music becomes less interesting when compared to the matter of their obvious interest in the question of the nature of liturgical events in relation to the immediacy of the vision of commissioning people in the world, society, and culture. In other words, their theology becomes more interesting as it particularly relates to the question of the interconnection between the church and the world, between Sunday and weekday, and between liturgy and culture. This is much more interesting, so to speak, than the question of their personal musicality. When it comes to their appreciation of music, and their practice of music *outside* the liturgy, then the reformers cannot be played off against each other: they stand together in the same positive approach. Further, when we consider music *within* the liturgy, we need to remember that how close Luther could come to Zwingli. In the *Deutsche Messe* he says that in the special and prominent form of worship, for "those who mean to be real Christians.., the many and elaborate chants would be unnecessary."[2] Here music in this context is redundant. Thus we encounter a longstanding ecclesiastical tradition which also played a fundamental role in the reformers' understanding of music.

In the early church, whether on good grounds or not, instrumental music had already been emphatically removed from the worship of the church.   Undoubtedly, an increasing desire for non-Christian and pagan worship played a role in the prohibition, as did the argument that instrumental music, as part of Old Testament ceremonial and thus being provisional, was superseded. This exclusion of instrumental music from the worship of the church was deeply-rooted within the theological convictions of the ecclesiastical leaders, and was continuously repeated and defended by the leaders and teachers of the church. One can see that there is an ecclesiastical line that includes Zwingli and Calvin (it can also be detected in Luther), and Thomas Aquinas, for example, which marks a resolute exclusion of organ music (as instrumental music) from the worship of the church. A centuries-old tradition was continued. But it was renewed, "re-formed," honored and put into practice, and insidious changes and abuses that had gradually entered the church had to be eliminated in accordance with the long-standing tradition.

From its beginnings, and also in later times, the organ was the instrument of nobles and secular authorities rather than an ecclesiastical instrument of leadership. It was only dragged into the church as a tolerable substitute for the human voice (or voices), which might not be available from time to time. The instrument was a substitute for the human voice, an alternative *vox humana*. Only in this way could the organ be legitimized. Luther, however, with his sensitive pastoral generosity, was inclined to allow organs to continue, especially for the sake of the young and the simple, "as a man gives apples and pears to children," as he says somewhere. In his liberality, he had no scruples against bringing extra-liturgical elements into the liturgy for the sake of the people and the youth. He would allow the liturgy to fill up, while others would be bailing out the water that was pouring into the ship.

In connection with what has been expressed here, it must be stated that from the beginning music in the worship of the church has been exclusively vocal (think also of Eastern Orthodoxy). It is in this light especially that

Zwingli's attempt to import "Sprechgesang" [recitative] into the church service should be seen and appreciated.[3] It is the attempt, musically speaking, to return to basics and to keep with the age-old tradition of the church. We need to be aware that what he meant by antiphonal speech is a pronounced musical expression, as is recitation on a monotone. This recitation speech is an event that is fundamentally and essentially musical. The notion that Zwingli banned music from worship, therefore, is a superficial judgment. Along with this musical "Sprechgesang," is his inclination to "hear" in the silence. Silence, even in the liturgy, is part of the musical event.

I remember very clearly how instructive it was in the 1960s to read Howard Hageman's fine and vivid book, *Pulpit and Table*.[4] All kinds of ideas and expressions impressed me, such as this sentence: "From the beginning the Reformed churches, though modest in their ceremonial, were fully liturgical."[5] That rang like a clarion call in my ears. There were other observations. Some were, naturally, thought-provoking; others raised some doubts. I think, for example, of what Hageman wrote concerning Zwingli's liturgy. I cite: "Strangest of all, there is no music... The strangeness of this prohibition becomes apparent when we remember that Zwingli was well-educated and gifted musically. Possibly if music other than Gregorian chant or the bawdy tunes with religious words which were then popular had been available, Zwingli would have been less rigid."[6]

We have now returned to the observations with which I began these "reflections on church music." That Zwingli was "well-educated and gifted musically" we can certainly underline. But I would like to ask Howard if we might not now abandon and altogether put aside that notion about "strangeness"...?

May my proposal testify to my everlasting admiration and friendship for Howard. And—let me add in the same breath—for Carol.

Endnotes

1. See Walter Blankenburg, "Luther und die Musik," in Walter Blankenburg, *Kirche und Musik*, ed. Renate Steiger and Erich Hubner (Göttingen, Germany: Vandenhoeck & Ruprecht, 1979), 17-30; Charles Garside, "The Origins of Calvin's Theology of Music, 1536-1543," in *Transactions of the American Philosophical Society*, 4 (1969): 1-36; Charles Garside, *Zwingli and the Arts* (New Haven: Yale University Press, 1966); Insititut für Kirchenmusik, *Musik in der evangelisch-reformierten Kirche: eine Kirche: eine Standortbestimmung*. 2nd ed. (Zurich: Zwingli-Verlag, 1989); Markus Jenny, *Zwinglis Stellung zur Musik im Gottesdienst* (Zurich: Zwingli Verlag, 1966); Winfried Kurzschenkel, *Die theologische Bestimmung der Musik: neuere Beiträge zur Deutung und Wertung des Musizierens im christlichen Leben* (Trier, Germany: Paulinus-Verlag, 1971); Jan R. Luth, *"Daer wert om't seerste uytgekreten..."*: *Bijdragen tot een geschiedenis van de gemeentezang in het Nederlandse Gereformeerde protestantisme ca. 1550 - ca. 1852* (Kampen: Uitgeverij van den Berg, 1986); Ross James Miller, *"John Calvin and the Reformation of Church Music in the Sixteenth Century."* Ph.D. dissertation, Claremont Graduate School, 1971; and Oskar Söhngen, *Theologie der Musik* (Kassel, Germany: Stauda Verlag, 1967). See also the articles on Luther, Calvin, Zwingli, etc., in such standard reference works as *Die Musik in Geschichte und Gegenwart*, ed. Friedrich Blume (Kassel, Germany: Bärenreiter, 1949-86) and *The New Grove Dictionary of Music and Musicians*, ed. Stanley Sadie (London and New York: Grove's Dictionaries of Music, 1980).

2. Bard Thompson, ed., *Liturgies of the Western Church* (Philadelphia: Fortress Press, 1980), 125-26. The German "Hier bedürfte es nicht viel und gross Gesänges" can also be translated: "Here there would not be the need for much or extensive singing."

3. See, for example, Thompson, *Ibid.*, 152-53.

4. Howard G. Hageman, *Pulpit and Table: Some Chapters in the History of Worship in the Reformed Churches* (Richmond, VA: John Knox Press, 1962).

5. *Ibid.*, 14.

6. *Ibid.*

THE PALATINATE LITURGY
AND THE PENNSYLVANIA GERMANS[1]

Kenneth E. Rowe
Drew University

The Palatinate Church Order of 1563, containing the Heidelberg Catechism and the Palatinate liturgy, introduced a permanent Reformed tradition to Germany. The *Kirchenordnung* represented the effort of a moderate Lutheran (Melanchthonian) church to maintain its evangelical consciousness against the pressure of high Lutherans in the late Reformation period. Two centuries later the document continued to set the liturgical and doctrinal pattern for the Reformed branch of the German Protestant family who migrated to Pennsylvania in large numbers in the early eighteenth century.

The Heidelberg Catechism is well known and often studied. Its companion liturgy has been overlooked by liturgical scholars. Yet the liturgy is a formative text for three American denominations, the United Church of Christ, the Reformed Church of America, and the United Methodist Church (through the Church of the United Brethren in Christ). The text is not included in standard anthologies, such as Thompson's *Liturgies of the Western Church*. Neither is it mentioned in Jones, Wainwright, and Yarnold's *Study of Liturgy* or in White's *Protestant Worship: Traditions in Transition*. Bard Thompson translated the eucharistic liturgy in 1963 but published it in an obscure

United Church of Christ journal.[2] Apart from brief
discussion in two of his articles I can find only one doctoral
dissertation that tackles the liturgy, and it is a comparative
study of Episcopal, Presbyterian, Methodist, and German
Reformed rites spread over three centuries.[3]

My purpose in this paper is simply to whet appetites
for further research. The paper unfolds in four parts: 1) the
origin of the liturgy, 2) the shape of the liturgy, 3) the role
of music in the liturgy, and 4) its use among the
Pennsylvania Germans in the eighteenth century.

The Origin of the Liturgy

The Reformation came late to the Palatinate and its
capital city Heidelberg—so late that some scholars refer to
the movement as the second German reformation. Luther's
1518 lecture on justification by faith at Heidelberg
impressed few faculty and students.[4] Prince Ludwig kept
his province and his cathedral city Catholic until his death
in 1544. Within a year under a new prince there were signs
of change. At mass the Sunday before Christmas both the
new prince (Frederick II) and the preacher were startled
when the congregation struck up a Protestant hymn : "Es is
das Heil uns kommen her."

> Salvation hath come down to us
> Of freest grace and love.
> Works cannot stand before God's law,
> A broken reed they prove.
> Faith looks to Jesus Christ alone,
> He must for all our sins atone,
> He is our one Redeemer.[5]

Henceforth Frederick ordered the mass to be celebrated in
German and allowed priests to marry. Additional Protestant

doctrines and practices were introduced when the next elector Otto Henry came to the throne in 1554. Otto Henry's chief theological adviser was the moderate Lutheran, ecumenical statesman Melanchthon, who was trying to form a via media between the high Lutherans and the Calvinist sympathizers.

By the time Frederick III succeeded Otto Henry in 1559, the Reformation was firmly established in the Palatinate but the church was seriously divided as were many other "Lutheran" provinces in Germany.[6] The bishop (Tilemann Hesshus) was a high Lutheran (Gnesio-Lutheran), but Otto Henry had packed the university faculty with several prominent Reformed-leaning professors—e.g., Peter Boquin and Thomas Erastus—dubbed Crypto-Calvinists by the high Lutheran cabal. The court preacher was Michael Diller, a middle-of-the-road Melanchthonian. Matters came to a head later that year (1559) when, during a communion service in the Cathedral Church of the Holy Ghost, Bishop Hesshus snatched the cup from a young celebrant (deacon Wilhelm Klebitz) saying he was unworthy to administer it because he was a Zwinglian.[7] Weary of such strife, Frederick dismissed both the contentious bishop and the young deacon, but sided with the Reformed sympathizers. He hired additional Reformed-leaning young faculty for his university, notably Zacharias Ursinus and Caspar Olevianus. He simplified Heidelberg's public worship—altars, chalices, and wafers were set aside. He sought the counsel of Melanchthon. Finally, to avoid the old disputes and to bring harmony to the church, in 1562 Frederick appointed a theological commission to draft a new confession of faith and a new liturgy for the Palatinate.

Two young faculty members dominated the drafting, Zacharius Ursinus and Caspar Olevianus. Ursinus (1534-1583) studied with Melanchthon at Wittenberg.[8] Even in his student days he leaned toward Reformed doctrines, which was deepened by travel. He lost his first teaching job at Breslau for being a crypto-Calvinist and fled to Zurich where he took up with Heinrich Bullinger and Peter Martyr. Ursinus was appointed to the theological faculty at Heidelberg in 1561. Caspar Olevianus (1536-1587), though German, studied law at the University of Bourges in France and theology at Geneva under Calvin. He returned to teach in the Catholic-dominated city of his birth, Treves. Within a few months he was imprisoned and then banished for preaching a sermon on justification by faith. Frederick invited him to Heidelberg first as professor and then as bishop. Ursinus apparently chaired the catechism subcommittee and Olevianus chaired the liturgy sub-committee. The new liturgy and catechism were published in a single Church Order in 1563 along with directives for swift implementation in the university and in the parishes.

Matters came to a crisis three years later (1566) when Frederick was summoned to appear before the Diet in Augsburg in May 1566 to answer for the publication of his catechism and liturgy. The enemies of Frederick looked upon the catechism and liturgy as an infringement of German law, which permitted Protestantism only of the Lutheran variety as expressed in the Augsburg Confession. Frederick's passionate defense of his catechism and liturgy as truly biblical before his peers was persuasive. Fritz and his people were permitted to keep their new liturgy and catechism, although the Reformed Church did not have legal standing in Germany until the middle of the next century (1648) at the end of the Thirty Years' War.

The liturgy was widely used in the Reformed part of Germany through the seventeenth and into the eighteenth centuries, though frequent celebrations were discouraged by the inroads of Pietism on the one hand (due to the awesomeness of the occasion) and of Rationalism on the other (due to the embarrassing irrationality of the supper).[9]

The Shape of the Liturgy

1. *The Setting of the Liturgy*

Under the now kosher *Kirchenordnung* the churches of Heidelberg and other Palatinate towns and villages shed ornaments of any kind. Pictures were painted out, statues covered in black cloth, crosses removed, altars replaced by tables, and organs silenced. Psalms were no longer sung in Latin but in German and hymns were gradually introduced into public worship.[10] Ministers (no longer called priests) were directed to shun vestments (unlike their Lutheran neighbors who retained them) and use "genteel and plain apparel" in the discharge of their official duties.[11] Heidelbergers no longer spoke of the Mass but of "the Holy Lord's Supper," and no longer of the "altar" but of "the Table of the Lord." Holy days were reduced from over thirty to under ten (Christmas and the day after, New Year's, Easter and the day after, Ascension, Pentecost and the day after).[12] "At least once a month in the towns, once every two months in the villages, and on Easter, Pentecost and Christmas in both places" the church order directed the Lord's Supper to be celebrated. However, "where the edification, custom, or need of the churches may necessitate," a rubric suggested, "it is Christian and proper to observe it more often."[13]

2. *Liturgy of Preparation*[14]

On Saturday afternoons before communion Sundays a preparatory service was required as Bucer had done in

Strasbourg.[15]   After preaching a sermon "on the true understanding of the sacrament," the minister left the pulpit and stood in front of the table. Young persons wishing to be admitted to the sacrament were required to stand with the minister before the Holy Table and to recite the Creed, Ten Commandments, and the Lord's Prayer and to answer questions from the Catechism concerning the Lord's Supper. A general congregational examination then followed based on the three-fold structure of the Heidelberg Catechism (sin, redemption, duty) requiring the people's assent by the words, "We do" and "It is." The service concluded with an assurance of pardon, congregational repetition of the Lord's Prayer (said kneeling) and a blessing. Those who wished private confession and absolution spoke to the Minister who provided an opportunity, a practice that Melanchthon commended.

3. *Liturgy of the Word*

As the people gathered on Communion Sundays, they would have seen a wooden cup and a common plate or platter on the Table. The Minister opened the service with Scriptural sentences and began the Prayer Before the Sermon, which is a lengthy confession of sins adapted from the Genevan rite. In "well-ordered churches" wrote Calvin, confession is the proper beginning of worship, for its brings folk to "a true estimation" of themselves.   And by acknowledging their wretchedness, they also acknowledge "the goodness and mercy of our God." Thus, as Calvin put it, "the gate of prayer is opened."[16]   The last paragraph borrows heavily from Calvin's Collect for Illumination.[17] All prayed the Lord's Prayer. A Psalm would have been sung in German. A lection "on the Lord's death and on His Supper"[18] would have been read and a sermon preached.

According to a rubric at the head of the Lord's Supper
portion of the liturgy, the sermon that day was to be brief
and to set forth the "institution, order, reasons, profit and
fruit of the Holy Supper."[19]   Following the sermon the
Minister exhorted the people to a second Confession. All
prayed the classic prayer of the German Reformation from
the 1536 Lutheran Wurttemberg rite,[20] though in the first
person singular:

> I poor sinner, confess before thee, my God and
> Creator, that I, alas, have sinned against thee
> grievously and in manifold ways....

Using the first person singular the Minister pronounced
pardon. "I proclaim [declare] at God's command that [you]
are released in heaven from all [your] sins...."   The
Palatinate Absolution was more than a statement of
comfortable words. Following the tradition of Bucer and
Melanchthon, the minister, by the power of the keys,
personally repeated the promise of the Gospel.[21]   Calvin,
too, insisted that confession deserved to be followed by
absolution.   When people throw themselves on God's
mercy, he wrote, "it is no mean or trivial consolation to
have Christ's ambassador present, furnished with the
mandate of reconciliation."[22]   In this respect the Palatinate
Liturgy succeeded where Calvin failed, for the magistrates
of Geneva refused to countenance an absolution.

        The concluding prayers consist of intercessions from
Calvin's rite,[23] followed by the Lord's Prayer.   Festival
prayers and prayers for special occasions may be
substituted. The alternate prayer as printed in the liturgy is
inspired by Calvin's paraphrase of the Lord's Prayer[24] No
provision was made anywhere in the rite for "free" prayer.

4. *The Liturgy of the Table*

Standing "by the Table" the minister began the liturgy of with the recitation of the Pauline version of the Words of Institution (I Corinthians 11), followed by a lengthy Fencing of the Table from Calvin's liturgy and the 1554 edition of à Lasco's liturgy published by Micronius.[25] In the second part of the exhortation the promises of Christ are rehearsed in considerable detail. They were literally "preached" to use Calvin's term. The Word, he said, must be added to the sacrament for the sake of its efficacy. Not the elements but the people are to be consecrated.[26] A Prayer of Approach, with similarities to Anglican, Lutheran (Württemberg), and Calvinist usage, introduces the administration. In a genuine epiclesis the Minister invokes the presence and power of the Holy Spirit:

> Merciful God and Father, ... act upon our hearts by the Holy Spirit in this Supper, at which we keep the glorious memorial of the bitter death of thy dear Son Jesus Christ, that with true faith we may ever more yield ourselves to Him, and that through the power of the Holy Spirit our weary and contrite hearts may be fed and quickened by His true body and blood....

The people join in the "Our Father" and ask to be confirmed through the Supper "in the universal and undoubted Christian faith" which they then confess using the words of the Apostles' Creed.

Immediately before the distribution, paraphrasing the *Sursum Corda* in such a way as to concisely review the Calvinist doctrine of the supper, the minister continues:

> That we may now be fed with Christ, the true bread
> of heaven, let us not cleave with our hearts to this
> external bread and wine, but lift up our hearts and
> faith into heaven, where Jesus Christ is our
> Intercessor [Advocate, *Fursprecher*] at the right hand
> of His heavenly Father...and doubt not that through
> the action of the Holy Spirit, our souls shall be fed
> and nourished with His body and blood, as truly as
> we receive the holy bread and cup in remembrance of
> Him.

Thus the earthly signs of God's "coming down" to us—plain bread and wine—become vehicles to transport us above all things earthly and visible. Then the Minister breaks the bread and places it on a platter. Lutherans rejected the fraction; Calvinists insisted upon it as a symbolic denial of Christ's physical presence in the sacrament. Heidelberg Professor Thomas Erastus' classic statement of the Calvinist view on the breaking of the bread, *Das Buchlein vom Brotbrechen*, was published in 1563 concurrently with the Heidelberg Catechism.[27]

The communicants left their pews and walked to the Table where they remained standing, unlike the Lutherans who knelt before the table and the Dutch who sat around it. The minister delivered a piece of bread to each communicant using Words of Delivery similar to those found in the liturgies of Calvin, Farel, Knox and à Lasco: "The bread which we break is a communion of the body of Christ."[28] While giving the cup to each, the minister said, "The cup of blessing which we bless is the communion of the blood of Christ." During the communion of the people some churches sang psalms and hymns, a practice popularized by Bucer through his Strasbourg Liturgy. In other churches a minister (or lay reader?) read portions of

Scripture "helpful to the remembrance of Christ's death," such as John 14-18 and Isaiah 53 as specified in the rubrics. When all had communed the Minister prayed a thanksgiving. Two texts are given. The first thanksgiving is a skillful interweaving of Psalm 103 and Romans 5.[29] I have been unable to identify the source of the second thanksgiving (Almighty, merciful God and Father, we give thee most hearty thanks...).[30] With the words "Praise ye the Lord with your song" the Minister announced a concluding Psalm. The Minister then pronounced the Aaronic blessing. Following à Lasco's practice, the people placed alms in a basin or basket at the door as they went out in peace.

Music in the Liturgy

Music was integral to Luther's *Deutsche Messe*. The lections, though in the vernacular, continued to be sung and the congregation was expected to join in singing hymns and psalms, a practical expression of the doctrine of the priesthood of all believers.[31] Although the chanting of lections was rejected by Olevianus and Frederick's liturgical commission, the Lutheran practice of congregational singing was considered essential. But in selecting what was proper to be sung, the liturgical commission followed Calvin and specified Psalms. An early rubric titled "Of Ecclesiastical Singing" made indebtedness to Calvin on the matter of music in the liturgy clear:

> With reference to the singing of Psalms, the Apostle Paul admonishes that it be done not only with the mouth, but the with the heart as well; and that all of it should be useful to the edification of the churches. But as the heart cannot praise God by that which it does not understand, we herewith require that none

other than German Psalms be sung in our churches.[32]

The liturgy prescribed psalms to be sung at the opening and closing of "Common Prayer" and during the reception on communion days. Although Calvin's Genevan Psalter was completed and published in 1562 it was Ambrosius Lobwasser's *Psalter des koniglichen Propheten Davids* (Leipzig, 1573) which long dominated Reformed church music books. To the 1593 Herborn edition of Lobwasser an appendix of "geistliche Lieder" were added. Lutherans labelled Lobwasser's psalter Calvinistic, calling it a mere rhymer's work, which obscured the evangelical spirit of the Psalms. The Lutherans countered with Cornelius Becker's 1602 psalter set to Lutheran tunes. Lutheran hymnals from the 1520s routinely mixed hymns with psalms. Not till the latter half of the seventeenth century did the German Reformed Church relax the exclusive use of Psalms and produce hymns equal to the best Lutheran hymns—notably hymns by Joachim Neander, Frederich Lampe and Gerhard Tersteegen.[33]

The Use of the Liturgy by the Pennsylvania Germans

Germans began to settle in English America in significant numbers in the late-seventeenth and early-eighteenth centuries. The great majority came to Pennsylvania, where by 1750 they numbered approximately 100,000, constituting one-third to one-half of the colony's population.[34] Three religious groups predominated-Lutheran, Reformed, and sectarian (Mennonites, Dunkards, Amish, and Moravians). Pennsylvania also had several

small and widely-scattered communities of German
Catholics in the eighteenth century. All except the sectarians, who relied on lay
ministers, were short of ordained clergy.[35]   For the
Lutherans and Reformed, liturgical books and hymnals were
also scarce. But there is no reason to doubt the tradition
that the Palatinate Liturgy was used for German Reformed
celebrations of the Lord's Supper in colonial America.[36]
The liturgy, though not published in America until 1798,
did not demand a large number of copies for congregational
use and German Reformed hymnals containing significant
liturgical materials were published beginning in 1752 and
steadily thereafter in revised editions.

In the absence of ordained ministers, lay leaders,
(often the community's school teacher) read the Palatinate
liturgy of the Word and a sermon accompanied by songs on
Sundays and holy days and also conducted funerals, but
congregations had to live without Baptism or the
Lord's Supper. Johann Philip Boehm, a schoolteacher,
exercised such a lay ministry among the German Reformed
in eastern Pennsylvania from 1720 until he was ordained in
1729.[37] In his reports to the Synod of Holland[38] Boehm
reported that his sacramental services were conducted
according to the "High German Church Order."[39]

In 1746 the Reformed Classis of Amsterdam, which
supervised both German and Dutch Reformed missions in
the colonies, sent Michael Schlatter (1716-1790)[40] to the
colonies to bring order to Pennsylvania's German
Reformed.[41]   The organizing coetus (synod) which met in
Philadelphia in 1747 adopted the Heidelberg Catechism and
the Canons of Dort, but did not bind itself to the use of a
particular liturgy.[42] Controversy soon broke out between
Boehm and Schlatter over liturgy—Boehm preferred the
Palatinate rite; Schlatter preferred the Swiss Reformed rite

of St. Gall.[43] Boehm complained that Schlatter's use of
the St. Gall rite was strange to the people and requested the
Dutch authorities to "give instruction to adhere only to all
the formulas which are ... in the Palatinate Church Order."
Boehm requested that copies of the Palatinate Church Order
be sent so each parish could have one for its minister or lay
leader.[44]   According   to   Richards,   Boehm's   view
prevailed.[45] In 1794 the Coetus censured a minister who
"had administered the sacraments of Baptism and the Lord's
Supper contrary to the set orders of the Church."[46] Thus
the Palatinate Liturgy was informally established by custom,
if not precept, as the most commonly used sacramental
liturgy of both Dutch and German Reformed in America
during the colonial period. The number of required
celebrations of the Lord's Supper, however, was reduced
probably more for practical then theological reasons. The
second German Reformed Coetus of 1748 prescribed twice-
yearly celebrations versus monthly/bi-monthly plus holy
days as prescribed by the 1563 church order.[47]

By the middle of the century, Great Awakening-style
revivals were sweeping Pennsylvania Dutch country.[48]
Unlike nineteenth-century revivals, the Lord's supper was
invested with great spiritual importance, for often as not the
sacramental observance might be the occasion of an
outpouring of revival fervor. The German Reformed, like
their Presbyterian and Methodist neighbors, administered
the Lord's Supper in the context of annual or semiannual
"sacramental seasons," often four-day affairs beginning on
Friday and lasting till Monday.[49] German Reformed—like
Methodists—used forms for the administration of the
sacraments and other general services, while practicing
extemporaneous prayer for their preaching services.

At the time of their organization as a self-governing
American church in 1793, the liturgical and sacramental life

of the German Reformed Church in the United States was not precisely defined. The Church had traditionally honored the Heidelberg Catechism and the Palatinate Liturgy. Both of these standards presented the Holy Communion as a theologically substantive rite to be observed frequently. Yet the Church was hampered in the effort to be faithful to its liturgical tradition by shortages of books and ministers.

Soon after gaining independence from Dutch oversight, the German Reformed Church had solved problems of clergy recruitment and support and in 1798 published the Palatinate Liturgy.[50] The *Kirchen Formularien der Evangelisch Reformirten Gemeinden* contained no order for Sunday services, but did provide forms for baptism, preparation for communion, and the Lord's Supper, as well as services for excommunication and restoration, marriage and ordination. Together with the revised hymnbook, which was published the previous year, the newly independent church now had the liturgical books it needed.

As in Germany, the singing of Psalms and hymns in public worship and especially at the communion became common practice in Pennsylvania. The earliest piece of German Reformed liturgical literature printed in America was a hymnal published by Christopher Sauer in Philadelphia in 1752, *Kern Alter und Neuer in 700. Bestehender, Geistreicher Lieder* (The Best Old and New Spiritual Songs).[51] Its publication may have been arranged to counter the growing popularity of the deeply Pietist Dunkard/Brethren hymnal *Das Kleine Davidische Psalter-Spiel* (The Small Davidic Psaltery) published by Sauer eight years earlier.[52] The title page of the new hymnal stated that the book was designed for use in the "Reformed churches in Hesse, Hanover, the Palatinate and

Pennsylvania." Its first 168 hymns are arranged according to a calendar more Lutheran than "reformed" since hymns were given for Advent, Christmas, New Year's, Epiphany, Presentation of Christ, Annunciation, Visitation of the Blessed Virgin Mary, the Passion, Easter, Ascension, and Pentecost. Sixteen hymns on the Lord's Supper are included. The remaining 532 hymns, arranged under headings according to the *ordo salutis*, indicate a shift in German hymnody from confessional hymns (*Bekentnisslied*) to pietistic and devotional hymns (*Erbauungslied*). In addition to hymns, the book contains liturgical collects, epistles and gospels for every Sunday as well as for festival and saints' days, plus a collection of daily prayers (including prayers for use before and after the sacrament), the Apostles' and Nicene Creeds and the Heidelberg Catechism, but no liturgy.

The next year (1753) Saur published Lobwasser's Psalter[53] for the German Reformed. These two books, the hymnal and psalter, were routinely bound together into one fat volume. Together they were the people's liturgy book. The Palatinate liturgy was essentially a ministerial liturgy; extensive congregational responses were not required. The Lord's Prayer and the Apostles' Creed, along with a few expressions of assent were all that was required. Winter is wrong, in my judgment, in concluding that since the first American printing of the Palatinate liturgy did not occur until 1798, it was rarely used.[54] Only one copy per parish would have been required for its full use and the official hymnal/psalter was clearly designed for a liturgical church.

Hymnals were in short supply. During the Revolutionary War Saur's publishing house was confiscated so hymnals were scarce. The organizing synod of 1793 appointed a committee of six clergy to revise the hymnal and psalter and to oversee their speedy printing. Four years later (1797), the revised psalter and hymnal were finally published. The new 148-page Psalter, *Das Neue und Verbesserte Gesang-buch, Worinnen die Psalmen Davids,* was based on Psalm paraphrases by Lobwasser, Spreng and the new "Herborner gesangbuch."[55] Its companion was a 585-page *Sammlung Alter und Neuer Geistreicher Lieder, zur Offentlichen und Besondern Erbauung der Evangelisch-Reformirten Gemeinen in den Vereinigten Staaten von America* compiled from the "Marburger und Pfalzer [i.e. Palatinate] gesangbuch" with additions from various other German hymnals.[56]

> We have chosen the most edifying and best known hymns in the Marburg and Palatinate hymn-books, composed by Joachim Neander, Friedrich Adolph Lampe, Caspar Zollikofer, and other godly men among the Protestants. To these we have added a number of edifying spiritual songs, taken from the hymn-books recently published in various parts of Germany. The metres are arranged throughout according to the Palatinate hymn-book. (preface)

Five editions of each were published by Germantown (Philadelphia) printers Melchoir Steiner and Michael Billmeyer through 1814, routinely bound together as one hymnal.[57] The liturgical material of the 1752 edition was retained in each successive edition.

As the wayward "Dutch" of colonial Pennsylvania were being formed into independent denominations, the Reformed branch of the family, despite heavy Pietist influence, kept the Palatinate liturgy in place. In the early national period (early years of the nineteenth century) as support for revivalist practices grew among German Reformed pastors and congregations, their commitment to the old liturgy waned.

Endnotes

1. An earlier draft of this paper was delivered to the History of Modern Liturgy section at the 1991 annual meeting of the North American Academy of Liturgy, Minneapolis, January, 1991.

2. "The Palatinate Liturgy, Heidelberg, 1563," [translated with notes by Bard Thompson] *Theology and Life* 6/1 (Spring 1963), 49-67.

3. Robert Milton Winter, *American Churches and the Holy Communion: a Comparative Study in Sacramental Theology, Practice and Piety in the Episcopal, Presbyterian, Methodist and German Reformed Traditions 1607-1875*. Unpublished doctoral dissertation, Union Theological Seminary, Richmond, VA, 1988.

4. Graduate student Martin Bucer was a notable exception. For essential background see Bard Thompson's two chapters "Historical Background of the Catechism" and "The Reformed Church in the Palatinate" in *Essays on the Heidelberg Catechism*. Philadelphia : United Church Press, 1963, 8-30; and Bard Thompson, "The Palatinate Church Order of 1563," *Church History* 23/4 (December 1954), 339-354.

5. Written by Paul Speratus in 1523, this hymn was sung in a number of German cities when the Reformation was introduced. Luther included it in his first hymnbook *Etlich christlich lieder*, 1524. To reinforce the notion that these hymns were the Word of God in song, every line was given its Scriptural source. See Robin A. Leaver, "'Then the Whole Congregation Sings" : The Sung Word in Reformation Worship," *Drew Gateway* 60/1 (Fall 1990), 61.

6. Frederick led the Palatinate from 1559 until 1576. See Owen Chadwick, "The Making of a Reforming Prince : Frederick III, Elector Palatine," in *Reformation, Conformity and Dissent: Essays in Honour of Geoffrey Nuttall*, edited by R. Buick Knox. London : Epworth Press, 1977, 44-69; and Henry J. Cohn, "The Territorial Princes in Germany's Second Reformation, 1559-1622," in *International Calvinism*, edited by Menna Prestwich. Oxford: Clarendon Press, 1985, [135]-165.

7. Klebitz published *Seven Theses on the Eucharist* that year in which he insisted upon the necessity of faith for a valid eucharist.

8. The most important recent work on Ursinus has been done by Derk Visser: *Zacharias Ursinus, The Reluctant Reformer* (New York: United Church Press, 1983). See also his essay "Zacharias Ursinus and the Palatinate Reformation" and another by Howard G. Hageman, "The Lasting Significance of Ursinus," in *Controversy and Conciliation, The Reformation and the Palatinate 1559-1583* edited by Derk Visser (Allison Park, PA: Pickwick Publications, 1986), 1-20 and 229-238.

9. The 1728 General Synod of the Reformed Church in Germany declared: "It does not become any individual minister, yea, not even a provincial Synod, to make any changes in the administration of the Word of God, the Holy Supper, Holy Baptism, and the form of conducting worship, as handed down to us...."

10. Bard Thompson, ed.,"The Palatinate Liturgy, Heidelberg, 1563," *Theology and Life* 6/1 (Spring 1963), 51, note 3.

11. Thompson, "The Palatinate Liturgy," 52, note 3.

12. Scripture lections and the content of sermons were prescribed for each festival day. See Thompson, "Palatinate Liturgy," 49f, note 2.

13. Thompson, "Palatinate Liturgy," 56.

14. For a full English translation of "The Preparation for the Holy Supper," see Thompson, "The Palatinate Liturgy," pages 56ff. My reconstruction of the liturgy that follows is heavily dependent on the pioneering work of Bard Thompson and the more recent descriptions of the rite by Robert M. Winter, *American Churches and the Holy Communion*, 683ff.

15. Hermann von Wied's 1545 Cologne Church Order (*A Simple and Religious Consultation*) called for a Saturday evening service of preparation. Bucer played a major part in drafting von Wied's Church Order.

16. *Institutes* 3:4:10f.

17. For a full English translation of the liturgy, see Bard Thompson, "The Palatinate Liturgy" cited above.

18. Epistles and Gospels for each Sunday in the church year and for festival and saints' days were provided in the earliest German Reformed hymnals.

19. Thompson, "Palatinate Liturgy," 59.

20. Edition 1536. See A. L. Richter, *Die evangelischen Kirchenordnungen des sechszehnten Jarhhunderts*, II (Leipzig : Gunther, 1871), 277.

21. Compare the Cologne formula.

22. *Institutes* 3:4:12ff.

23. Both structure and content agree with Pollanus' 1554 edition of Calvin's Strasbourg rite, *Liturgia Sacra*.

24. *Calvini opera* VI, 178-179.

25. See Calvin's Great Thanksgiving in Pollanus' edition of *Liturgia sacra*.

26. *Institutes* 4:14; see also 4:17:39.

27. See Bodo Nischan, "The 'Fractio Panis' : A Reformed Communion Practice in Late Reformation Germany," *Church History* 3/1 (March 1984), 17-29.

28. In some cases the platter is passed and each communicant breaks off a piece of bread.

29. John à Lasco's *Forma ac Ratio* specified Psalm 103 to be sung or said as a post-communion Thanksgiving.

30. Perhaps based on the practice of Marian exiles in Frankfurt?

31. See Leaver, note #5 above.

32. See Calvin's preface to his 1547 (?) rite; see also Thompson, "The Palatinate Liturgy," 51f, note 3.

33. See "Psalters, Versions in German," appendix I, in John Julian, *A Dictionary of Hymnology*, Revised edition with a new supplement (London : John Murray, 1915 [c1907]), 1543.

34. See Marianne Wokeck, *A Tide of Alien Tongues: The Flow and Ebb of German Immigration to Pennsylvania, 1683-1776*. Unpublished doctoral dissertation, Temple University, 1982.

35. A major reason for the small number of ministers was inadequate fianancial support, for unlike their counterparts in Europe, the German religious groups in America received no financial aid from the state and voluntary contributions were rarely adequate to meet the churches' needs.

36. Early documentation for the use of the Palatinate Liturgy in Pennsylvania is the Mayer MS (I.15) cited in Joseph Henry Dubbs, *Historic Manual of the Reformed Church in the United States* (Lancaster, PA: Inquirer Printing Co., 1885), 256.

37. Some families took their children to Philadelphia to be baptized by the Presbyterian pastor. The nearest Reformed clergy were Freylinghusen and his Dutch Reformed associates in New Jersey, but their revivalism repelled Boehm. So Boehm traveled to New York in 1729 to be ordained by the Dutch Calvinists. By the early 1740s Boehm was filling five pulpits simultaneously while itinerating to outlying congregations in southeastern Pennsylvania.

38. The Dutch, through the Classis of Amsterdam, exercised oversight of the German Reformed in America until they became an independent church body in 1793. The result was a warm friendship between German and Dutch Reformed in the colonies, for in spite of geographic and linguistic differences, both bodies used the Heidelberg Catechism

and the Palatinate Liturgy. The Palatinate Liturgy was translated into Dutch by Petrus Dathenus in 1566, taken out of the Church Order and appended to the metrical Psalter in the Genevan fashion. Modified and expanded, the Netherlands Liturgy reached its definitive form in 1619 as adopted by the Synod of Dort. An English translation was published in New York in 1767, but would hardly have been used by German Reformed pastors. For a full study of the Dutch liturgy see Daniel James Meeter, *The North American Liturgy: A Critical Edition of the Liturgy of the Reformed Dutch Church in North American, 1793*, unpublished doctoral dissertation, Drew University, 1989.

39. Citations in George W. Richards, *History of the Theological Seminary of the Reformed Church in the United States* (Lancaster, PA: Rudisill, 1952), 28-30.

40. A native of St. Gall in Switzerland, Schlatter had obtained his early education there, was confirmed in its Reformed Church, and had become a Pietist. Before going to America he held two brief pastorates in Switzerland. From his arrival in August of 1746 the thirty-year-old Schlatter visited widely scattered German Reformed congregations in Pennsylvania, New Jersey, Maryland and Virginia instructing them in the doctrines of the Heidelberg Catechism. In 1751 he returned to Europe for additional funds and personnel. In the following year he brought back from the German Reformed university at Herborn six ordained ministers, the most effective of whom was Philip William Otterbein, later founder of the Church of the United Brethren in Christ. See Henry Harbaugh, *The Life of Rev. Michael Schlatter* (Philadelphia: Lindsay and Blakiston, 1857).

41. The Classis' Committee of Deputies for External Affairs acted as a foreign mission board for the whole Dutch church, executing all the duties which, for example, the Church of England had given to the Bishop of London and to the Society for the Propagation of the Gospel in Foreign Parts.

42. *Minutes and Letters of the Coetus of the German Reformed Congregations* (Philadelphia : Reformed Church Publication Board, 1903), 40. See also "Church Order of 1748" in William J. Hinke, ed., *Life and Letters of the Rev. John Philip Boehm, Founder of the*

Reformed Church in Pennsylvania, 1683-1749 (New York: Arno Press, 1972), 463-467.

43. Schlatter was an enthusiastic Pietist; Boehm was not.

44. William J. Hinke, ed., *Life and Letters of the Rev. John Philip Boehm*, 452.

45. George W. Richards, *History of the Theological Seminary of the Reformed Church in the United States* (Lancaster, PA: Rudisill, 1952), 332-333.

46. *Acts and Proceedings of the Coetus and Synod of the German Reformed Church in the United States from 1791 to 1816 inclusive*, translated from the German (Allentown, PA: Zion's Reformed Church, 1930). Originally printed at Chambersburg, PA by M. Kieffer & Co., 1854, 11.

47. See *Minutes and Letters of the Coetus of the German Reformed Congregations in Pennsylvania 1747-1972* (Philadelphia: Reformed Church Publication Board, 1903), 50. See also H.M.J.Klein, *The History of the Eastern Synod of the Reformed Church in the United States* (Lancaster, PA: Eastern Synod, 1943), 41-43. John Philip Boehm's January 1739 report to the Classis of Amsterdam suggests twice-yearly celebrations of communion in several Pennsylvania congregations, *Minutes and Letters of the Coetus of the German Reformed Congregations in Pennsylvania 1747-1792* (Philadelphia: Reformed Church Publication Board, 1903), 6.

48. John B. Frantz uses the phrase "German Awakening" in "The Awakening of Religion among the German Settlers in the Middle Colonies," *William and Mary Quarterly* 33 (April 1976), 266-288. See also Frantz's unpublished doctoral dissertation on which this article is based: *Revivalism in the German Reformed Church in the United States to 1850, with emphasis on the Eastern Synod* (University of Pennsylvania), 1961. See also Stephen L. Longenecker, *Piety and Tolerance: Pennsylvania German Religion, 1700-1850* (Metuchen, N.J., Scarecrow Press), 1994, chapters 5 and 6.

49. See Leigh Eric Schmidt, *Holy Fairs: Scottish Communions and American Revivals in the Early Modern Period* (Princeton: Princeton University Press, 1989).

50. *Kirchen-formularien der Evangelisch-Reformirten Gemeinen.* Germantaun [Philadelphia]: Michael Billmeyer, 1798. 60p. In 1767 an English translation of the Netherlands Liturgy (Drathenus' Dutch translation of the Palatinate liturgy) was published in New York City and was used by both Dutch and German Reformed ministers in the colonies. See David D. Demarest, *The Reformed Church in America.* (New York: Board of Publication of the Reformed Church in America, 1889), 146-147. But Pennsylvania's German pastors and congregations preferred the text in German.

51. *Kern alter und neuer, in 700. bestehender geistreicher lieder, welche sowohl bey dem offentlichen Gottesdienste in denen Reformirten kirchen der hessisch-hanauisch-pfaltzisch-pensilvanischen und mehren andern angrantzenden landen, als auch zur privatandacht und erbauung nutzlich konnen gebraucht werden. Nebst Joachimi Neandri bundesliedern, mit beygefugten morgen- und abend- und communion-gebatern, wie auch Catechismo und Simbolis. Nach dem neuesten gesangbuch, welches gedruckt zu Marburg bey Johann Henrich Stock, nun zum ersten mahl gedruckt zu Germanton bey C. Saur,* 1752. 562p. Saur published four editions, a second in 1763, a third in 1772 and a fourth in 1774. The hymnal was first published in Marburg in 1746 and again in 1750. I am indebted to my colleague Howard Hageman for pointing me to this hymnal. See also Howard Hageman, *Pulpit and Table*, 49. The hymnal included some of the most popular hymns recently written by Joachim Neander, "Lobe dem Herren, den machtigen Konig der Ehren," "Sich, hier bin ich Ehrenkonig," and "Unser Herrscher, unser Konig."

52. See Hedwig T. Durnbaugh, *The German Hymnody of the Brethren, 1720-1903* (Philadelphia: Brethren Encyclopedia, Inc., 1986), 41-57.

53. *Neu-vermehrt- und vollstandiges gesang-buch, worinnen sowohl die Psalmen Davids, nach d. Ambrosii Lobwassers ubersetzung hin und wieder verbessert* (Germantown [Philadelphia]: Christoph Saur, 1753), 214p. Four editions were published through 1774.

54. Winter, *American Churches and the Holy Communion*, 691.

55. The title-page reference to the new "Herborner gesangbuch" may refer to Wilhelm Heinrich Seel, *Psalmen* (Herborn: 1787); the first edition of Johann Jacob Spreng's *Neue Ubersetzung der Psalmen Davids* was published in Basel in 1741.

56. The 1793 Coetus agreed that "improvements should be made in a Hymn book which is to be used in all our churches and congregations." Six clergy were appointed a committee "to attend to this duty." *Acts and Proceedings of the Coetus and Synod of the German Reformed Church in the United States from 1791 to 1816 inclusive* (Allentown, PA: Zion's Reformed Church, 1930), 8-9. Three years later the Synod minutes reported an interview with Germantown printer Melchoir Steiner in reference to printing of the new Hymn book. "Mr. Steiner proposes to print it by next fall at the most reasonable price. It was resolved by the majority of the ministers that they would support it." *Acts and Proceedings*, 19. Steiner's successor, Michael Billmeyer, asked the 1799 Synod for, and received an advance toward, the publication of a revised edition of the hymn book. *Acts and Proceedings*, 25. The 1800 Synod transferred the copyright for the Hymn book to Billmeyer, *Acts and Proceedings*, 27.

57. A second edition in 1799, a third in 1806, a fourth in 1813, and a fifth in 1814.

LECTION, SERMON, AND CONGREGATIONAL SONG: A PREACHING LECTIONARY OF THE DUTCH REFORMED CHURCH (1782) AND ITS IMPLICATIONS

Robin A. Leaver
Westminster Choir College of Rider College
and Drew University

In 1960 Howard Hageman, then pastor of the North Reformed Dutch Church, Newark, New Jersey, was invited to give the Stone Lectures at Princeton Theological Seminary. One primary concern of these lectures, which were later published,[1] was to investigate the paradox that in English-speaking Reformed churches, while Calvin's liturgical legacy had been the subject of exhaustive study, very little of that legacy was observable in the practice of worship in those churches. Hageman wrote in the preface: "This question is all the more enticing when we consider Calvin's enormous influence in almost every other area of the life of the Reformed churches."[2] Hageman's Stone Lectures were principally concerned with the recovery of liturgical form in the Reformed tradition, but, as his later writings and teaching amply demonstrate, liturgical form in the Reformed tradition cannot exist without a high regard for liturgical preaching within the context of liturgical time.[3]

Hageman's liturgical perspectives were formed by the heritage of the church in which he grew up, and later served as a minister and theological teacher. The Reformed Church in America has its origins in the Dutch West-India Company, chartered to develop the Dutch colony of the New Netherlands along the Hudson River valley in the early seventeenth century.[4] For nearly a century and a half these American Dutch churches were supervised by the Classis, clergy ministerium, in Amsterdam. A separate Classis for these North American churches was not formed until 1747, although theological training and ordination continued to take place only in the Netherlands. After protracted negotiations, which were extended by the Revolutionary War, these Dutch churches in America resolved, in 1784, to establish a theological seminary. In 1810 this theological institution, initially situated in New York, moved to New Jersey, to become the New Brunswick Seminary—still known today as "the Dutch Reformed Seminary." Howard Hageman was first a student then a teacher of this seminary, and ultimately became its president and historian.[5]

The Dutch Reformed Churches in the Netherlands have continued to influence the Reformed Church in America throughout its existence, but that influence was particularly marked during the immediate post-Revolutionary years, the first period of independence from Britain. In April 1782 John Adams was received in The Hague as the official representative of the newly-founded United States of America, and a few months later the Dutch envoy to America was warmly received by the Continental Congress, then in session in what is now Nassau Hall of Princeton University, New Jersey.[6] All the ministers of the Dutch churches in the New World had been theologically trained and ordained half a world away in the Netherlands, but in thought and action they remained close to their mentors and colleagues in the Old World.

In the same year that John Adams arrived in the Netherlands, an interesting preaching lectionary, based on the church year, was issued by the Dutch Reformed Classis in Rotterdam:

> TEXT- | BOEKJE, | Waer in | Alle de Texten der H. Schrifture | begrepen zyn, dewelke to Ge- | dagtenis van CHRISTI GE- | BOORTE, BESNYDENIS | LYDEN en STERVEN | OPSTANDINGE en | HEMELVAART. | Mitsgaders | Zendinge des H. Geestes op | den Pinxterdag; jaerlyks | worden verklaerd en | toegeëigend aen de | GEMIENTE CHRISTI | BINNEN ROTTERDAM | Met Consent van den E. Herkenraed. | TE ROTTERDAM. | Gedrukt by JOHANNES RUYS, | Boekdrukker en Boekverkoper/ in de | West-Wagestraat. | Met Privilegie 1782.

The title can be translated thus: "Text-Book, Wherein is comprehended all the Texts of Holy Scripture in which is recorded the Birth, Circumcision, Passion and Death, Resurrection and Ascension of Christ. Together with the Sending of the Holy Spirit at Pentecost; annually expounded and appropriated in the Parish of Christ within Rotterdam."[7]

The publishing of such annual cycles of Biblical preaching texts was an established practice in the Dutch Reformed Church. Thus the preface to the Rotterdam *Text-Boekje* of 1782 indicates that it is a "new edition," implying an earlier Rotterdam imprint, and that other cities, such as Dordrecht, The Hague, Amsterdam, and Utrecht, also published such text-books.[8]

There were four Dutch Reformed churches in Rotterdam: the Grote, Prince, Zuider, and Ooster churches.

In 1782 these four churches were served by fourteen Domines (ministers), who between them had amassed almost 230 years of preaching experience in Rotterdam![9] The weekly pattern of preaching in the four Rotterdam churches was as follows:[10]

Sunday
  Grote Kerk:
        7:00 a.m. Early Service
        Summer only; omitted on Communion Sundays[11]

        9:00 a.m. Morning Service
        On Communion Sundays the service begins at 8:00 a.m. in the Summer; 8:30 a.m. in Winter

        2:00 p.m. Afternoon Service

Zuider Kerk, Prince Kerk, and Ooster Kerk:
  Morning and Afternoon Services

Tuesday	5:00 p.m.	Evening Service (Grote Kerk)
Wednesday	9:00 p.m.	Morning Service (Grote Kerk)
Thursday	5:00 p.m.	Evening Service (Grote Kerk)
Friday	9:00 a.m.	Morning Service (Zuider Kerk)
Saturday	2:00 p.m.	Afternoon Service (Grote Kerk)

This pattern represents the minimal weekly pattern of preaching services. At specific times and seasons this basic pattern was modified by addition and subtraction, as the following notes illustrate:

> Of the sermons [i.e. preaching services] in the week, it should be remembered that on Thursday after a prayer day [Biddag], on the Tuesday after Easter and

Pentecost, on the Wednesday before and the Friday after Ascension, as well as on the day before Christmas [i.e. Christmas Eve], and before and after New Year's Day (with no Sunday in between) there is no service. Note also that the Wednesday Prayer services [Bedestonden] in time of war are usually held in the Grote, Zuider and Ooster churches in the evening at 7.00 pm... Lastly... on New Year's Day (where no Sunday intervenes) on the second day of Easter [= Easter Monday], the second day of Pentecost [= Monday] and on the second day of Christmas [= 26 December] (when there is no Sunday coming) there are services... NB. On Ascension Day there is a service in the morning only in the Grote and Zuider churches.[12]

The *Text-Boekje* gives verbatim the texts that are to be read and preached upon throughout the course of a year, and comprises some 167 pages. Its readings are structured around the principal festivals and seasons of the church year: Christmas, New Year [= Circumcision and Naming of Jesus], Passion, Easter, Ascension, and Pentecost. With the exception of the Passion texts, the pericopes are not simply given in a sequential pattern, but are assigned to particular services on specific days (see below). In contrast, the Passion texts are given in a sequence, numbered from I to XLIX, and covers chronologically the history of the passion of Christ. In many respects these readings parallel the history of the Passion and Resurrection extracted from all four Gospels, compiled by Bugenhagen in the sixteenth century for Lutheran liturgical use.[13] The Dutch text books for the principal seasons of the church year appear to have evolved from similar compilations of the Biblical history of the passion.[14]

The Rotterdam *Text-Boekje* usually gives more than one or two references in each numbered section. The exceptions are those primary passages that stand on their own, such as Jesus sweating drops of blood (XI), "My kingdom is not of this world" (XXV), "Behold the Man!" (XXXIII) and "Father, forgive them" (XL).

The preface to the *Text-Boekje* indicates that these Passion readings are to be used at the discretion of the preacher "during the season when the history of the Passion is preached,"[15] that is, pre-Easter. This implies that not all the Passion texts would be covered in a single year, although it would be possible to do so. With two services on a Sunday, and one daily, from Tuesday to Saturday, each week in Rotterdam, a total of seven services, the entire cycle of Passion texts could have been expounded consecutively in seven weeks, which is just a little longer than the traditional season of Lent.

The lectionary of the *Text-Boekje* is as follows:

Texts Concerning the Birth of Christ

Christmas	Morning:	Luke 2.1-7
Day	Afternoon:	Luke 2.8-12
	Evening:	Luke 2.13-14
26 December	Morning:	Luke 2.15-16
	Afternoon:	Luke 2.17-20

Texts Concerning the Circumcision of Christ

| New Year's | Morning: | Luke 2.21^a |
| Day | Evening: | Luke 2.21^b |

Texts Concerning the Passion of Christ

| [I.] | Matt. 26.1-5; Mark 14.1-2; Luke 22.1-2 |
| II. | Matt 26.6-9; Mark 14.3-5; John 12.1-6 |

III.	Matt. 26.10-13; Mark 14.6-9; John 12.7-8
IV.	Matt. 26.14-16; Mark 14.10-11; Luke 22.3-6; John 13.2
V.	Matt. 26.17-19; Mark 14.12-16; Luke 22.7-13
VI.	Matt. 26.20-25; Mark 14.17-21; John 13.21-30
VII.	Matt. 26.30-32; Mark 14.26-28; Luke 22. 31-32,39; John 18.1^a
VIII.	Matt. 26.33-35; Mark 14.29-31; Luke 22.33-34
IX.	Matt. 26.36-38; Mark 14.32-24; Luke 22.39; John 18.1^b-2
X.	Matt. 26.39-46; Mark 14.25-42; Luke 22.40-42, 45-46
XI.	Luke 22.43-44
XII.	John 18.3-9; Matt. 26.47; Mark 14.43; Luke 22.47^a
XIII.	Matt. 26.48-50; Mark 14.44-46; Luke 22.47-48
XIV.	Matt. 26.51-54; Mark 14.47; Luke 22.49-51; John 18.10-11
XV.	Matt. 26.55-56; Mark 14.48-52; Luke 22.52-53
XVI.	John 18.12-14, 19, 24; Matt. 26.57; Mark 14.53
XVII.	Matt. 26.59-63; Mark 14.55-61^a
XVIII.	Matt. 26.63^b-64; Mark 14.61^b-62
XIX.	Matt. 26.65-68; Mark 14.63-65; Luke 22.63-65, 71
XX.	Matt. 26.69-74; Mark 14.54, 66-71; Luke 22.54^b-60^a; John 18.15-18, 25-27
XXI.	Luke 22.60^b-62; Matt. 26.75; Mark 14.72; John 18.27^b

XXII.	John 18.28-32; Matt. 27.1-2; Mark 14.1; Luke 23.1
XXIII.	Matt. 27.3-10; Acts 1.18
XXIV.	Matt. 27.11-14; Mark 15.2-5; Luke 23.2-3, 5
XXV.	John 18.33-36
XXVI.	John 18.37-38; Luke 23.4;
XXVII.	Luke 23.6-12
XXVIII.	Luke 23.13-16
XXIX.	Matt. 27.15-18; Mark 15.6-10; Luke 23.17-19; John 18.39-40[b]
XXX.	Matt. 27.19-23; Mark 15.11-14; Luke 23.20-23; John 18.40
XXXI.	Matt. 27. 24-26[a]; Mark 15.15[a]; Luke 23.24-25[a]
XXXII.	John 19.1-4; Matt. 27.27-30; Mark 15.15[b]-19; Luke 23.25[b]
XXXIII.	John 19.5-7
XXXIV.	John 19.8-12
XXXV.	John 19.13-16[a]
XXXVI.	Matt. 27.31-32; Mark 15.20-21; Luke 23.26; John 19.16[a]-17[b]
XXXVII.	Luke 23.27-31
XXXVIII.	Mark 15.22-25; Matt. 27.33-36, 38; Luke 23.33; John 19.17[b]-18, 23-24
XXXIX.	John 19.19-22; Matt. 27.37; Mark 15.26; Luke 23.38
XL.	Luke 23.34[a]
XLI.	Matt. 27.39-43; Mark 15.29-32; Luke 23.35-37
XLII.	Luke 23.39-43; Matt. 27.44
XLIII.	John 19.25-27
XLIV.	Matt. 27.45-49; Mark 15.33-36; Luke 23.44-45[a]

XLV.	John 19.28-30; Matt. 27.50; Mark 15.37; Luke 23.46
XLVI.	Matt 27.51-54; Mark 15.38-41; Luke 23.45^b,47-49
XLVII.	John 19.31-37
XLVIII.	Matt. 27.57-61; Mark 15.42-47; Luke 23.50-56; John 19.38-42
XLIX.	Matt. 26.62-66

Texts Concerning the Resurrection of Christ
Easter Day
Morning: Matt. 28.1-7; Mark 16.1-7; Luke 24.1-7; John 20.1
Evening: John 20.11-18; Mark 16.9-11

Easter Monday
Morning: Luke 24.13-24; Mark 16.12
Afternoon: Luke 24.25-53; Mark 14.13

Texts Concerning the Ascension of Christ
Thursday
Morning: Acts 1.9-11; Mark 16.19; Luke 24.50-52

Texts Concerning the Sending of the Holy Spirit at Pentecost
Pentecost
Early: Free Text
Morning: Acts 2.1-4
Afternoon: Acts 2.5-13

Pentecost Monday
Morning: Acts 2.14-18
Evening: Acts 2.19-21

Although the structure of the readings is based on the major seasons of the church year, a close inspection of the references reveals that the Reformed principle of *lectio continua*, established in early liturgies of the Reformation era, is fundamental for this sequence of pericopes. Thus the *Text-Boekje* represents a distinctively Reformed variant of a lectionary for the church year.

On the reverse of the title page is the following: "Volgens Kerken-Ordre" [Follows the Church-Order]. The new official metrical psalter, *Het Boek der Psalmen, nevens de Gezangen bij de Hervormde Kerk van Nederland in gebruik... Uit drei Berymingen, In den jaare 1773, gekooren*, Amsterdam, et al, 1775, following the long-standing tradition of the earlier psalter of Petrus Datheen,[16] included an appendix of confessional and liturgical material, that is, the "Kerken-Ordre." The *Text-Boekje* was, therefore, designed to be bound-up with copies of the new metrical psalter.[17] The first implication is that the pericopes of the *Text-Boekje* were to be read and expounded within the context of the Service of the Word and, especially on the principal festivals, within the context of the Lord's Supper. The second implication is that this preaching throughout the church year was accompanied by metrical psalmody. Although the Rotterdam *Text-Boekje* does not indicate which psalms were to be sung at the specific services at festivals, other collections of pericopes did include such listings. One example is *Ordre der Texten Dewelke Jaarlykes op de Feest-Dagen, Ter Gedagtenisse van Christi Geboorte, Besnydinge, Lyden en Sterven, Opstandinge, Hemelvaart en Zendinge van den H. Geest, worden verklaart en toeeëeigent aan de Gemeente J. Christi te Leeuwarden... Derde Druk* [Third edition] *Leeuwarden 1773*. Since this textbook was issued before the publication of the new official psalter of 1775, the metrical psalms

listed for use at the major festivals in Leeuwarden are those
of Petrus Datheen:[18]

Christmas Day
Morning: Psalm 2, part 2 (st. 4-7)
Noon: Psalm 89, part 3 (st. 9-12)
Evening: Psalm 148 (st.1-5)

26 December
Morning: Psalm 132, part 2 (vs. 7-12)
Noon: Psalm 98 (st. 1-4)

New Year's Day
Morning: Psalm 90, part 1 (st. 1-4)
Noon: Psalm 90, part 2 (st. 5-9)

Easter Day
Morning: Psalm 16, part 2 (st. 4-6)
Noon: Psalm 2, part 2 (st. 4-7)
Evening: Psalm 118, part 4 (st. 11-14)

Easter Monday
Morning: Psalm 110 (st. 1-7)
Noon: Psalm 98 (st. 1-4)

Ascension
Morning: Psalm 68, part 3 (st. 8-10)
Noon: Psalm 47 (st. 1-5)

Pentecost
Morning: Psalm 51, part 2 (st. 5-10)
Noon: Psalm 119, part 6 (st. 21-24)
Evening: Psalm 87 (st. 1-5)

Pentecost Monday
Morning: Psalm 119, part 7 (st. 25-28)
Noon: Psalm 98 (st. 1-4)

Although no such listing of congregational psalms appears in the Rotterdam *Text-Boekje,* it is clear psalms were sung in connection with this church-year cycle of preaching texts. The earliest liturgical order in the Dutch Reformed tradition, the liturgy of the Dutch stranger church in London, based on the *Forma ac Ratio* of Johannes à Lasco, 1552-54,[19] included direct reference to congregational psalmody, specifically the psalms of Jan Utenhove.[20] The same primary concern for metrical psalmody within the liturgy continued in subsequent generations, and discussions of the liturgies of the Dutch Reformed tradition usually include some account of congregational psalmody.[21]

Despite the lack of information regarding which psalms were sung at the principal festivals in Rotterdam, there is a reference in a published open letter, written by Domine Petrus Hofstede concerning the introduction of the new metrical psalter into the Rotterdam churches in 1775, that indicates that the singing of one particular congregational song continued in Rotterdam: the "Bedezang voor de Predikatie" [Prayer-song before the sermon].[22] This "Prayer-song," a metrical version of a prayer found in the sixteenth-century London Dutch liturgy, was written Jan Utenhove.[23] The earliest printed source is Utenhove's *25 Psalmen,* Emden, 1557. Datheen included it in the appendix to his metrical psalms, first printed in Heidelberg in 1566, and thereafter was regularly sung, with the psalms of Datheen, by Dutch congregations for more than two hundred years. Its popularity was such that when the new metrical psalms were issued in 1775, replacing the psalms of Datheen, the "Bedezang voor de Predikatie" could not be excluded from its appendix:

> O God, thou art our Father through Jesus Christ,
> give thy Spirit on us all ,
> that we may be led into the truth.
> So that we may hear, open the mouth
> of thy servant that he may purely
> and courageously declare thy Word.
> Therefore, O Lord, graciously
> open our hearts and ears,
> that we who hear may remain
> diligent, faithful and fruitful,
> and declare thy praise.[24]

The "Bedezang," which in many respects is a congregational version of Calvin's ministerial prayer for illumination before the sermon,[25] enunciates a Reformed epiclesis: the invocation of the Holy Spirit on the gathered community at worship.   In particular it expresses the conviction that an inspired preacher will lead to an inspired congregation, whose response is to live worthy lives that respond to the Word of God with the praise of God.   In the Dutch Reformed tradition the Word of God was received primarily by preaching and the praise of God fundamentally proclaimed in congregational metrical psalmody.

In the latter part of the eighteenth century, when this Rotterdam *Text-Boekje* was issued, there were moves to expand congregational song considerably beyond the confines of metrical psalmody.   There was, of course, the small number of items of non-psalmic song, such as the "Bedezang," in the appendix to the official metrical psalter, and there was a long-standing tradition of locally produced collections of hymns.   Many of these were directly related to the published collections of church-year pericopes.   For example, in Leeuwarden the following two booklets were issued: *Gezangen die op het Paasch-Feest invallende op Zondag den 8ste April 1792. Zullen gesongen worden op Zondag nademiddag in de Wester Kerk, en 's avonds in de Grote Kerk, en s' Maandags nademiddags in de Wester Kerk...* [Hymns for Pentecost falling on Sunday the 8th April 1792, which shall be sung on Sunday afternoon in the Wester Kerk, and in the evening in the Grote Kerk, and on Monday afternoon in the Wester Kerk]; *Gezangen, welken op Woensdag den Tweeden Dag des Kers-Feests. Invallende op den 26. December 1798. 's Avonds ten vyf Uuren in de Groote Kerk* [Hymns for Wednesday the Second Day of Christmas, falling on the 26 December 1798, in the evening at 5 o'clock in the Grote Kerk].[26]

As the century drew to a close there were voices raised in favor of the compilation of an official collection of hymns to supplement the new psalter of 1775, for use in all the churches of the provincial synods that comprised the Dutch Reformed Church. Foremost among the campaigners for such a hymnal was Petrus Hofstede, senior Domine of Rotterdam.[27] The possibility for such a hymnal was first discussed at the synod of Noord-Holland, meeting in Amsterdam in 1796. Ultimately a commission was formed and the hymnal was eventually published as: *Evangelische Gezangen om nevens het Boek der Psalmen bij den openbaren Godsdienst in de Nederlandsche Hervormde Gemeenten gebruike te worden; op uitdrukkelijken Last van alle de Synoden der voornoemde Gemeenten, bijeen verzameld en in orde gebracht in de jaren 1803, 1804, en 1805*, Amsterdam: Johannes Allart, 1806.

The hymnal contained 192 hymns, gathered together in ten main sections. Section 7 (Nos. 88-110) comprised liturgical hymns, including six for before the sermon— supplementing Utenhove's "Bedezang" in the appendix of the 1775 psalter—and two for after the sermon. Section 8 (Nos. 111-158), "On Christian Festival Days," was effectively a collection of hymns to be sung with the church-year collections of pericopes, such as the Rotterdam *Text-Boekje*, which continued to be issued.[28] The hymns were compiled in the following subsections:

A. Hymns on the Birth of Jesus
B. Passion Hymns
C. Hymns on the Resurrection of Jesus
D. Hymns on the Ascension of Jesus
E. Hymns on the Outpouring of the Holy Spirit

There was no subsection devoted to the Circumcision of Jesus but since this was celebrated on January 1, suitable hymns could be found in Section 9, "On Special Times and Occasions," which began with four hymns for the New Year (Nos. 159-62).

The *Evangelische Gezangen* thus gave the Dutch Reformed Church as a whole a unified collection of hymns for use at the principal festivals of the church year. But it was the culmination rather than the initiation of a tradition of liturgical congregational song. As early 1610 the Church Regulations of the Provincial Synod of Utrecht had decreed what could be sung in its churches: "The one hundred and fifty Psalms of David, the songs of praise of Mary, Zachariah, and Simeon, the Articles of Belief [Apostles' Creed by Utenhove], the Ten Commandments, the Lord's Prayer, and the evening hymn "Christe dei du bist dagh en Licht [Dutch version of the Latin *Christe qui lux es et dies*], and also the prayer before the sermon, "O Godt die on onse Vader bist" [by Utenhove]." All these items were to be found in editions of Datheen's psalms. But the Church Regulations went further and indicated that other "Scriptural

songs of praise, and Christian hymns, which deal with the
Birth, Circumcision, Suffering, Passion, Death, Resurrection
from the Dead, Ascension into Heaven, Sending of the Holy
Spirit, etc." were also permissible.[29] These Utrecht
Regulations led directly to the publication of *Hymni ofte
Loff-sangen op de Christelijcke Feest-Dagen* [Hymns or
Songs of Praise for the Festival Days of Christ], The
Hague: Hillebrant Jacobsz, 1615.[30] This collection, the
first Dutch Reformed hymnal, contained 58 hymns,
arranged for the major festivals of the church year:
Christmas (Nos. 1-13); New Year (Nos. 14-16); Passion
(Nos. 17-37); Easter (Nos. 38-43); Ascension (Nos. 44-45);
and Pentecost (Nos. 46-51), with a final section of morning
and evening hymns (Nos. 52-58). A significant number of
the hymns were translations from Latin and German: the
translations from Latin include, *Conditor alme siderum* (No.
1), *A solus ortus cardine* (No. 3), *Te lucis ante terminum*
(No. 57), and others; German translations include Luther's
Vom Himmel hoch (No. 12),   and *Christ lag in
Todesbanden* (No. 39), along with hymns by others. The
hymns were given specific Biblical references in their
headings, allowing them to be selected for use with specific
church-year pericopes found in the various published text
books that became normative for Dutch Reformed worship.

This liturgical tradition of Biblical readings,
preaching, and congregational song was transplanted into
North American soil. Hageman cites the report that Domine
Henry Selyns—who served the New York congregation
from 1682 to 1701—sent to the Amsterdam Classis in
September 1698, to the effect that it was customary for the
reception of catechumens to take place on Easter Monday,
Ascension Day, and Pentecost Monday.[31] This confirms
that the church year festivals were being observed in these
North American Dutch Reformed churches. Hageman was,

therefore, right to take to task the Lutheran liturgical scholar, Luther D. Reed, who asserted that "the strongest Lutheran settlements were made in soil thoroughly uncongenial to liturgical worship...among the Dutch Reformed of New York."[32] Hageman comments: "Here in New York at the end of the seventeenth century the life of the Reformed Church was liturgical. The liturgy was used for Sunday worship and weekday instruction. The Christian year was still observed with services not only on Easter and Whitsunday, but on Easter Monday and Whitmonday as well."[33]

This liturgical tradition was continued to some degree at the end of the eighteenth century, although the influences of Rationalism and Pietism had made their mark on Dutch Reformed thought and action.[34] The demise of the tradition was accelerated by the decline of Dutch and the rise of English as the primary language of worship.[35] The combined influence of New England Puritanism, American Pietism, and New World Rationalism, eliminated specific liturgical elements from Reformed worship. Thus by the nineteenth century Hageman concludes:

> The liturgy had almost entirely disappeared. A few sacramental forms and skeletal remains of an order of service survived in some churches to witness to the fact, increasingly incredible with the passing of time, that the Reformed churches had once a liturgical life.... The Christian year had almost entirely disappeared.[36]

In the twentieth century it has been Reformed liturgical scholars, such as Gerardus van der Leeuw in the Netherlands,[37] and Howard Hageman in the United States, who have rediscovered and reinterpreted for their own generation the liturgical tradition of the Dutch Reformed

Church. But their work has been part of the much wider, ecumenical liturgical movement of this century. We have been learning anew what Dutch-speaking worshippers experienced around the turn of the eighteenth century. They discovered that a concern for a church-year lectionary led to new developments in congregational song, especially the publication of the *Evangelische Gezangen* of 1806. We, too, have made a similar discovery, that our use of the Common Three-Year Lectionary, introduced in the 1970s, has given rise to a new generation of hymn-writing, as is witnessed by such hymnals as *The Episcopal Hymnal 1982* (1985), the Roman Catholic *Worship III* (1986), *The United Methodist Hymnal* (1989), *The Presbyterian Hymnal* (1990), and especially *Rejoice in the Lord* (1985), the hymnal of the Reformed Church in America, and the *Psalter Hymnal* (1989), issued by the Christian Reformed Church in North America, which continue the metrical psalm tradition of the Dutch Reformed Church.

Endnotes

1. Howard G. Hageman, *Pulpit and Table: Some Chapters in the History of Worship in the Reformed Churches* (Richmond, VA: John Knox Press, 1962).

2. Hageman, *Ibid.*, 9.

3. See, for example, Hageman's, *We call This Friday Good* (Philadelphia: Fortress Press, 1961), and (with J. C. Becker) *Easter. Proclamation: Aids for Interpreting the Lessons of the Church Year. Series C. 5* (Philadelphia: Fortress Press, 1974).

4. On the background, see Arthur Carl Piepkorn, *Profiles in Belief: The Religious Bodies of the United States and Canada*, Vol. 2: *Protestant Denominations* (San Francisco: Harper and Row, 1978), 327-29.

5. See Howard G. Hageman, *Two Centuries Plus: The Story of New Brunswick Seminary*, with an additional chapter by Benjamin Alicea, (Grand Rapids, MI: Eerdmans, 1984).

6. On the general background see the catalog prepared by Daniel J. Meeter: *The Dutch in Two Worlds: An Exhibition of Rare Books, Manuscripts, and Engravings from the Gardner Sage Library of New Brunswick Theological Seminary, Celebrating the Seminary's Bicentennial (1784-1984) and the Bicentennial of Peaceful Diplomatic Relations between the Netherlands and United States (1782-1982)* ([New Brunswick, N. J.: New Brunswick Theological Seminary, 1982]).

7. All translations from Dutch sources are my own.

8. *Text-Boekje*, fol. A3^r.

9. The following list of the current preachers in 1782 is taken from the *Text-Boekje*, 153-64. The preceding number in parentheses indicates the numerical sequence of Reformed preachers in Rotterdam since the founding of the Reformed church in the city in 1573.

> (78) Dr. Johannes Patyn, Professor of Emblematics, installed 10 May 1739, retired 2 September 1777, but apparently continued to preach.
> (81) Dr. Petrus Hofstede, Professor of Ecclesiastical History, installed 22 June 1749, the senior Domine in 1782.
> (82) Johannes Wilh. de Heyde, installed 1751.
> (84) Paulus Bonnet, installed 7 August 1757.
> (85) Wesselus Knock, installed 30 April 1758.
> (88) Dr. Barthol. van Velsen, installed 16 November 1766.
> (90) Dr. Johannes Habbema, installed 16 August 1767.
> (92) Johannes Zuidhoek van Laren, installed 28 June 1772.
> (93) Daniel Barbe, installed 13 December 1772.
> (95) Dingeman Wouter Smits, installed 31 March 1776.
> (96) Jean Louis Verster, installed 25 May 1777.

(97) Joh. Jacob le Sage ten Broek, installed 22 February
    1778.
(98) Arnoldus Voorduin, installed 13 December 1778.
(99) Petrus Godefried Sprenger van Eyk, installed 25
    November 1781.

On the reverse of the title page of the *Text-Boekje* there is a kind of
imprimatur: "By my signature [below] this *Text-Boekje* has been
properly inspected. Rotterdam 1782." My own personal copy is signed
"J. Habbema" (No. 90 above). It was customary for such
official church books to be so authenticated.

10. This following information is derived from the Winter and Summer
preaching rosters given in the *Text-Boekje*, 164-66.

11. *Text-Boekje*, 129.

12. *Text-Boekje*, 166-67.

13. At the end of his commentary of the letters of St. Paul, issued in
March 1524, Bugenhagen included composite history of the Passion and
Resurrection in Latin. A revised version in High German was issued
in Wittenberg in 1530 with the title: *Historia des leidens und
Afferstehung unsers Herrn Jhesu Christi/ aus der vier Euangelisten/
durch Joh. Bugenhagen Pomer auffs new vleissig zusamen bracht.* The
following year it appeared in a Low German edition; thereafter it was
incorporated into hymnals and liturgical orders, forming basic readings
of the Passion and Resurrection.

14. See, for example, Johannes Martini, *De Gecrucigde Christus Ofte
XXXV Texten van't Lyden ende Sterven Jesu Christi In dewelcke
datselve uyt de vier Euangelisten jaerlicks verclaert wort in de
Gemeynte des Heeren tot Groningen* (Groningen, 1649); cited in Jan
Roelof Luth, *"Daer wert om't seerste uytgekreten...": Bijdragen toteen
geschiedenis van de gemeentezang in het Nederlandse Gereformeerde
protestantisme ca. 1550 - ca. 1852* (Kampen: Van den Berg, 1986), 525.

15. *Text-Boekje*, fol. A3^r.

16. The official psalter of Dutch Reformed congregations since the Synod of Wesel of 1568.

17. On the use of the 1775 psalter in Rotterdam, see Luth, op. cit., 250, 286-87, 300.

18. The listing, cited in Luth, op. cit., 254, has been collated with *De Psalmen Des Propheten Davids, Met eenige andere Lof-zangen: Uyt den Francoyschen in Nederlantschen Dichte overgeset, door Petrum Dathenum* (Amsterdam: Ph. Losel, et al, 1757).

19. See Dirk W. Rodgers, "John à Lasco in England," Ph.D dissertation, Drew University, 1991, esp. 55-161.

20. See Robin A. Leaver, *'Goostly psalmes and spirituall songes': English and Dutch Metrical Psalms from Coverdale to Utenhove 1535-1566* (Oxford: Clarendon Press, 1991), 170-73.

21. See, for example, *Kort Historisch Berigt Van de Publieke Schriften, Rakende de Leer en Dienst der Nederduytze Kerken van de Vereenigde Nederlanden: Zynde de Formulieren van Eenigheyt en de Liturgie, Doorgaans gevoegt agter de Psalmboeken, die zelve Kerken gebruykt worden* (Amsterdam: Schouten & de Jonge, 1746).

22. Petrus Hofstede, *Brief aan den Hoogeleerden Heer, J. J. le Sage den Broek... Behelzende een Berigt van de middelen, door welke men, in de Hervormde Gemeente te Rotterdam. met de niewe Psalm-beryming te gelyk een Nieuwe Manier van Zingen, zoo spoedig als gelukkig heef ingevoerd* (Rotterdam: J. Bosch & R. Arrenberg, 1775), 7. For a discussion of this document, see Jan Pieter de Bie, *Het Leven en de Werken van Petrus Hofstede* (Rotterdam: Daamen, 1899), 291-306.

23. Leaver, *Ibid.*, 178, 180.

24. A literal translation; for the original Dutch, see Leaver, *Ibid.*, 180.

25. The rubric in Calvin's 1542 Geneva liturgy reads: "...a psalm is sung by the Congregation. Then the Minister commences again to pray, beseeching God for the grace of his Holy Spirit, that his Word may be

faithfully expressed to the honor of his name and the edification of the Church, and be received with such humility and obedience which it deserves. The form is left to the discretion of the Minister"; Bard Thompson, ed., *The Liturgies of the Western Church* (Philadelphia: Fortress Press, 1980), 198-99.

26. See Luth, *Ibid.*, 517-18.

27. Cornelis P. van Andel, *Tussen de Regels: De samenhang van kerkgeschiedenis en kerklied* (The Hague: Boekcentrum, 1982), 172; Bie, loc. cit.

28. See, for example, *De Historie van des Heeren Jezus Christus Geboorte, Besnydenis, Lyden en Sterven, Opstandinge, Hemelvaart, en uitstortinge des Heiligen Geestes op het Pinxterfeest, welke jaarlyks wordt verklaart en toegeëigent aan de Gereformeerde Gemeente van de Here Jezus Christus in Groningen* (Groningen [1790]); cited Luth, op. cit., 530.

29. Cited in H. Hasper, *Een Reformatorsich Kerkboek* (Leeuwarden: Jongbloed, 1941), 65.

30. *Hymni ofte Loff-sangen op de Christelijcke Feest-Dagen*, facsimile ed. J. van Biezen and Marie Veldhuyzen (Hilversum: Frits Knuf, 1967).

31. Hageman, *Pulpit and Table*, 39.

32. Luther D. Reed, *Worship* (Philadelphia: Muhlenberg Press, 1959), 56.

33. Hageman, *Pulpit and Table*, 40.

34. For the effect of Pietism and Rationalism on Dutch hymnody, see van Andel, *Ibid.*, 159-77.

35. The liturgical transition from Dutch to English has been investigated by Daniel J. Meeter, "The North American Liturgy: A Critical Edition of the Liturgy of the Reformed Dutch in North America, 1793," Ph.D dissertation, Drew University, 1989, and English hymnals by James L.

H. Brumm, *Singing the Lord's Song: A History of the English-Language Hymnals of the Reformed Church in America* (New Brunswick, NJ: Reformed Church Historical Society, 1990).

36. Hageman, *Pulpit and Table*, 58.

37. Gerardus van der Leeuw, *Liturgiek* (Nijkerk: Callendbach [ca. 1940]).

THE HISTORIOGRAPHICAL NEGLECT OF RELIGION IN THE MIDDLE COLONIES

Randall Balmer
Columbia University

While Alistair Cooke would not be counted a member of the historians' guild, his comments about settlements in the New World, appearing in the 1973 volume *America*, capture the operative assumptions of many historians. "Between the two strong and opposing cultures of Virginia and New England, the only continuous highway was the sea," he wrote. "So there came into being a string of Middle Colonies—New York, Pennsylvania, Maryland, Delaware—whose only original links were the English language, the English common law, and an itch to start afresh, for various reasons, in the New World."[1] I think it would be safe to assume that the burghers of New Amsterdam, already busy establishing a commercial empire in the 1620s, might be a trifle surprised to learn that theirs was an English colony with an English common-law tradition that had sprung up out of the wilderness as a kind of link between Virginia and Puritan New England. Their astonishment would likely be compounded by the fact that Puritans had yet to arrive in the New World.

Cooke's declaration, often quoted by Howard Hageman as an example of widespread disregard for the Middle Colonies, is all too characteristic of colonial historiography. Indeed, far too often the Middle

Colonies—defined, for our purposes, as New York, New Jersey, Delaware, and Pennsylvania—have been treated as a cipher in colonial America. Ever since Perry Miller "rediscovered" the Puritans in the 1930s, historians intent on understanding the colonial experience have cast their eyes upon New England. And not without reason. Puritanism certainly represented a bold—even noble—experiment in social planning, one that left its imprint on the American character.[2] Miller's spadework into the intellectual terrain of colonial New England uncovered a deep and complex substratum of belief and conviction that animated Puritan consciousness. Miller's doctoral dissertation at the University of Chicago, published in 1933 as *Orthodoxy in Massachusetts*, coupled with his appointment at Harvard stimulated an outpouring of scholarship on Puritan life, thought, and culture that only recently has shown any signs of abating. Miller's own seminal works on *The Puritan Mind* and *Jonathan Edwards*, among others, showed the way, followed by those of his students, principally Edmund S. Morgan, and then a succession of others, many of them lesser lights.

Every extant shred of evidence from the Puritans, it would seem, has been scrutinized, analyzed, interpreted, and debated. We can now speak confidently about Puritan attitudes toward death, their political ideology, patterns of child-rearing, church polity, and their behavior on the Sabbath. We have studied their towns, their wills, their diet, their ministry, their piety, their relation to the Indians, and their attitudes toward deviance. We have speculated on the reasons for their demise and have posited connections between the spirit of Puritanism and the spirit of 1776. In short, as one weary soul put it, we know more about the Puritans than they knew about themselves.

Finally Edmund Morgan, who had himself made so many vital contributions to the literature, threw up his hands and cried, "Enough!" In 1966 he observed that "we already know more about the Puritans than sane men should want to know."[3] Morgan's pronouncement failed to stanch completely the outpouring of scholarship on New England, but his own turn to the Chesapeake (exemplified in his fine study, *American Slavery, American Freedom*, published in 1975) signaled a shift in historiographical concerns for colonial historians.

But for students of American religion this change of venue has proven less than satisfying, for the simple reason that the settlers of colonial Virginia (to put it delicately) were not noted for their religious convictions. In contrast to the stable family life in New England, early Virginia was populated overwhelmingly by males—many of whom could fairly be called rogues—who were bent on securing economic advancement, not pursuing some quixotic religious ideal. This is not to say that religion has been lacking altogether from the literature. Various studies have explored the nominal Anglicanism of the early settlers or the vestry system, which functioned in fact, if not in theory, as the local government and provided endless occasions for wrangling and acrimony, and Rhys Isaac's important study, *The Transformation of Virginia, 1740-1790*, examined the effects of the evangelical awakening.

All of this leads us back to the Middle Colonies as a kind of frontier of colonial religious historiography. And, indeed, there is a richness of unexplored possibilities here. The last major work on colonial Presbyterianism appeared in 1949. Anglicanism in the region, an important element of both religious and political life after 1700, has gone virtually unnoticed. Only recently (with the publication of Jon Butler's *The Huguenots in America*) have French

Protestants received anything like the attention they deserve. The Puritan and Quaker cultures on Long Island have, oddly enough, escaped the notice of New England historians. The German Palatines have no religious history, attempts to understand the religious life of New Sweden have been desultory at best, and the Dutch, whose culture formed the earliest European settlement and shaped colonial life in New York City, have also, until very recently, passed virtually unnoticed.[4] (Colonial Pennsylvania has fared considerably better in the literature, much of which has centered around the Quakers and their attempts to maintain the reins of government in an increasingly bellicose age.)

There are, of course, good—even obvious—reasons for this neglect. The first has to do with the extent that colonial culture did, in fact, emanate from New England and that institutions like Harvard and Yale have sought, self-consciously and quite successfully, to perpetuate that tradition. Other explanations have more to do with logistics and the availability of source materials. The various religious traditions in the Middle Colonies are no match for the compulsive literacy that characterized the Puritans. The Puritans' penchant for introspection and their emphasis on the printed word gave rise to a vast literature of diaries and sermons not found in the middle Atlantic region. The plethora of languages in the Middle Colonies also has proved a barrier, and whereas Puritan New England was a homogeneous culture, the religious culture to the south was notoriously—and confusingly—heterogeneous.

But, at another level, this neglect is curious for several reasons. From a contemporary perspective it strikes me as an oddity that the heart of the very region that functions as the center of influence in the twentieth century—the "power alley" between Boston and Washington—has yet to muster the will to record, let alone interpret, its colonial origins. Furthermore, from a seventeenth-century view the neglect is even more glaring. The European society taking root in present-day New York City came directly from the Netherlands, considered at that time the nexus of northern European culture and probably the most modern society in the seventeenth century. The Dutch mercantile empire was the envy of Europe, their inheritance customs rejected the primogeniture of England and elsewhere in favor of a system that apportioned a man's estate first to his widow and then more or less equally among his children. Dutch and Flemish artists of this era are still counted among the masters of all time. The Dutch configuration of church and state, forged in the bitter struggle between the Netherlands States-General and Spain, in many ways anticipated the formulation of the United States.

Why bother with the Middle Colonies and resist the historiographical stampede to New England? What can a historian of religion hope to find in the middle Atlantic region? Let me suggest several lines of inquiry. First, with its fabled diversity, the Middle Colonies provide a veritable laboratory of both English and European religions: Swedish, Finnish, and German Lutherans, Dutch Reformed, French Huguenots, English Quakers and Dissenters of all stripes, Roman Catholics, Jews, Scots-Irish Presbyterians, Mennonites, Hutterites, Schwenckfelders, Moravians, Anglicans, Baptists, and Methodists. The middle Atlantic also included its share of visionaries. In 1663 a young, enigmatic Anabaptist named Pieter Corneliszoon Plockhoy arrived at the mouth of the Delaware River to establish a communal experiment, the principles of which anticipated some of the New England transcendentalist communities two centuries later—Brook Farm, Hopedale Community,

Bronson Alcott's experiment at Fruitlands—before its untimely demise at the hands of the English in 1664. All of this suggests the variegated pattern of religious development in the Middle Colonies. Unlike the Puritans who feared religious diversity (as a succession of Quakers who were jailed, pilloried, banished, and sometimes hanged could well attest) the Middle Colonies fairly thrived on it, and the patterns of acculturation and assimilation formed therein anticipated those of the new nation in the nineteenth century.[5]

Such a cornucopia of religions offers virtually limitless possibilities to examine the interaction of religious and ethnic cultures. Various discrete Old World traditions suddenly were thrust together into the cauldron of the Middle Colonies. What happened then? We know surprisingly little, except that by the late eighteenth-century this smattering of Continental groups had become English in language, culture, and religion. How did this come about? What events transpired to prompt this transformation? How did religion and politics interact to affect ethnic identity? These are all, it seems to me, vexing and largely unanswered questions.

The second line of inquiry concerns the Great Awakening and its relation to the American Revolution. When historians write about the earliest harbingers of colonial revival, they usually refer to Solomon Stoddard's "harvests" at Northampton, Massachusetts, in the 1690s. Here, once again, the New England bias of colonial historiography obscures some equally important developments to the south. Contemporaneous with Stoddard's "harvests," a cooper-turned-minister named Guiliam Bertholf began his itinerancy in northern New Jersey. Bertholf openly flaunted his independence from Dutch ecclesiastical authorities, and his machinations gave rise to several pietistic congregations.[6]   In 1702 (the year before Jonathan Edwards was born) a young Swede named Lars Tolstadius arrived in New Jersey. Tolstadius lacked certification from the Swedish Lutheran Church authorities in Uppsala, but he succeeded nevertheless in gathering a congregation in Raccoon, New Jersey, in the face of active opposition from the established clergy.[7]   Both ministers rejected the formalism of their more traditionalist adversaries in favor of a warm "heart religion." Among the Dutch, Bertholf's work prepared the ground for the arrival of Theodorus Jacobus Frelinghuysen in 1720, whose labors along the Raritan River won recognition from both Jonathan Edwards and George Whitefield (and, later, Henry Melchior Muhlenberg) as the catalyst for the Great Awakening in the Middle Colonies.

Yet, strangely, the role of New York and New Jersey in the colonial revival has passed virtually unnoticed. The only systematic treatment of the Awakening in the Middle Colonies is Charles Maxson's 1920 study, which has not stood the test of time. All of this is unfortunate because many of the explanations given for the Great Awakening in New England actually work as well, and perhaps better, in the Middle Colonies. Like New England and even the Welsh Revival in Britain, the Awakening in New Jersey represented a protest on the part of rural settlers against the urban elite. Revival in the Middle Colonies, moreover, grew quite decidedly out of specific economic, demographic, and political dislocations, dating back to Leisler's Rebellion in 1691 and even to the English Conquest of 1664.[8] The Awakening, moreover, appears to be transcultural in that it appealed to disparate ethnic groups and knitted them together within either revivalist or antirevivalist camps.

All of this brings us around to the relation of the Great Awakening to the American Revolution. Perhaps no question has vexed New England historiography more than this one. Picking up on the suggestion of Perry Miller, various historians have sought to explore the connection between revivalist and Patriot. None was more systematic and exhaustive in his approach than Alan Heimert, whose *Religion and the American Mind* examined the writings of the revivalists, seeking, in the author's words, to "read between the lines" to find affinities between revivalist and Patriot rhetoric. Heimert's work was savaged in the reviews, with the result that others have been a trifle chary about taking up the topic. Several less ambitious (and, hence, more successful) attempts to posit connections between the two events include Nathan Hatch's *The Sacred Cause of Liberty*, which charts the evolution of millennial rhetoric surrounding the Awakening into the Whiggish rhetoric of the Revolution, and Richard Bushman's *From Puritan to Yankee*. Others, notably Harry Stout and Edmund Morgan, have seen in the revival the emergence of patterns of communication and leadership styles, respectively, that played themselves out in the Revolution.

Once again, some of this theorizing might profitably be applied to the Middle Colonies. Like New England with its James Davenports and Andrew Crosswells, the middle Atlantic had more than its share of itinerants—Bertholf, Johann Bernhard van Dieren, Gilbert Tennent, Henry Melchior Mühlenberg, Frelinghuysen himself, a renegade preacher named John Henry Goetschius—all of whom altered forever the social, religious, and political fabric of eighteenth-century life.[9] As for the relation between revivalist and Patriot, the Middle Colonies show a strong correlation between the two.

The final line of inquiry, one especially relevant to a twentieth-century agenda, concerns the relation of church and state. If asked to name the individuals responsible for the Constitutional configuration of religion and politics, theorists like Roger Williams, Isaac Backus, Thomas Jefferson, and perhaps William Penn undoubtedly leap to mind. But the separation doctrine had one of its earliest incarnations in colonial New York. Building upon the two kingdoms model of church and state back in the Netherlands, the colony's first minister, Jonas Michaδlius, advocated a careful distance between civil and ecclesiastical government. In 1628 Michaδlius conceded that although "political and ecclesiastical persons can greatly assist each other, nevertheless the matters and offices belonging together must not be mixed but kept separate, in order to prevent all confusion and disorder."[10] Although the Dutch Reformed Church maintained a nominal establishment, in fact the Dutch directors-general granted broad toleration throughout the New Netherland period.

The English resolutely challenged this configuration for a century after the Conquest of 1664. The Ministry Act of 1693 legally—if not effectively—established the Church of England in New York City and the surrounding counties. At the turn of the century the intrigues of Governor Cornbury, coupled with the onslaught of the Society for the Propagation of the Gospel, combined to place all "Dissenting" religions on the defensive. By the middle of the eighteenth century the battleground of church and state shifted to King's College and the circumstances surrounding its establishment. Should King's College be chartered as an Anglican school with the support of public money? The Anglicans, who held the reins of power, thought so. Others, including William Livingston, detected grave dangers in such a scheme. Livingston's several treatises on the issue, published in *The Independent Reflector*, argued intelligently and passionately against any such establishment as inimical to religious freedom, and his efforts certainly earned him a rightful place in the pantheon along side of Williams, Backus, Penn, and Jefferson.

The middle Atlantic holds, I think, great promise as the frontier of colonial historiography. The diversity of its religious and ethnic traditions, its critical role in the Great Awakening and the American Revolution, and the religious toleration it fostered early in its history--all of these topics have yet to receive the attention they deserve. But such an undertaking is not without its pitfalls. Language barriers and the paucity of sources relative to New England mean that the historian of religion in the Middle Colonies must very often turn to sociology and anthropology for assistance in reconstructing religious life and experience.

But will such an enterprise yield anything of value beyond an elucidation of religion in a long-neglected recess of colonial America? I think so. Let me suggest (however tentatively) one way in which an understanding of the Middle Colonies, drawn in greater or lesser degrees from the questions I have posed in this essay, might well broaden our interpretation of the American experience beyond the eighteenth century.

Perhaps no motif has dominated both Puritan and post-Puritan life in America more than the theme of declension. The Puritan jeremiad, of course, established the mold. Beginning in the seventeenth century a succession of Puritan divines implored their auditors to renounce wickedness and return to the piety of the founders. Perry Miller and Sacvan Bercovitch, among many others, have applied this declension theme to the whole of American history. Even civil religion, to the extent you are inclined, as I am, to view it as a revitalization movement—although

I hasten to add that that interpretation is, by no means, original to me—can be seen as an attempt to recover the sense of America's mission and destiny. In the years since Vietnam and Watergate people like Jerry Falwell and Ronald Reagan have taken the religious rhetoric of declension at face value and have exploited the jeremiad to great personal and political advantage. They have bemoaned this nation's fall from grace, castigated Americans for failing to live up to the religious standards of the founders (who include, oddly enough, Thomas Jefferson and Benjamin Franklin), and they have even managed to conjure the specter of something they call "secular humanism" as the source of the nation's ills. But if the results of the 1980 and 1984 presidential elections are any indication, appeals to America's mythic origins still resonate with many Americans.

But the anomaly that the declension motif does not explain is the remarkable extent to which Americans, in the face of all this secularization, are still such a religious people. Here I wonder if an interpretation of American religion might better be served by setting down firm roots in the Middle Colonies and seeing how its branches affected the American experience. Unlike New England, which granted only a grudging toleration well into the nineteenth century, the Middle Colonies' tradition of religious diversity and open cultures prompted an early accommodation to pluralism, a recognition that toleration was the surest route to guaranteeing individual liberties. Unlike New England, the Middle Colonies sought not to contain or stifle the various religious traditions within its bounds, but rather adopted a strategy of toleration, which it bequeathed to the new nation. An interpretation of the American experience, then, that draws not from the exceptional insularity of New England, but rather from the more normative pattern of religious life in the Middle Colonies may bring us closer to the true genius of the American constellation of church and state. Colonial New England has enjoyed a rich harvest of scholarship over the past half-century, and there can be no question that students of American religion have gleaned their share from the bounty. Yet there are, I think, good reasons to shift our historiographical sights to the south. The Middle Colonies hold out the promise of rich rewards for those willing to brave its complexities.

Endnotes

1. Alistair Cooke, *Alistair Cooke's America* (New York, Alfred A. Knopf, 1974), 88.

2. See, for example, Edmund S. Morgan, "The Puritan Ethic and the American Revolution," *William and Mary Quarterly*, 3d Ser., XXIV (1967), 3-43; Sacvan Bercovitch, *The Puritan Origins of the American Self* (New Haven: Yale University Press, 1975).

3. Edmund S. Morgan, "The Historians of Early New England," in Ray Allen Billington, ed., *The Reinterpretation of Early American History* (San Marino, CA: Huntington Library, 1966), 41-42.

4. Recent studies include Randall Balmer, *A Perfect Babel of Confusion: Dutch Religion and English Culture in the Middle Colonies* (New York: Oxford University Press, 1989); and David G. Hackett, *The Rude Hand of Innovation: Religion and Social Order in Albany, New York, 1652-1836* (New York: Oxford University Press, 1991).

5. See Richard W. Pointer, *Protestant Pluralism and the New York Experience: A Study of Eighteenth-Century Religious Diversity* (Bloomington and Indianapolis: Indiana University Press, 1988).

6. Howard G. Hageman, "William Bertholf: Pioneer Dominie of New Jersey," *Reformed Review*, XXIX (1976), 73-80.

7. Donald Einar Bjarnson, "Swedish-Finnish Settlements in New Jersey in the Seventeenth Century," *Swedish Pioneer Quarterly*, XXVII (1976), 239-240; Suzanne B. Geissler, "A Step upon the Swedish Lutheran Road to Anglicanism," *Historical Magazine of the Protestant Episcopal Church, LIV (1985), 39-49.*

8. Randall Balmer, "The Social Roots of Dutch Pietism in the Middle Colonies," *Church History*, LIII (1984), 187-199.

9. Randall Balmer, "John Henry Goetschius and *The Unknown God*: Eighteenth-Century Pietism in the Middle Colonies," *Pennsylvania Magazine of History and Biography*, CXIII (1989), 575-608.

10. Edward T. Corwin, ed., *Ecclesiastical Records: State of New York*, 7 vols. (Albany, 1901-1916),I, 55.

THE CATHOLIC APOSTOLIC CHURCH AND REFORMED LITURGICAL RENEWALS OF THE NINETEENTH CENTURY

Gregg Alan Mast
Reformed Church in America

The Catholic Apostolic Church, often called the Irvingites because of their early dependence on Edward Irving, is an intriguing but little-studied movement of nineteenth-century England. In a time when evangelical zeal abounded and liturgical emphasis and practice faded, the Catholic Apostolic Church stood as a strangely luminous star. Having borrowed heavily not only from the *Book of Common Prayer*, but also from the riches of both the Eastern and Western liturgical traditions, it constructed a liturgy "higher" than any Anglican service in use at the time. The liturgical work of the charismatic, highly skilled liturgist of the Catholic Apostolic Church provided an invisible link between some of the riches of east and west and the liturgical renewals of the latter half of the nineteenth century. In particular, the liturgical reformers of the German Reformed Church of the United States and the Church of Scotland, and to a lesser degree, the Dutch Reformed Church in North America, were influenced by the Catholic Apostolic Church.

The Church of Scotland, like many American Protestant denominations, entered the nineteenth century with a sparse order of service. The sermon dominated

Sunday worship, surrounded by prayers and hymns. Weddings and baptisms were celebrated in the home, burials without prayers, and the sacrament of Holy Communion annually in the midst of great social fanfare.[1] The time was ripe for what John Kerr called a "second reformation."

Edward Irving was baptized, nurtured, ordained, served, and finally defrocked in the Church of Scotland. He served with the most famous of the early-nineteenth-century Scottish preachers, Thomas Chalmers, at St. John's in Glasgow between 1819 and 1821. He was then called to serve a struggling Scottish congregation in London, which he built into the Scottish National Church by the end of the 1820s. It was in the Church of Scotland that the charismatic outbreaks first occurred which would finally lead Irving and much of his congregation out of the church. The church on Regent Square, Irving's monument not only to his own popular ministry but also to the presence of the Church of Scotland in England, formed the embryo of the Catholic Apostolic Church. Remarkably, it is to this sectarian movement that the Church Service Society, a Scottish liturgical society, would look when searching for resources for its *Euchologion* of 1867. The influence of the Eucharistic service of the Catholic Apostolic Church on the liturgical renewal of the Church of Scotland through the Church Service Society will be the primary focus of this essay.

The Renewal of Scottish Worship

The liturgical renewal in the Church of Scotland did not take place until late in the nineteenth century, but the groundwork was laid by individuals and churches beginning with the first decade. One of the most important initial publications was Robertson's *Scotch Minister's Assistant* (1802), reissued in 1822 under the title *Forms of Prayer for use in the Church of Scotland.* In 1812 an injunction was issued by the church reminding parish pastors of their responsibility to read the scriptures each Sunday. Apparently this mandate, reflecting the *Westminster Directory*, was so thoroughly ignored that another edict was issued in 1856 directing that a portion of both the Old and New Testaments should be read at each service.[2] As early as 1829, George Burns, serving St. John's Church in New Brunswick, Canada, had published a volume of prayers for those of the Scottish church scattered throughout the world. In 1840, John Cumming, minister of the Scottish church in London, republished Knox's liturgy, the 1564 Scottish *Book of Common Order.* In his preface Cumming directed his concern toward the majority of the church which had forgotten its liturgical character. Eight years later, in 1848, Cumming also published an edition of the *Psalms and Paraphrases*, with prayers and services from the *Book of Common Order* prefixed to it. Other curious volumes included an 1842 volume of sermons which had eleven baptismal addresses among them and a communion service by Dr. Brichan of Dyke and Moy. The Rev. W. Liston of Redgorton published *The Service of the House of God* in 1843, and a Dr. Brunton produced *Forms for Public Worship* in 1848.[3] These are just a few of the examples cited by George Sprott, a primary mover in the liturgical renewal to come, to illustrate a church in which the liturgical soil was being slowly but surely tilled.

The Duke of Argyll, in his *Presbytery Examined*, published in 1848, was the first parson to publicly call the church to task concerning its defective worship. Lamenting the secession of Scottish pastors to the Anglican fold after the Disruption of 1843, he observed that "a partial use of liturgical forms of prayer...would along, I think have been of immense value in engaging the affections and preventing the straying."[4] In the General Assembly of 1849, an overture was adopted to provide those who lived in the Highlands and Islands, and in foreign countries, with an appropriate liturgical tool so they could worship regularly through a printed "Book of Devotion." A committee was appointed to carry the project, with a Dr. Crawford as convener. A pamphlet was published by Principal Campbell in Aberdeen in 1851 entitled, "Scattered Sheep: How to Reunite Them." Campbell again pointed to a defective form of public worship as the grounds on which many were defecting to the Episcopal Church. In April of 1852 an article was published by Professor Lorimer of Edinburgh on Knox's Liturgy. It was after republished under the title "A National Church Demands a National Liturgy."[5]

The reaction to Anglican defections and a growing concern to enrich Reformed liturgical life escalated into open controversy by a sermon preached by Marshall Lang, minister of the East Church, Aberdeen, in 1857. At the early age of twenty-three, Lang was an unlikely candidate to lead an uprising. The cause of the uproar, and Lang's censure by his presbytery, was his suggestion that it would be more appropriate for the congregation to stand for singing, instead of the traditional posture of sitting. He was encouraged to appeal his censure, a suggestion he did not heed, by another liturgical maverick, Robert Lee of Greyfriars' Church in Edinburgh. Lee had been ordained in 1833, and his church at Greyfriars' has been gutted by fire in 1845. After a lapse of twelve years, the church was restored in 1857. In November of the same year, Lee published his own service book, *Prayers for Public Worship*. The congregation was encouraged to stand to sing (as Lang had suggested), kneel to pray, and participate in the service through audible responses. New editions of Lee's book appeared in 1858 and 1863. A harmonium was utilized in 1863, and a pipe organ, a radically new step for the Scottish church, in 1864.[6]

In 1858, Andrew Bonar also published anonymously a volume entitled *Presbyterian Liturgies.* Borrowing heavily from an English edition of Baird's *Eutaxia,* Bonar promoted liturgical reform without embracing Lee's radical new steps. He also printed a liturgy for the Lord's Supper and the Burial of the Dead from a revised *Liturgy* of the American Dutch Reformed Church of 1857, and some liturgical specimens from the *Mercersburg Review.*[7] The liturgical renewals in both the German and Dutch Reformed churches in the United States had traversed the Atlantic to appear in Scotland at a critical time in its own liturgical renaissance. Indeed, when the *Euchologion* would be finally produced a decade later in 1867, the liturgies published by the Catholic Apostolic Church and the German Reformed Church in the United States were the primary models.

In 1859, the Church of Scotland, through one of its committees, published *Prayers for Social and Family Worship.* This volume, reprinted in 1863, recommended prayers to be used by soldiers, sailors, emigrants and all who were deprived of regular services of Christian worship. It was the first liturgical document produced by the Church of Scotland since the Westminster Directory of 1645. However, it was also in 1859 that the General Assembly ruled that reading prayers from a book was not permissible in public worship. This ruling caused Lee to be condemned, not for his innovations in music, liturgical postures, or stained glass windows, but for his printed book of prayers. Although Lee wanted his book to be endorsed by the Church Service Society, he was disappointed. Consequently, his liturgical forms were not nearly as important as his role as a liturgical innovator during these difficult years at the beginning of the Scottish liturgical revival. The Presbytery of Edinburgh continued to harass Lee until his untimely death in 1868. During 1867, Robert Story, one of the founders with Lee of the Church Service Society, and convener of its editorial committee, was also brought under the ban of the presbytery for having read prayers out of Lee's book while conducting a service at Greyfriars'.[8]

The Assembly appointed a committee to study worship in 1863, and the following year they reported that "almost universally the order is as follows: Praise, Prayer, Reading of Scripture, Praise, Prayer, Lecture or Sermon, Prayer, Praise, Benediction."[9] The same year the Assembly vested the control of worship in the presbyteries, a blow for both local and national reform. In 1866, Lee published *The Reform of the Church of Scotland* in which he argued for a new reformation in the worship, government, and doctrine in the Church of Scotland.[10] The pressure for liturgical change was growing and Robert Lee was readying the troops. On May 22, 1867, a day before the Assembly was to decide his fate, Lee fell from his horse in Edinburgh, suffered a cerebral hemorrhage and was paralyzed on the left side. While his case was postponed, Lee lingered almost a year, and finally died on March 12, 1868.[11] It could be said that Lee was a martyr in the cause of liturgical reform, for it was Lee who experimented and enthusiastically promoted the renaissance to come. One commentator has suggested that Lee's service book of 1857 owed much to the liturgy of the Catholic Apostolic Church.[12] Since I have been unable to locate a copy of the book, it is impossible to ascertain the truth of this assertion. However, it will be suggested that it was through the Church Service Society, and its publication, the *Euchologion*, in 1867, that the Catholic Apostolic Church has a substantial impact on liturgical renewal in Scotland. The impetus for the Church Service Society came in 1863 with the publication of a pamphlet entitled, "The Worship, Rites, and Ceremonies of the Church of Scotland," by George W. Sprott. Sprott was born in Nova Scotia in 1829, the son of a Presbyterian minister who had emigrated from Scotland. He was educated at Glasgow University, licensed and ordained by the Presbytery of Dunoon in 1852 "for work overseas."[13] Following his ordination he served as assistant at Halifax, Nova Scotia, at Greenock, and at Dumfries. From 1857 to 1864 he served as chaplain to the Scots Church in Kandy, Ceylon; in 1865 as the acting chaplain at Portsmouth; from 1866 to 1873 at the chapel in Garioch; and thereafter at the parish church of North Berwick.[14] Sprott was obviously aware of the liturgical needs of Scots living abroad, and his initial concerns with worship were stimulated by this knowledge.

Sprott was the first to publicly endorse a society of liturgical scholars in the church. He expected that after study and consideration, the society would publish a Book of Prayer for Public Worship which would include forms for the administration of the sacraments and serve as a guide in liturgical matters for clergy. Sprott encouraged investigation not only of Reformation liturgies, but those of antiquity as well, so that the published document would be based on the best the universal and historic church had to offer. Perhaps because of the great vacuum of liturgical resources, he had high hopes that such a book would be widely embraced by both clergy and laity.[15] He also lamented the loss to the church of "Irvingite men (members of the Catholic Apostolic Church), who would have corrected the Zwinglian notions of the sacraments, and the hard austerities of a Calvinism which is not Calvin's and restored the authority of the ministry."[16]   Sprott highlighted a primary concern of both the Irvingites and Mercersburg, that is, the re-establishment of the ministry and sacraments as integral parts of the worship of the church.

On January 31, 1865, three young pastors met in Glasgow and formed the Church Service Society. The Rev. Robert Herbert Story, the pastor at Rosneath, where he had followed the long pastorate of his father, was only thirty when the Society was formed. J. Cameron Lees, a minister at Paisley Abbey, was also thirty, and George Campbell, minister of the Parish of Eastwood, was thirty-seven. In spite of the fact that Sprott had initiated the idea of such a society, his presence in Ceylon made his attendance at the initial meeting impossible.

Following the January session, an invitation was issued to interested clergy to attend an open meeting on March 21, 1865. At that time, Principal Thomas Barclay of Glasgow University was appointed the first president. Principal John Tulloch of St. Mary's College, St. Andrews, Principal P. C. Campbell of Aberdeen University, Professor Robert Lee of Edinburgh University (formerly of Greyfriars'), and Professor John Caird of Glasgow University were all named as vice-presidents of the new society. Thirty-one ministers were in attendance at the first meeting.

Speaking twenty-five years after its formation, at the annual meeting of 1889, Dr. Story remembered the early days of the Church Service Society:

I remember when we began the Society—myself and two other friends—in a small back room in Glasgow. I remember when we first began to meet in Edinburgh in a small vestry. I remember how, on one occasion, the small vestry, owing to some mistake, was found to be locked, and we had to look about the High Street for any vacant chamber we could find. We were directed to one where Evangelical meetings were held on Sundays, and as the small and rather disconsolate band entered they were confronted by the inscription about the door of the hall: "The wicked shall be turned into hell." When I look at our present locality, or present numbers, I feel that such a meeting as this is one of the most emphatic testimonies that can be borne to the great progress the Society has made.[17]

At the initial open meeting in March, a report was offered to the group for adoption by Story, Lees, and Campbell. In this first report, the Society was made fully aware of the misconceptions it had to confront in the church of its birth. It was already widely believed that the Society had been formed to introduce a Liturgy into the Church of Scotland. This was emphatically denied as the constitutional apparatus of the church was acknowledged as the only appropriate means for the introduction of such a document. Rather, the Society established its work as "constructive" and "eclectic" in nature. Its constructive goals were to compile and compose forms for special services which were, at least initially, the celebration of the sacraments, a marriage service, and the burial of the dead. The Reformed churches of the Continent and the *Directory* were held up as models to be consulted and followed as the report clearly distanced itself from the Episcopal Church. The eclectic focus of the Society affirmed free prayer in the

life of the church, but at the same time, the report lauded
a compilation of prayers which would assist the pastor in
his work. Hoping they would not be perceived as crypto-
Catholics, the society confessed they could not ignore the
liturgical riches to be found in the Greek, Latin, Reformed,
Lutheran and Anglican communions.[18] Members
consulted the liturgical collections in the University libraries
of Edinburgh, St. Andrews, Glasgow, and Aberdeen.
Current liturgical volumes were also sought out and
examined.

> Such are the already mentioned work by Dr. Lee, and
> that issued in the name of the General Assembly; "A
> Chapter on Liturgies," by Mr. Baird, an American
> Presbyterian minister, and edited in this country by
> Dr. Binney, of London; the "Liturgy of the Dutch
> Church of North America;" the "Liturgy of the
> German Reformed Church of North America;" the
> "Liturgy of the Lutheran Church in America,"
> translated into English; "The Book of Common
> Prayer, as amended by the Presbyterian Divines of the
> Savoy Conference," edited by Dr. Shields of
> Philadelphia; the "Liturgy of the Holy Catholic
> Apostolic Church" (vulgarly called the "Irvingite");
> Dr. Cumming's Edition of "John Knox's Book of
> Prayer;" Hall's "Reliquiae Liturgicae," in 5 small
> vols.; and some others. These are mentioned as
> being, for the most part, comparatively recent
> publications, and so cheap as to be accessible to
> all.[19]

The inclusion of both the Irvingite and the Liturgy of the
German Reformed Church should be noted, for it will be to
these two liturgies that the Society will look in the
production of the *Euchologion* in 1867.

The constitution of the Society promoted the study and republication of the historic liturgies of the church. To that end, the Society published a series of volumes of reprints: *The Book of Common Order, Commonly Called Knox's "Liturgy,"* edited by G.W. Sprott; *Scottish Liturgies of the Reign of James VI*, edited by G.W. Sprott; *The Westminster Directory*, edited by Thomas Leishman; *The Second Liturgy of Edward VI*, edited by H.J. Witherspoon; and *The Liturgy of 1637, Commonly Called "Laud's Liturgy,"* edited by James Cooper. The most important volume published under the area of "constructive" publication however, was the *Euchologion*. Before focusing specifically on this volume, the convener of the initial subcommittee of 1865 and the editorial committee, Robert Herbert Story, should be introduced.

Robert Herbert Story was born in 1835, the same year the twelve apostles were called to form the Catholic Apostolic Church, and one year after the death of Edward Irving. Irving and Story's father, Robert Story, were boyhood friends. They corresponded and visited often throughout Irving's short lifetime. When Drummond invited those interested in prophecy to Albury in 1826, Story was among those who attended. He was initially impressed with the sincerity with which the meetings were conducted and the spirituality which permeated its members. Subsequently, he became disenchanted with the direction the annual meetings were taking, and removed himself. It was in Rosneath, Scotland, Story's parish, that the first stirrings of the charismatic movement began. Story wrote the *Memoir of Isabella Campbell* which publicized Campbell's quasi-mystic communion with the Divine. The book was widely read in England and Scotland, and reprinted in America.[20] In 1831, Story received a small group of interested laypeople led by John Bate Cardale and convinced them of the integrity of the events of healing and glossolalia in his parish. The miraculous healing of Mary Campbell, Isabella's sister, in 1831, ultimately led the London group to form local prayer meetings to plead for a similar outpouring of the Spirit in England. Mary Campbell later married W.R. Caird, who became a prominent member of the Catholic Apostolic Church. Story later questioned Mrs. Caird's motives in her subsequent use of the healing experience, which led to a series of accusatory letters between him and Drummond, under whose care she had settled. Story and Irving were also at odds concerning the events in London which would finally spell Irving's downfall and death. Irving encouraged Story not to hold back from the work of the Lord, and to stop standing aloof from God's new age.[21]

In spite of these tensions, Robert Herbert Story recounts in his father's biography that throughout his entire life, members of the Catholic Apostolic Church were among his dearest friends. His father knew their beliefs and their principles, and when time and schedule permitted, he joined readily in their public worship.[22] There appears to be little doubt concerning Story's continuing relationship with, and knowledge of, the Catholic Apostolic Church. Undoubtedly, his son gleaned a great deal of information concerning the church through his father's experiences.

Robert Story was born in 1790, ordained in 1818, and having served the parish of Rosneath his entire ministerial career, died in 1859 to be followed in his ministry by his son and biographer. Among the letters of condolence received at his death and printed in his biography, was one from one of the "Angels" of the "Holy, Catholic, Apostolic Church."[23]   Included in the same volume, penned in 1862, just three years after his death, was the account of Henry Drummond's ordination on December 28, 1832 in Albury Park.

The above information clearly demonstrates not only Robert Story's relationship with the initial events which led to the formation of the Catholic Apostolic Church and his association with the major personalities of the movement, but also his lifelong connection with the church. His occasional attendance at its worship undoubtedly included his son, who is the focus of these pages. Robert Herbert Story, convener of the initial subcommittee of the Church Service Society in 1865, recommended that the Society look closely at the Liturgy of the Catholic Apostolic Church. When the *Euchologion* was produced in 1867, it was Story who served as the chief compiler of the document. When Robert Herbert Story's own daughter wrote his biography in 1909, she further highlighted this most important connection by including Margaret Oliphant's recollection of travelling to the Story home to study correspondence for her biography of Edward Irving:

> Mr. Story told me of his father's long intimacy with Irving, and promised me many letters if I would go to the manse of Rosneath to see them. I went accordingly, rather unwillingly in cold February weather, grudging the absence from my children for few days very much. I did not know anything about the West of Scotland, and, winter as it was, the lonely little loch was a revelation to me, with the wonderful line of hills called the Duke's Bowling Green, which I afterwards came to know so well. The family at the manse was a very interesting one....[24]

The Story family and the Catholic Apostolic Church were far from strangers. Story entered his liturgical tasks with a knowledge of the formation and worship of the church, and a certain family loyalty to its work.

The Euchologion

The major responsibility for compiling the *Euchologion* was given to G.W. Sprott, Principal Tulloch, and the convener of the Editorial committee, Robert Herbert Story. The report to the Society in 1866-1867 indicated that the committee had drafted forms for the administration of both the Lord's Supper and Baptism, the celebration of marriage and a lectionary and materials helpful in the planning of a Lord's Day service. However, one of the marriage services and one table of lessons were borrowed directly from liturgical books published in America.[25] The committee played a dominant role in compiling contributions from individual members of the committee, and editing them to meet the perceived needs of the church.

The first edition of the *Euchologion*, also called the *Book of Common Order*, was published by the Church Service Society in 1867. This edition had a printing of 750 copies, thus making it now a fairly rare volume. It contained a large number of footnotes indicating sources, and a lengthy appendix consisting of a bibliography of the liturgical works found in Scottish Universities. The preface reminds the reader of the liturgical tradition of the church dating back to the Reformation and introduces the work to come. The book contains forms for baptism, for the Lord's Supper (with an introductory section analyzing different Communion Services), for marriage and burial, a lectionary of psalms and lessons, a selection of prayers for public worship, and the appendix of liturgical works.

The second edition in 1869, the first to use the title, *Euchologion*, added our complete services of public worship, forms for the admission of catechumens and for ordination. The sacramental services, which were in the front of the initial volume, were placed towards the back with the table of lessons and the "Materials for the Construction of a Service for Public Worship on the Lord's Day" taking an introductory position. The first two services were taken largely from the works of Jeremy Taylor, while the second two depend more heavily on the Catholic Apostolic Church. The third edition appeared in 1874, with the only new service being a form for the baptism of adults. In 1877, a fourth edition displayed few changes, but the fifth contained many new items. For the first time the Apostles' Creed was provided for use at every service, the *Sursum Corda* in the service for Holy Communion, and new orders were included for the Visitation of the Sick, the Admission of Elders, the Laying of the Foundation Stone, and the Dedication of a Church. The Nicene Creed was also printed for use in the Communion Service, with the Apostles' Creed still provided as an alternative. A controversial sixth edition was published in 1890 which placed the Lord's Prayer, the intercessions and commemorations before, instead of after, the sermon. This "Anglican" re-ordering of the prayers caused a great outcry from some members of the Society (it appears Sprott and Leishmann were particularly opposed) who perceived that Anglicanizing of the order of service as a move away from the primitive practice and toward a morning prayer format. Over such objections, the changes were voted and were maintained for many years to come. The sixth edition also made the Nicene Creed the confession for exclusive use in communion services and the *Agnus Dei* was introduced before the prayer of access. A seventh edition was issued in 1896, with the total number of copies printed in the seven edition being 10,557.[26]

A special edition was published in 1905 under the editorship of G.W. Sprott. The text of this special edition is that of the seventh edition, but includes a full history of the reintroduction of liturgical forms into the Scottish church. More importantly, the appendix identifies the sources of the prayers utilized in the *Euchologion*. It appears obvious from the sources cited that the prayerbook drew from a wide range of liturgical texts, with the early Reformed services being most prominent. The names of Luther, Calvin, Hermann, and Jeremy Taylor also are frequently listed, and this listing reflects a dependence on Knox's *Liturgy* and Lee's "Prayers for Public Worship." Such a list only scratches the surface of the works and people listed by Sprott in the appendix. The preface of the appendix lists the following abbreviations utilized in the text revealing their frequent use:

A.	For the Greek Liturgies, Latin Sacramentaries, Leonine, Gelasian, Gregorian, the Ambrosian, and Mozarabicrites--and all pre-Reformation prayers.
R.	For the Genevan and other Continental Liturgies of that type.
E.	For the English Book of Common Prayer.
S.	For Knox's Liturgy and Church of Scotland Prayers for Social and Family Worship (1st edition).
D.	For the American (Dutch) Reformed Liturgy.
CA.	For the Liturgy of the Catholic Apostolic Church.
G.	For the Provisional Liturgy of the America German Reformed Church, 1857.
P.	For the Book of Common Worship, printed by authority of the Presbyterian Church, U.S.A., 1905.[27]

However, it is the influence of the Catholic Apostolic Church, a considerable one according to Sprott, that is of particular interest.[28] Horton Davies has observed that it took brave men to borrow from the liturgical treasures not only of the Greek, Roman, Anglican, and Reformed traditions, but also from the Catholic Apostolic Church, a sect founded by a Scottish pastor ostracized by the Church of Scotland a mere generation before.[29]

The first *Euchologion* introduced its service for the Lord's Supper with an analysis of communion services. These rites began with the service of Justin Martyr and the *Apostolic Constitutions*, an Eastern service translated by Neale, and the Roman Mass. The Reformed Services, described or outlined, include the old French and Genevan order, the present Genevan form, the Neufchatel service (utilized in Charleston, South Carolina), the Dutch service, the service in the *Book of Common Order*, the Anglican service, and the Order of the Westminster *Directory*. There were two modern services listed, the Liturgy of the "Holy Catholic and Apostolic" Church and the American German Reformed Service, the latter of which was introduced with the words: "This follows the 'Irvingite', and both the ancient order."[30] Following an analysis of each section of the Eucharistic liturgy common to most of the rites, the compiler of the *Euchologion* states:

> The ancient and Catholic devotional material is to be found in modernized forms which can scarcely be improved upon in the "Irvingite" liturgy, and the American German Reformed service. The prayers on the annexed Communion Service are, with a few, chiefly verbal, exceptions, taken from these sources, and arranged differently.[31]

G. W. Sprott, a member of the Editorial Committee, fifteen years later, reiterated the fact that the *Euchologion* was drawn from many sources, but then observed: "...but it is based ultimately upon the Eastern Liturgies, like the American (German) Reformed, and Catholic Apostolic Services, from which it is largely borrowed."[32] The Irvingites had never claimed to have created a new liturgy, but rather to have re-created the worship of the church from the best it had to offer consistent with divine revelation.

The Order for Communion in the *Euchologion* begins with an exhortation after the prayer following the sermon. The exhortation is primarily from the *Book of Common Order* and the *Book of Common Prayer*, which at times have identical wording. It ends with the phrase, "Holy things which are for holy persons," and then dismisses those who do not intend to commune. After the collection of alms and during the singing of a hymn, the minister and elders bring in the elements and place them on the communion table. The communicants move to the table or tables, and the communion service proper is ready to begin. The minister pronounces the Apostolic Benediction and then reads the words of institution following the order of the *Directory*. An Address is then offered calling the congregation to remember Christ in the Supper. The compilers of the *Euchologion* point to the Dutch Liturgy as being influential in the writing of the address. They then observe concerning the next section:

> The wording is a compilation; what is said of the communion of saints after the text of Scripture is compiled from Dr. Lee's Order of Public Worship, the "Irvingite," German Reformed, and the ancient prayers of commemoration.[33]

The address is followed by a profession of faith, which in the initial volume was the Apostles' Creed, but altered to become the Nicene in later editions. Then comes a "Prayer of Access" which is largely borrowed from the Liturgy of the Catholic Apostolic Church:

Irvingite Liturgy

Almighty God, our heavenly Father, who admittest Thy people unto such wonderful communion, that, partaking by a divine mystery of the Body and Blood of Thy dear Son, they should dwell in Him, and He in them; We unworthy sinners, approaching to Thy presence and beholding Thy Divine glory, do abhor ourselves, and repent in dust and ashes. We have sinned, we have grievously sinned against Thee, in thought, in word, and in deed, provoking most justly Thy wrath and indignation against us. We have broken our past vows, we have dishonoured Thy holy Name, and profaned Thy holy sanctuary.

Yet now, most merciful Father, have mercy upon us; for the sake of Jesus Christ, forgive us all our sins; deliver us, by the inspiration of Thy Holy Spirit, from all uncleannes in spirit and in flesh; and give unto us heartily to forgive others, as we beseech Thee to forgive us, and to serve Thee hence forth in newness of life, to the glory of Thy holy Name; through Jesus Christ our Lord. AMEN.[34]

Euchologion

Almighty God, our heavenly Father, who admittest Thy people into such wonderful communion, that partaking of the body and blood of Thy dear Son, they should dwell in Him, and He in them; we unworthy sinners, approaching Thy presence, and beholding Thy glory, do abhor ourselves, and repent in dust and ashes. We have grievously sinned against Thee in thought, in word, and in deed, provoking most justly Thy wrath and indignation against us. We have broken our past vows, we have dishonoured Thy Holy name, and are unworthy of the least of all Thy mercies.

Yet now, most gracious Father, have mercy upon us; for the sake of Jesus Christ forgive us all our sins; purify us from all uncleanness in spirit and in flesh; enable us heartily to forgive others as we beseech Thee to forgive us; and grant that we may hereafter serve Thee in newness of life to the glory of Thy holy Name; through Jesus Christ our Lord. AMEN.[35]

The Absolution is omitted in the Scottish rite and then the "prayer of the veil" is offered:

Irvingite Liturgy

O God, who by the blood of Thy dear Son hast consecrated unto us a new and living way into the holiest of all; grant unto us, we beseech Thee, the assurance of Thy mercy, and sanctify us by Thy heavenly grace: that we approaching unto Thee with pure heart and undefiled conscience, may offer unto Thee a sacrifice in righteousness, and duly celebrate these holy mysteries, to the glory of Thy name; through Jesus Christ our Lord. AMEN.[36]

Euchologion

O God, who by the blood of Thy dear Son has consecrated for us a new and living way into the holiest of all, grant unto us, we beseech Thee, the assurance of Thy mercy, and sanctify us by Thy Holy spirit that drawing near unto Thee in these holy mysteries with a pure heart and undefiled conscience, we may offer unto Thee a sacrifice in righteousness, through Jesus Christ our Lord. AMEN.[37]

Later editions add the *Agnus Dei* and *Sursum Corda*, with the Eucharistic prayer following. Although the two prayers are not a word-for-word rendition, the dependence remains clear:

Irvingite Liturgy

It is very meet, right, and our bounden duty, that we should at all times and in all places give thanks unto Thee, O Lord, Father Almighty, Eternal God; who, together with Thine Only-begotten Son and the Holy Ghost, are ONE GOD AND ONE LORD.

For Thou didst create heaven and earth, and all things that are therein. Thou hast given unto us life and being. By Thy providence are the fruits of the earth preserved; and by Thy blessing we, and all things living, are sustained:...

For all Thy bounties known to us, for all unknown, we give Thee thanks. But chiefly that, when through disobedience we had fallen from Thee, Thou didst not suffer us to depart from Thee forever; Thou hast ransomed us from eternal death, and given us the joyful hope of everlasting life, through Jesus Christ; who, being very and eternal God, dwelling with Thee before all time in glory and blessedness unspeakable, came down from heaven in perfect love, from perfect Love, and became very Man for our salvation.

We bless thee for His holy Incarnation; for His life on earth; for His precious sufferings and death upon the cross; for His resurrection from the dead; and for His glorious ascension to Thy right hand.

We bless Thee for the giving of the Holy
Ghost; for all the sacraments and ordinances of Thy
church; and for the most blessed communion of all
saints in these holy mysteries. We bless Thee for the
hope of everlasting life, and of the glory which shall
be brought unto us at the coming, and in the
kingdom, of Thy dear Son.

Thee, mighty God, heavenly King, we
magnify and praise. We worship and adore Thy
glorious Name; the Name of the Father, and of the
Son, and of the Holy Ghost; joining in the hymn of
angels, and archangels, and all the hosts of heaven,
the cherubim and seraphim before Thy throne, and
singing unto Thee,...[38]

Euchologion

It is very meet and right, above all things, to give
thanks unto Thee, O eternal God: who, by Thy word,
didst create heaven and earth, and all things therein;
who didst, at the first, make man after Thine own
image and likeness, and by whose providence we and
all things living are sustained.

For all Thy bounties known to us, for all
unknown, we give Thee thanks; but chiefly that when,
through disobedience, we had fallen from Thee, Thou
didst not suffer us to depart from Thee for ever, but
has ransomed us from eternal death, and given us the
joyful hope of everlasting life, through Jesus Christ
Thy son; who, being Very and Eternal God, dwelling
with Thee before all time, in glory and blessedness
unspeakable, came down from heaven and became
Man for us men, and for our salvation. Not as we
ought, but as we are able, we bless Thee for His holy
incarnation; for His life on earth; for His precious
sufferings and death upon the cross; for His
resurrection from the dead; and for His glorious
ascension to Thy right hand.

> We bless Thee for the giving of the Holy
> Ghost; for the sacraments and ordinances of the
> Church; for the communion of Christ's body and
> blood; for the great hope of everlasting life, and of an
> eternal weight of glory.
> Thee, mighty God, heavenly King, we
> magnify and praise. With angels and archangels, and
> all the hosts of heaven, we worship and adore Thy
> glorious name, joining in the song of Cherubim and
> Seraphim, and saying,...[39]

Both texts then proceed to the *Sanctus*, which is
again almost word-for-word the same. Next, the
Euchologion prints an Invocation followed by the Lord's
Prayer, while the Irvingites place the Lord's Prayer before
their Consecration.

At this critical point in the liturgy the place of
consecration, the *Euchologion* echoes more clearly the *Book
of Common Prayer* with the major addition of an epiclesis.
The compilers of the *Euchologion* pointedly ask God to
sanctify with Word and Spirit the gifts of bread and wine.
After this explicit epiclesis the *Euchologion* borrows
directly from the *Book of Common Prayer* with the words:
"that we, receiving them, according to our Savior's
Institution, in thankful remembrance of His death and
passion, may, through the power of the Holy Ghost, be
partakers of His body and blood, with all His benefits, to
our salvation and the glory of Thy most holy name."[40]

The Communion is initiated with the Words of
Institution including the manual actions of breaking the
bread and taking the cup. The celebrant first communes,
then the elders, and finally the people. When all have
received, the minister shares the peace. The first prayer of
thanksgiving is dependent on the *Book of Common Prayer*,

but channeled through the Irvingite Liturgy to the *Euchologion.* A careful study of the texts reveal the prayer in the *Euchologion* to be an almost exact duplication of the one found in the Catholic Apostolic rite, indicating the mediating role played by the sect.

The First Prayer Book of King Edward VI (1549)

Almightye and euerlyuyng GOD, we moste hartely thanke thee, for that thou hast vouchsafed to feede us in these holy Misteries, with the spirituall foode of the most precious body and bloud of thy sonne, our savior Jesus Christ, and hast assured us (duely receiuing the same) of thy faour and goodnes toward us, and that we be very membres incorporate in thy Misticall bodye, whiche is the blessed companye of all faythfull people: and heyres through hope of thy euerlasting kingdome, by the merites of the most precious death and passion, of thy dere soone. Wee therefore most humbly beseche thee, O heauenly father, so to assist us with thy grace, that we may continue in that holy felowship, and doe all suche good woorkes, as thou hast prepared for us to walke in, through Hesus Christe our Lorde, to whome with thee, and the holy goste, bee all honor and glory, world without ende.[41]

Irvingite Liturgy

ALMIGHTY and everlasting God, we most heartily thank Thee, that Thou hast now vouchsafed to feed us with the spiritual food of the most precious Body and Blood of Thy Son our Saviour Jesus Christ, assuring us thereby that we are very members incorporate in the mystical body of Thy Son, and heirs through hope of Thine everlasting kingdom. And we most humbly beseech Thee, O heavenly Father, so to assist us with Thy grace, that we may continue in that holy fellowship, and do all such good works as Thou hast prepared for us to walk in; through Jesus Christ our Lord, (to whom, with Thee and the Holy Ghost, be all honour and glory, world without end). R. AMEN.[42]

Euchologion

ALMIGHTY and everlasting God, we most heartily thank Thee that Thous hast now vouchsafed to feed us with the spiritual food of the most precious body and blood of Thy Son our Saviour Jesus Christ, assuring us thereby that we are very members incorporate in the mystical body of thy Son, and heirs through hope of Thine everlasting kingdom. And we beseech Thee, O heavenly Father, so to assist us with Thy grace that we may continue in that holy fellowship, and do all such good works as Thou has before ordained that we should walk in them; through Jesus Christ our Lord....[43]

The second prayer of thanksgiving and self-dedication which follows is similar in tone to the Prayer of Oblation after Communion printed in the Irvingite Liturgy. As in the *Provisional Liturgy* of the German Reformed Church of 1857, the *Euchologion* ends the prayer with a self-oblation of "souls and bodies." Intercessions for the Church Militant follow the style and substance of both the German and Irvingite ties as well. The prayer for thanks for the Church Triumphant echoes the Irvingite liturgy:

Irvingite Liturgy

Hasten, O God, the time when Thou shalt send...but with unveiled face we shall then behold Him, rejoicing in His glory, made like unto Him in

His glory; and by Him we, with all Thy Church, holy
and unspotted, shall be presented with exceeding joy
before the presence of Thy glory.   Hear us, O
heavenly Father, for His sake, to whom, with Thee
and the Holy Ghost, One living and true God, be
glory for ever and ever. AMEN.[44]

Euchologion

And rejoicing in the communion of Thy
saints... when, made like unto Christ, we shall behold
Him with unveiled face, rejoicing in His glory, and by
Him we, with all Thy church, holy and unspotted,
shall be presented with exceeding joy before the
presence of Thy glory. Hear us, O heavenly Father,
for His sake; to whom, with Thee and the Holy
Ghost, be glory for ever and ever. AMEN.[45]

This last prayer is followed by the *Nunc Dimittis* as
prescribed in Calvin's Strasbourg Liturgy. The service ends
with the Benediction.

The *Order of the Provisional Liturgy* of the
American German Reformed Church of 1857 clearly
followed much more closely the Irvingite rite than the
Euchologion. However, the evidence remains convincing,
that the *Euchologion* looked to the Irvingites for a great
deal of the substance of their prayers. As clearly stated in
the analysis of communion services in the preface of the
Euchologion, it was the Irvingite and Mercersburg liturgies
which most clearly transformed the ancient traditions into
modern rites for the Scottish compilers. The reintroduction
of the Eucharist as the central act of the worshipping
community, and the reintegration of traditional and catholic
sources into their worship, were two of the main goals of

the compilers of the *Euchologion*. A considerable amount of borrowing of additional material from the Irvingites also appears in other services of the *Euchologion*, a dependence which lies outside the scope of the essay.[46]

The Catholic Apostolic Church clearly mediated the liturgical riches of the East and West to the Scottish Church. The form for the celebration of Holy Communion found in the *Euchologion* was used by Church of Scotland parishes from 1890 to 1923.[47] No book, in its several editions, has played a more critical role in the development of Presbyterian worship since the *Directory*. The prayers of the church, instead of rambling and often repetitious, were written in the liturgical prose of the church universal. The marriage and burial services were greatly improved, along with a service for dedication of churches. The Christian year was again observed, and most importantly, the Eucharist returned to a normative role in Sunday worship, consequently making its celebration more frequent.

The work of the Church Service Society served as an inspiration in the creation of other Reformed liturgical societies in the final years of the nineteenth century. In 1882 "The United Presbyterian Devotional Service Association" was formed, and in 1891 it published *Presbyterian Forms of Service*. In the same year, ministers of the Free Church formed "The Public Worship Association," and seven years later published *A New Directory for the Public Worship of God*.[48] In 1900 the two were fused into the "Church Worship Association" of the United Free Church. Finally in 1923, the reconstituted Church Service Society was formed from all three of the liturgical associations. In addition to these associations, certain individuals should also be cited as important in developing the liturgical consciousness of the church. John Hunter, pastor of the Trinity Congregational Church in

Glasgow, produced an influential volume in 1887 entitled, *Devotional Services for Public Worship*. Dr. Cameron Lees of the Church of Scotland, wrote and compiled the *St. Giles Book of Common Order* which was used in the cathedral between 1884 and 1926 and also had great influence on the rest of the kirk.

The Church of Scotland entered the nineteenth century like most other Presbyterians and Reformed churches, with a sermon-dominated worship. The Lord's Supper was celebrated infrequently. Baptism was celebrated in the home and with a minimum of liturgy. Through the energetic leadership of pastors like Robert Lee, Marshall Lang, Robert Herbert Story, G.W. Sprott, and many others, the Church of Scotland's liturgical life was renewed with the formation of the Church Service Society and the publication of the *Euchologion* in 1867.

A renewed commitment to the centrality of both word and sacrament became the cornerstone of public worship. While carefully guarding the freedom treasured by the Scottish people, the Church Service Society at the same time presented model sacramental and occasional services that reflected the best of both the Catholic and Reformed traditions. From an almost exclusive focus on the sermon as the means of grace in weekly worship, the Church of Scotland, by the end of the century, had again embraced a vision of worship and the sacraments that was Evangelical, Reformed and Catholic.

Endnotes

1. John Kerr, *The Renascence of Worship* (Edinburgh: J. Gardner Hitt, 1909).

2. Sprott, G., *Euchologion*, xv.

3. *Ibid.*, xii.

4. *Ibid.*, xiii.

5. *Ibid.*, xiv.

6. Alastair K. Robertson, "The Place of Robert Lee in the Developments in the Public Worship of the Church of Scotland 1840-1940:" *Church Service Society Annual* (May, 1958), 33.

7. Howard G. Hageman, *Pulpit and Table: Some Chapters in the History of Worship in the Reformed Churches* (London: SCM Press, 1962), 70-73.

8. Elizabeth Story, *Memoir of Robert Herbert Story* (Glasgow: James Maclehose & Sons, 1909), 64.

9. Sprott, G., *Euchologion*, xvi.

10. Robert Lee, *The Reform of the Church of Scotland in Worship*, Government and Doctrine (Edinburgh: Edmonston & Sons, 1866).

11. Andrew L. Drummond and James Bulloch, *The Church in Victorian Scotland 1843-1874* (Edinburgh: Saint Andrew Press, 1975), 196.

12. Stephen A. Hurlbut (ed.), *The Liturgy of the Church of Scotland*, Vol. 4 (Charleston: St. Albans Press, 1952), 94.

13. Alastair K. Robertson, "George Washington Sprott: 1829-1909," *Church Service Society Annual (1966)*, 10.

14. *Ibid.*

15. Sprott, G. *Euchologion*, xvii-xviii.

16. A. Robertson, "George Washington Sprott: 1829-1909," 11.

17. E. Story, 68.

18. Kerr, 59.

19. *Ibid.*

20. Robert H. Story, *Memoir of the Life of The Reverend Robert Story,* (Cambridge: Macmillan & Co., 1862), 139.

21. *Ibid.*, 227. Perhaps one of the most curious stories involving Story and Irving included Joseph Wolff, the Jewish convert, as well. On one of the Wolff's many travels he rescued from danger two Greek lads, whom he sent to Irving in London to be educated. Irving, in turn, wrote to Story a letter of introduction which described one of the "lads" as a twenty-four-year-old Deacon in the Greek church and the other a thirteen- or fourteen-year-old son of a Cypriot merchant. Irving encouraged Story to educate the youths in Scotland, and in the Scottish church, so they might be returned to their homes as "teachers and preachers." (Story, 249) The two young men did come to the small village of Rosneath, boarded with the schoolmaster, and caused quite an uproar in the quiet provincial countryside.

22. *Ibid.*, 236.

23. *Ibid.*, 375.

24. E. Story, 44.

25. William McMillan, "Euchologion: The Book of Common Order" *Church Service Society Annual* (May, 1936-1937): 24-25.

26. Kerr, 33.

27. Sprott, G., *Euchologion*, 419.

28. This thesis is defended most clearly by W. McMillan; Stuart Louden, "Centenary Reflections," *Church Service Society Annual* (May, 1965), 3-17; John M. Barkley, "The Liturgical Movement and Reformed Worship," *Church Service Society Annual* (May, 1961), 13-22.

29. Horton Davies, *Worship and Theology in England From Newman to Martineau 1850-1900* (Princeton: Princeton University Press, 1962), 98.

30. *Euchologion of Book of prayers*, issued by The Church Service Society, (Edinburgh and London: William Blackwood & Sons, 1867), 42.

31. *Ibid.*, 43. The *order* of the Communion Service, however, is primarily taken from the *Directory*.

32. George W. Sprott, *The Worship and Offices of the Church of Scotland* (London: William Blackwood & Sons, 1882), 118.

33. *Euchologion* (1867), 49.

34. *The Liturgy of the Catholic Apostolic Church*, 1-2.

35. *Euchologion* (1867), 52-53.

36. *The Liturgy of the Catholic Apostolic Church*, 2-3.

37. *Euchologion* (1867), 53-54.

38. *The Liturgy of the Catholic Apostolic Church*, 8-9.

39. *Euchologion* (1867), 53-54.

40. *Euchologion* (1867), 55.

41. As cited in Bard Thompson, ed., *Liturgies of the Western Church* (Cleveland: Meridian Books, 1961), 263-264.

42. *The Liturgy of the Catholic Apostolic Church* , 22.

43. *Euchologion* (1867), 61.

44. *The Liturgy of the Catholic Apostolic Church*, 17.

45. *Euchologion* (1867), 58.

46. See G.W. Sprott, *Euchologion* (1905).

47. William D. Maxwell, *A History of Worship In the Church of Scotland*, (New York: Oxford University Press, 1955), 177.

48. These societies are described in Charles G. McCrie, *The Public Worship of Presbyterian Scotland* (Edinburgh and London: William Blackwood & Sons, 1892), 349-353.

STORMING THE FORTS OF DARKNESS: ANGLO-CATHOLIC SACRAMENTAL REVIVALISM IN MID-VICTORIAN ENGLAND

Martin L. Cox, Jr.
United Methodist Church

"Brothers," he said, "Let us go to Calvary! In the contemplation of the Passion we best learn the secrets of mission work." He then went through some of the utterances on the Cross. "Christ thirsts," he said, "thirsts for the tears of the penitents. Jesus, as one with the Father, yearns for the return of prodigals." This was mission work—to satisfy the thirst, the loving thirst, of God, by speaking to men the one name of Jesus; not speaking mere doctrines, but revealing a personal Saviour. We had to tell men of the love of Jesus crucified, risen, ascending. Have much faith in preaching. Strike the rock and the waters shall gush out to slake the thirst of God. Tell the old, old story. The name of Jesus is mighty as ever. Don't work yourselves up, or try to work others up, to a state of excitement; but tell the old plain story. Conversion, we must remember, is the direct work of the Holy Spirit, and cannot be forced. We must go forth on the simple dependence on that, and then wait calmly and patiently.[1]

One might have expected these words to come from Dwight L. Moody, but they come from Fr. George Body, missioner, slum-priest, and Ritualist. Revivalism takes many forms in Victorian England, but one of the most intriguing was the expression of revivalism found within the Anglo-Catholic branch of the Church of England. The intent of this paper is to make a brief examination of the second generation Tractarians, and to see how they demonstrated a concern for revival, but revival along sacramental lines. The Twelve Day London Mission, of November 1869, will be used as an illustration of the sacramental revivalism exhibited by the Ritualists.

In order to see the unfolding of sacramental revivalism it is important to trace the roots of this movement back to its origins in the Tractarian Movement. It would not be an overstatement to say that names such as Keble, Pusey, and Newman took on a "holy aura" for the Ritualists. Fr. Desmond Morse-Boycott, in his less than objective study of the Tractarians and Sub-Tractarians, *They Shine Like Stars*, notes that, "Newman's influence will be felt in a thousand years' time. His books will be read and his life studied, his character will be loved and his hymns sung."[2] The Oxford Movement dawned upon a church divided into two theological parties: Cambridge's Evangelicals and Oxford's deists. Neither extreme would satisfy the commons room of Oriel College. To replace the atonement theology of the Evangelicals, the Tractarians offered an incarnational theology made apparent through the Church and the sacraments. To counter arid deism the Tractarians offered an imminent God present in bread and wine.

The Reformation was for the Tractarians an embarrassment. The glory of the Church could be found in the Fathers or the medieval church. They maintained that the sacraments were visible signs of God present in the church, not merely tokens of grace. Often overlooked is that the Tractarians saw the pulpit as a means of setting forth their tenets. It may be true that Newman was ". . .

essentially a writer for the pulpit rather than a great preacher."[3] Yet it is significant that one of the means used to get the Tractarian message across was the pulpit as well as the *Tracts for the Times.*

In turning to the second generation of Tractarians what first catches one's attention is their seeming absorption with ritual and all its trappings, earning for them the title "Ritualists." In truth, they might better bear the name "ceremonialists." "A ritualist means a liturgical expert who knows the history of Rites and services. They [the Ritualists] should have been called ceremonialists."[4]

What prodded the ecclesial anxiety of the average Mid-Victorian was the importance the Anglo-Catholics placed upon what they, Evangelicals and Broad Churchmen, would have deemed the proper understanding and celebration of the liturgy. The Ritualists' fascination with ceremony was all the more arresting when one realizes that the first generation Tractarians took little note of ceremony in the liturgy.

> Newman and Pusey were not sympathetic to change
> of trivial detail which might offend, to coloured stoles
> or rich hangings or unaccustomed postures. Pusey
> thought that the reassertion of Catholic truth must not
> be hindered by unnecessary provocation in ceremony,
> and that the simplicity of English practice was
> appropriate to the penitential state of divided
> Christendom.[5]

For the Ritualists ceremony became a critical element of the theological expression of their faith. Their love of, and need for, ceremony may have helped *describe* who was or was not a member of this party, but it did not *define* who they were.

> Carpenter defines Ritualists as slum-priests who for
> the sake of the poor they loved and served devotedly,
> they desired very earnestly to set forth the glory of
> God and the beauty of holiness. It seemed to them
> intensely important that the Holy Communion should
> have the chief place in Christian worship. To this
> end they built churches with lofty and noble chancels,
> and they adorned and beautified their altars, and they
> multiplied the number of celebrations.[6]

There are two critical elements in Carpenter's definition. The first is the social commitment shared by the Ritualists. G. W. E. Russell, biographer of Arthur Stanton and Pusey, and also the author of a fifty-year history of St. Alban, the Martyr Church, Holborn, a Ritualist church and center of ritualist controversy, described the community into which St. Alban's was built as a place where "Decent people seldom ventured into its courts and alleys. If they did they ran the risk of being assailed with filthy missiles and filthier words from inhabitants who resented all intrusion. The very policemen appeared rarely, and then in pairs."[7] In assessing the East-end congregations of ritualist parishes in the 1880s, Maurice Davies, *The Times* of London religious editor, observed that, ". . . it must be remembered that it is not the fashion here to go to church, as it is at the West. Those who come to church mean something by it. They are earnest. Life is terribly earnest in the East-end of London."[8] The church he wrote about was yet another Ritualist church assaulted with controversy, St. George-in-the-East. This mission was started by Fr. Charles Lowder and drew to it the implacable Ritualist warrior Alexander Heriot Machonochie.

What attracted the Ritualists to the slums was a desire to reach and convert society's outcasts, and to do so using Ritualist methods. Anglo-Catholics believed that,

> What would attract the masses and penetrate their minds was the use of symbols, colour, processions, music, drama -- a pattern which the sacramental system justified theologically. The sacraments of the Church, which Ritualists did not limit to those of Baptism and the Lord's Supper, offered the proper basis, not only for a symbolic presentation of Christianity which was to communicate where language had failed, but which was to communicate the reality of what was symbolized, for the Anglo-Catholics believed that the symbols of bread and wine made available not only the idea of God, but the presence of God.[9]

The slums became the home mission field--a field ripe unto harvest, employing a Tractarian theological framework, and expressing itself in Anglo-Catholic ceremonial as reflected in their sacramental theology. Some figures from one of the efforts, St. Alban's Church, constructed in the 1860s and first pastored by Machonochie, indicated the success with the Ritualist's strategy.

> Within [sic] seven years from the consecration of the church [21 February 1863] . . . the number of baptisms had risen from 295 to 537, marriages from 5 to 8, Easter communicants from 291 to 596, and offertories from 541 pounds to 2,184 pounds. In brief, whatever may be thought of the theological lines on which it was conducted, the work of St. Alban's was earnest, was practical, and was eminently successful.[10]

The second element in Carpenter's definition of Ritualists was that Holy Communion should have the *chief* place in Christian worship. This distinguished Ritualism from other movements in the Church of England.

> By the 1860's advanced Anglo-Catholic churches could be recognized by whether or not they observed what were known as the 'six points': taking the eastward position at the Eucharist; wearing the full eucharistic vestments; mixing water with wine in the chalice; using lighted candles on the altar; using unleavened bread or wafer bread in the Eucharist; and using incense during the service.[11]

If one examines the charges brought against the Ritualists by their opponents, one will see that the ceremonials associated with Holy Communion became the telling issue. In 1867 Mochonochie was brought before the Court of Arches and charged with

> Having elevated the paten and the chalice, and with bowing, kneeling, or prostrating himself before the consecrated elements; with using lighted candles on the communion table during the celebration of Communion, although they were not necessary to provide light; with the ceremonial use of incense during the Communion Service; and with mixing water with wine in the Communion (intinction or the Mixed Chalice.)[12]

The danger is to assume that ceremonial was practiced because it was deemed to be the best and only way to celebrate the Eucharist; that the Ritualists looked "Roman" simply because they assumed Rome knew how properly to celebrate the Eucharist.

Whereas some Ritualists may have used ceremonials simply because Rome did, most took seriously the various ceremonials as an expression of their sacramental theology. As it pertains to the Ritualist's eucharistic theology, it can be said that

> . . . the profession of the doctrine of the Real Presence and the real Sacrifice in the Eucharist made it "impossible to be satisfied with the bare and denuded churches which at their best were but preaching halls, where there no longer was an altar, and where, behind the high-backed pews, the pulpit, and the reading desk, one could hardly catch a glimpse of the plain wooden table upon which on very rare occasions the communion Service was celebrated, without honour, and often without decency."[13]

Far too often we have looked at *what* the Ritualists did rather than *why*. The answer to "why" lay in the belief, outlined in Pusey's sermon, *The Holy Eucharist A Comfort to the Penitent*, preached in 1843. The sacrament of the Lord's Supper was no mere (bare) memorial by which Christ is at best symbolically present. In the celebration of the Eucharist Christ is really and powerfully present. The focal point, therefore, of the offering of the sacrifice must be the altar. Thus the altar, and all that drew attention to it, were of serious concern to the Ritualists. Again, Maurice Davies describes the altars found in Anglo-Catholic churches during Christmas 1874, in London.

> As regards the "Highest" churches a decided tendency on the part of the [Christmas] decorations to retire from the body of the church, not only in the sacrarium, but on the altar itself. Several churches had no decorations, either in the nave or chancel, but

exhausted all their efforts in vases of flowers and
profuse lights on the holy table. This is very
significant. As the sacramental system gains ground,
all interest gradually gathers to the altar as the focus
. . . the adornment converges to the altar as a fixed
point.[14]

The need for proper vestments for the celebration of
the Eucharist would seem a logical conclusion to such a
view of the Real Presence. The Ritualist's most
controversial activity, the introduction and use of
Confession, which shall be addressed shortly, can best be
explained in light of the Eucharist. "A high doctrine of the
Sacraments inevitably produced an emphasis on adequate
preparation by fasting and confession, the arts of mental
prayer, and the asceticism that was the proof of sacramental
living."[15] The full expression of Anglo-Catholic
sacramental theology was manifest during the Twelve Day
London Mission of 1869.

The Religious Census of 1851 proved to be a
shocking revelation to a nation that prided itself on its
religious heritage. Some of the results of the census were
as follows:

Total population of England and Wales	17,927,609
Attending the Church of England	5,292,551
Attending Roman Catholic Churches	383,630
Attending Main Protestant Churches	
(Presbyterian, Methodist, etc.)	4,536,264[16]

"About five and a quarter million people failed to do their
duty [attend church]—here was a great mission field in
England, which the churches must co-operate in
attacking."[17] What was also evident was that the large
urban areas were the haven for most of the nation's

unchurched. The Census indicated that ". . . the strength of the Church of England to be in the home counties and the east. In the big towns dissent was shown to be strong."[18]

The Ritualists' response to the unchurched in England, and London's inner city in particular, was not restricted to establishing mission outposts and building churches in slum areas. The idea of holding a twelve-day mission, centered in established parishes, bore fruition in November 1869. The mission lasted from 14 November to 23 November. "In central and west London, about sixty-four parishes with some degree of Anglo-Catholic sympathy took part; another forty-eight parishes, most of them in East London, took part after the mission had started, mostly confining their activity to preaching services of the traditional evangelical sort."[19] *The Times* of 24 November described the mission by quoting the Mission's printed material. "What is a mission? It is a call to the unconverted—to grow in grace! To the unconverted—to flee from the wrath to come! To all—to prepare to meet their God!" But what was the origin of a twelve-day mission?

On this question there are two differing opinions. Dieter Voll, in his work *Catholic Evangelicalism*, contends that the Twelve Day Mission traced its source from the evangelical tradition. He shows the evangelical heritage shared by many of the Tractarians and Ritualists. Voll then points out the common features between traditional evangelical concerns and Ritualist practices: the saving of souls, the power of the sermon, the call for response. Voll concludes that what one has in the Twelve Day Mission is a ritualistic expression of old evangelical revivalistic attitudes and practices—evangelism with a sacramental accent. Horton Davies shares a similar view by indicating not so much a direct link between the Evangelicals, but rather a "borrowing" of the Ritualists from the Evangelicals. "Perhaps the most conspicuous example of Tractarian borrowing from Evangelicalism is seen in the provision of evangelical missions in which passionate preaching and sacred songs predominated, after the example of those invincibly Protestant American evangelists, Moody and Sankey."[20]

Another suggestion is made concerning the origin of the London Mission by John Kent. In his volume, *Holding the Fort*, Kent argues that the Ritualists turned not to the old evangelical methods, but to a Roman Catholic mission model. "The movement did not draw on evangelical sources for its revivalistic technique . . . but turned to French Catholic precedents, in which preaching had always been as prominent as it was in Protestantism."[21]   Kent reinforces his position by indicating that Lowder, one of the planners of the Twelve Day London Mission, and the founder of the Anglican religious order, the Society of the Holy Cross, ran afoul of his bishop by involving himself in a rather embarrassing incident.   He encouraged some lads to bombard a vocal opponent with rotten eggs.   Lowder was suspended from his curacy for six weeks during which ". . . he went abroad and spent some days at the Petit Seminaire at Yvetot, in the diocese of Rouen, where he seems to have taken up in the library the *Life of St. Vincent de Paul*."[22] Lowder was attracted by the commitment St. Vincent de Paul had for the poor of the city, a commitment shared by Lowder.

> Anglo-catholics like Lowder were not in the mood to
> adapt Evangelism to their own purposes. They were
> much more easily impressed by Roman Catholic
> models, and St. Vincent de Paul was no minor figure
> in the history of the Roman Church.   He first
> conceived the plan of his congregation of Mission

Priests in 1617, began to hold missions himself in the French countryside in 1618, and first elaborated his Rule in 1626. Lowder, by the time that he returned from France, was already scheming to form a similar order; the immediate result was the Society of the Holy Cross, which dated from 1855.[23]

In truth, it would appear that Voll and Kent have identified in the London Mission of 1869 elements that are both evangelical and Roman Catholic, but similarities do not prove definitive origins. It might be better to accept Horton Davies' word "borrow" regarding the origin of the London Mission. The Ritualists appear to have "borrowed" from two traditions which, at first, seem antithetical to each other—Evangelical and Roman Catholic. Yet they merge these two traditions into a sacramental revival in Mid-Victorian London.

One of the principal motives for the establishment of the London Mission was the Ritualist's overpowering conviction of the need for conversion. The desire to convert the masses was paramount to the Ritualists.

The Evangelicals seem sometimes to fancy that they have a monopoly of the teaching of Conversion. If they would attend a mission-service at a Ritualistic church . . . they would know better. They would learn that Catholics insist, with all force of which they are capable, on the absolute need of an unconditional surrender of the will to the Will of God; and place the whole hope of salvation in pardon through the Precious Blood, definitely sought by the individual sinner, for sins actually done in his body. It was not a Low Churchman who wrote:—

> If some poor wandering child of Thine
> Have spurned to-day the Voice Divine,
> Now, Lord, the gracious work begin;

> Let him no more lie down to sin.
> According to all Catholic teaching, the sinner, in the
> work of repentance, is *solus cum Solo*. If "the Voice
> Divine" reaches him on a desert island, a thousand
> miles from priest, or altar, or bible, he has only to
> turn to the Crucified Lord in repentance and faith.
> Then and there he is forgiven; then and there he is at
> peace.[24]

Even Lord Shaftesbury, the evangelical leader, was quoted as saying that "All zeal for Christ seems to have passed away. The Ritualists have more of it than the Evangelicals."[25]   Such words are not always identified with Anglo-Catholics, yet the yearning for lost souls was one of the motivating factors in the Ritualists' urban strategy. *The Times* quoted one of the handbills from the mission by referring to it as ". . . the 12 days of prayer and preaching for the conversion of sinners."[26] There can be little doubt that conversion was in the hearts and minds of the London missioners.

A second factor which needs to be considered as to what motivated the Twelve Day Mission was that the Ritualists felt that they had the solution to reaching the inner city. As Kent noted in his work, the Anglo-Catholics were convinced they could offer the means of reaching the masses through the power of symbols, color, and the drama of the liturgy. The lines were drawn between the subjectivity of the traditional evangelical attitudes toward evangelism and the objectivity demonstrated by the Ritualists. "Where Evangelicals had talked to the poor about the Spirit, Anglo-Catholics should bring them the real presence of Christ in the Eucharist. Where the Evangelicals offered them a subjective kind of self-forgiveness for their sins, Anglo-Catholics should offer them the objectified

forgiveness of priestly absolution in the Confessional."[27]
The Ritualists felt that they would be able to accomplish
that which the Evangelicals had failed to do. They would
convert the city through the power of symbols and the
might of mystery.

A third factor that should be taken into consideration
as to a motive for the London Mission venture might be
traced back to the 1851 Census which drove home a
chilling point to the Church of England. The established
church was strongest in rural England and weakest in the
cities. The major urban areas were quickly becoming the
strongholds of dissent. In London alone people were
flocking not to St. Paul's but to the Metropolitan
Tabernacle to hear Charles Haddon Spurgeon. In 1861,

> . . . the Metropolitan Tabernacle was built for him
> [Spurgeon], at a cost of over 30,000 pounds, and
> there he preached to the end of his life, to
> congregations of five thousand and more . . . . The
> preacher was the attraction; there was no organ and
> the singing was led by a precentor. At the end of
> 1891, the membership of the church stood at 5,311.
> Spurgeon used to say there was not a seat in the
> Tabernacle but somebody had been converted in it.[28]

A similar story could be told of the building and filling of
Methodist "Central Halls" in many of England's larger
cities. Related to this was the success in America of
Moody and Sankey. It was not until 1874 that the two
Americans held the first crusades in England and Scotland,
but their exploits would set the Evangelicals' agenda for
years to come. Convinced that conversion was needed to
redeem the urban centers, certain that they had the means
to bring about conversion and alarmed by the success of

dissenters in the cities, the Ritualists set upon a plan to conduct the Twelve Day London Mission of 1869. Such a mission enterprise was not new to the Ritualists. George Howard Wilkinson, the rector of St. Peter's, Great Windmill Street, London, during the 1869 London Mission, and one of the organizers of the Mission itself, had conducted previous mission weeks involving other clergy who would find themselves as missioners during the Twelve Day Mission. The London Mission would be a more intentional and more coordinated venture than had be tried to date.

A reporter from *The Times* gave one an outline of what a day at a mission church looked like.

> The afternoon services commence with prayer, partly extemporary. The clergyman [George Body] then takes his position at the entrance to the altar, reads a portion of Scripture, and then gives an exposition. After the address a hymn is sung, while the congregation is kneeling. This is succeeded by a prayer and benediction, and the announcement is made that the "Bible class" will commence in about five minutes, the congregation being asked to remain. Another portion of Scripture is read, followed by a second address. A similar proceeding is adopted in the evening at 8 o'clock. Occasionally the first address (for it cannot properly be called sermon) is delivered from the pulpit. There is no regular choir nor instrumental music. The singing is led by some of the ministers and juvenile members of the choir, who are stationed in the body of the church.[29]

One other part of the service noted in *The Times* a few days later, and one of the most debated parts of the Ritualists' movement was the "after service." "The clergy, in most cases, after the end of the services, retired into the vestries or sacristies, and occupied themselves with receiving penitents in confession up to a later hour. A guide to Confession, with prayers to be said before and after, is contained in the *Book of the Mission*, which was published under authority of the clergy . . ."[30]

We, thus, have a skeletal outline of an average service conducted during the Twelve Day London Mission. Its critical elements were: (1) the setting was the Nave, not parish hall or Sunday School room, let alone on street corners or parks; (2) preaching/addressing the congregation from the altar, as well as from the pulpit; (3) prayers, both read and extemporary; (4) hymn singing; and (5) the "after service" which invited individual converts to make their confession in private to the priest.

One of the points Voll seeks to make in his book is the similarity between the Evangelicals and Ritualists. Whereas there are some striking points of similarity, which shall be noted shortly, there is one obvious point at which the two positions part. The Evangelicals did not always see the center of evangelism as being the church structure. Evangelism often went outside the church. There were attempts to rent theaters and convert them into preaching centers, much in the manner of Spurgeon and other dissenters. Such practices were criticized by the Tractarians who believed that the church was the proper center for evangelism.[31] During the Twelve Day London Mission it was the church building that became the center for evangelical endeavor.

The "borrowing" from Evangelicals can best be seen in the preaching, praying, and singing. Kent is correct in recognizing that there could easily be a Roman Catholic origin of the preaching, praying, and singing. But the striking similarity between *current* evangelical practices, as opposed to copying seventeenth-century French Roman

Catholic practices, and the common history shared by
Ritualists in the evangelical tradition would lead one to see
in the implementation of traditional evangelical revival
techniques in a sacred setting, the church, and hallowed by
the overall sacramental overtone to the entire event, a
syncretization of evangelical and Roman Catholic practices.
If we examine the practices of one of the
Missioners, as related in *The Times*, we get the picture of
a priest who seems more like a revivalist in the evangelical
tradition than a Ritualist.

> Mr. Body is most able, zealous, and devoted, and has
> been delivering addresses that would have done credit
> to George Whitefield, John Wesley, or Father
> Hyacinthe. His whole soul appears to be in his work;
> he speaks with great eloquence, power and intense
> earnestness. His appeal to his hearers when urging
> them to immediately decide for Christ are most
> pathetic and touching. Numbers of people are
> evidently deeply impressed. Many seem to be
> engaged on their knees in prayer while he is
> preaching, others are affected to tears, and all are
> listening with rapt attention to his earnest entreaty that
> they should one and all accept there and then God's
> offer of mercy. Although Mr. Body's address and
> mode of delivery may be some be termed to a degree
> sensational, they cannot truthfully be so designated.
> When he, in a winning and subdued voice,
> affectionately implores those who listen to the Lord,
> and subsequently thunders forth his anathemas against
> the apathetic sinner sleeping on the verge of a
> precipice, unconscious of his imminent dangers, and
> urges him to rouse himself from the slumber of death
> and the Lord will give him light, he is only doing
> what Whitefield and John Wesley did before him, and
> with such great results.[32]

The comparison of Body's preaching to Whitefield and Wesley would have given the average reader of the article the clear impression that Evangelicals were at work in the Twelve Day Mission. But the preaching, and the style of the preaching, were not the only items borrowed from the evangelical tradition.

The prayers, which one must assume were read from the Book of Common Prayer, and also extemporaneous, would again lead one to see a strong element of the evangelical tradition. It would be false to assume that the Ritualists, who appeared to stretch the Prayer Book to its extremes, did not value the Book. It was the Book of Common Prayer that, according to the Ritualists, gave them the latitude to practice their ceremonials. Rather than seeing the use of extemporaneous prayers as something to be avoided, the Ritualists saw the need for such prayers, and unabashedly added them to their mission services.

Regarding the music used in the London Mission we have the account of Maurice Davies who indicated that,

> The Penitential Psalms were chanted slowly to the most unmitigated Gregorians, and the prayers monotoned very low down in the gamut. One cannot help wondering whether a little cheerful music written in round notes on five lines would not suit these simple people as well as the dreadful squareheaded notes on four lines. Why must we go back to imperfect musical notation when we want to sing about religion? The hymns, however, were lively, and 'There is a fountain', followed by its refrain, 'I do believe, I will believe', put one in mind of the meeting-house.[33]

Davies has given us a more revealing picture of what the Ritualists offered London in November 1869 than he might have thought. They offered their congregations sacred song from ancient tradition of the Church, "the Gregorian," side by side with the gospel hymns of the present, "There is a Fountain, with refrain." Singing of traditional revival hymns, in spite of the fact that Ritualist churches were well known for their surpliced male choirs, points again to the inclusion of evangelical elements in the Revival Mission alongside Roman Catholic elements.

One final issue in the London Mission needs to be identified, and this is probably the item which attracts most attention. The Twelve Day London Mission was an event that was wrapped in a sacramental theology which saw expression in a daily eucharist, a closing service of a Renewal of the Baptismal covenant, and the use of private Confession.

For any group of people who are claiming the sacrament of the altar as the primary act of worship a daily Eucharist would surprise no one. But the concluding event of the Twelve Day Mission being a Renewal of one's Baptismal Covenant was a new twist. Again we have the witness of *The Times* as to the nature of this event.

> [The Mission] came to an end last evening, when the services were concluded in nearly all the churches that had taken part in the movement by a "solemn renewal of baptismal vows." For this service a special form had been prepared. It consisted of one of the forms of confession in the Prayer Book, and a hymn; after which the officiating clergyman asked the congregation some of the questions and answers to be found in the Baptismal and Confirmation Services. to which the people present replied, "I do" and "I will," in a hearty and solemn manner. This was followed by another prayer and the blessing after which in many churches one or another hymns were sung, either standing or in procession . . . . The "renewal of baptismal vows" formed a very striking and effective

finale to the Revival Services.[34]

Since it appears that no copies of the service booklet used during the Mission Week survived, one is left trying to imagine what the baptismal renewal service might have looked like. What is of interest is not simply the shape of the service, but also the fact that the means of tying together the Twelve Day London Mission was through a renewal of baptismal vows. Baptismal regeneration had been an accepted position by the Ritualists since it was set forth by E. B. Pusey in *Tract LXVII*, "The Scriptural View of Holy Baptism." One would have to surmise that even though converting the unsaved of London might have been one of the motivating factors for the London Mission, the Ritualists also wanted to call back to the church those persons who stood in need of being reminded of what had transpired during their baptism. Thus the Mission ended on a note of sacramental renewal and a ceremony of *re-initiation*.

The final sacramental element that must be mentioned is Confession. The use of private Confession in the Church of England in the nineteenth century was rare. The Ritualists, and not without support from the first generation Tractarians, saw confession as a vital pastoral tool. Confession was seen, " . . . as an essential part of the Tractarian [Ritualist] parochial programme, and individual priests regarded it as the best method of developing within their parishioners an understanding of spirituality."[35] But the practice of auricular confession drew much anger from those outside Ritualistic circles. James Froude, brother of Richard Hurrell Froude, and a onetime supporter of the Tractarians during his Oxford days, in later years felt that the " . . . father confessors were busy in our families, dictating conditions of marriage, dividing wives from husbands, and children from parents."[36] He, like many others, saw confession as a threat to the Victorian family structure. More than this, he thought that confession was a Roman Catholic plot to lure away members of the established Church to the Church of Rome. Froude again wrote: "[The Ritualist] invites the ladies of his congregation to confess to him and whispers his absolution and having led them away from their old moorings, and filled the with aspirations which he is unable to gratify, he passes them over in ever-gathering numbers to the hands of the genuine Roman, who waits to receive them."[37]

Confession was one of the "worst renewal facets" of the first London Mission of 1869, said Maurice Davies five years later. "Some years ago, when what came to be called the 'Twelve Days' Mission' was organized, the movement got very much into the hands of one extreme part in the Church, and the tone of the teaching was what would be loosely termed 'High,' confession itself being freely advocated by one of the prominent preachers of the Mission."[38] In truth, confession was espoused by more than one preacher in the Mission. Confession, as used in the 1869 Mission, took the form of an "after service."

The Times again describes Mr. Body's "after service" in some detail.

> After each service Mr. Body intimates that he is waiting all day in the vestry to see, converse, and pray with all penitents who may desire advice as to the salvation of their souls. He says plainly that he has no power in himself of absolving sins, and pointing to the image of Our Blessed Savior over the altar, he says it is to Him, and Him only, that the sinner must look for forgiveness of sin and for peace. He afterwards said, "If you come to me I don't ask

> you, if against your conscience, to confess your sins
> to me. I will receive and talk to you in your own
> way. I will not bind you to any particular forms. I
> will advise with you, read to you, pray with you. I
> desire not to interfere with the prejudices of any one.
> My only wish is to assist you on the road to peace
> with God through Jesus Christ.[39]

One might see little difference between such an after service as found in a Ritualistic Church and the altar calls offered by a Moody. Kent maintains that the seeming innocence of a mission priest counseling with a penitent may have been a subtle way of introducing sacramental confession into one's spiritual life. "Wilkinson thought of the process which began as the after-meeting as entailing the unremitting spiritual direction of the awakened person by the parish priest . . . his aim was to build up that peculiar kind of religious intimacy between priest and people which became the hallmark of the true Anglo-Catholic parish."[40] Some scholars see sacramental confession as the principal innovation brought by the Tractarians and their followers[41] while others see it as means of priestly control.[42] Whereas, both observations might well be true, what is certain is that revivalism, for the Ritualists, had a clear sacramental character about it—the eucharist, baptism, and confession.

Protestant revivalists saw a new vision of how the gospel might set the captive free when the Catholic Revivalists offered sacramental revivalism in Mid-Victorian England. The assessment of whether or not the movement was effective does not lie within the scope of this paper. What is significant is that Christians who place at the center of their piety the sacraments of the church, borrowed pastoral practices from their separated sisters and brother

Evangelicals as well as their Roman Catholic brethren. Revival ritualist-style was both evangelical and eucharistic. It might well be that R. W. Dale's comment to his assistant pastor has the ring of truth: "These High Churchmen with the use they make of the liturgical and devotional literature of many centuries, have much to teach us."[43]

Endnotes

1. Cited in Maurice Davies, *Orthodox London* (London: Tinsley Brothers, 1875), 290-91.

2. Desmond Morse-Boycott, *They Shine Like Stars* (London: Skeffington & Son, Ltd., 1947), 47.

3. Charles Smyth, *The Art of Preaching 1747-1939* (London: SPCK, 1953), 224.

4. S. C. Carpenter, *Church and People 1789-1889* (London: SPCK, 1937), 213.

5. Owen Chadwick, *The Victorian Church.* vol. 1 (London: Adam & Charles Black, 1970), 212.

6. Carpenter, 213.

7. G. W. E. Russell, *The Household of Faith* (London: Hodder and Stoughton, 1902), 80.

8. M. Davies, 107.

9. John Kent, *Holding the Fort* (London: Epworth Press, 1978), 265-66.

10. Russell, 85-86.

11. Nigel Yates, *The Oxford Movement and Anglican Ritualism* (London: The Historical Association, 1984), 26.

12. Horton Davies, *Worship in England: From Watts and Wesley to Maurice* (Princeton: Princeton University Press, 1961), 246.

13. H. Davies, 126.

14. M. Davies, 239.

15. H. Davies, 121.

16. Chadwick, 365.

17. Chadwick, 366.

18. Chadwick, 368.

19. Kent, 243.

20. H. Davies, 246.

21. Kent, 243.

22. Kent, 253.

23. Kent, 254.

24. Russell, 316-17. The verse cited is from John Keble's hymn "Sun of My Soul."

25. Quoted by L. Elliott-Binns, *Religion in Victorian England* (London: Lutterworth Press, 1936), 237.

26. Quoted in Elliott-Binns, *Religion in Victorian England,* 237.

27. *The Times,* 19 November 1869.

28. A. C. Underwood, *A History of the English Baptists* (London: The Baptist Union of Great Britain, 1970), 218.

29. *The Times*, 19 November 1869.

30. *The Times*, 24 November 1869.

31. L. Elliott-Binns, *The Evangelical Movement in the English Church* (Garden City, N.J.: Doubleday; Duran & Co, 1928), 58.

32. *The Times*, 19 November 1869. Father Hyacinthe, born Charles Loyson, was a Roman Catholic Carmelite who called for the reform of the Roman Catholic Church during the 1860s. He eventually married, moved to Switzerland, and founded the Christian Catholic Church of Switzerland.

33. Cited in Kent, 261.

34. *The Times of London*, 24 November 1869.

35. Yates, 27.

36. James A. Froude, *Short Subjects on Great   Subjects,* vol. IV (London: Longmans, Green & Co., 1896), 232.

37. Froude, vol. III, 173.

38. M. Davies, 276.

39. *The Times*, 19 November 1869.

40. Kent, 250-51.

41. Yates, 26.

42. Kent, 249f.

43. A. W. Dale, *The Life of R. W. Dale of Birmingham* (London: Hodder & Stoughton, 1902), 635.

"SING LUSTILY": HYMN TUNE FAVORITES IN THE METHODIST EPISCOPAL CHURCH OF THE NINETEENTH CENTURY[1]

Fred Kimball Graham
United Church of Canada

In the midst of the seminar on Mercersburg Theology, Howard Hageman brought Philip Schaff (1819-1893) to my attention. One of the pivotal figures of the Mercersburg movement, Schaff is renowned as a founder of the American Society for Church History, and for his ecumenical work and writings which include such landmarks as *Creeds of Christendom* and the *Schaff-Herzog Encyclopedia.* Perhaps less well-known is his involvement in the preparation of hymn poetry, particularly translations. He believed hymns to be beneficial to both the individual and the corporate gathering, and a means of promoting unity of faith. He included works of the Wesleys in his collections along with the classic hymns; he was determined to emphasize this "common property," belonging to and accessible to all.

John Wesley would have approved. He advocated hymns and tunes which would edify and include all the faithful, and advises singers: "... join with the congregation as frequently as you can. Sing lustily and with a good courage."[2]

He openly railed against the fuging tunes of his day,[3] and preferred plain tunes sung just as printed. His

"Directions" note: If you have learned to sing them [other than as printed] unlearn it as soon as you can.[4]

The Memorial of Choristers received by the General Conference of the Methodist Episcopal Church in May, 1864 underlined the importance of singing for all members of the congregation.

It has been the purpose of the Methodist church that music should be the medium and instrument of fervent spiritual devotions, adapted to all.[5]

This purpose was not new in the Methodist experience; John Wesley's preface to *A Collection of Hymns for the Use of the People Called Methodists* (1780) provides a strong indication of the value which he placed on the power of singing.[6] He exercised an almost intuitive musical intelligence[7] as he oversaw the publication of tunes beginning with the *Foundery Collection* in 1742.[8]

In the United States, the first official Methodist hymn book, *A Collection of Psalms and Hymns for the Lord's Day,* contained hymns and no tunes; it was adopted during the "Christmas Conference" of Baltimore in 1784. More popular in the American experience, however, was Robert Spence's *Collection of Hymns from Various Authors* (known as the *Pocket Hymn Book*) of 1786, of which Wesley disapproved. He issued his own *Pocket Hymn Book* (London, 1787) which was reprinted in Philadelphia, 1790 as *A Pocket Hymn-Book Designed as a Constant Companion for the Pious, Collected from Various Authors.* However, no collection containing tunes was granted official status until 1878, when a revised *Hymnal of the Methodist Episcopal Church*[9] was published. Until then, tunes had to be found in a separate book containing the melody, supported by one, two, or three harmony parts.

Early settlers had brought with them the *Ainsworth Psalter*[10] (Amsterdam, 1612), and the Sternhold and Hopkins psalter[11] (London, 1562.) The "usual way" of singing[12] included the practice of "lining out," whereby a minister or clerk would read or sing the metrical psalm line by line, with the congregation repeating it. As a result, many tunes were altered or varied.[13] John Wesley abhorred departure from the tunes as provided, and advised against altering or amending them. Over the strenuous objections of those who preferred the "usual way" of singing, Singing Schools were established in the 1700s to assist singers to sing by note. The first instructional material is found in a set of psalms compiled by John Tufts, *An Introduction to the Singing of Psalm Tunes* (Boston, 1721). Working with the principles of British solmization (*fa, sol, la, mi*), he had devised a system of notation which disregarded the usual style of rounded musical notation, and utilized varying shapes. Later, music was published utilizing differently-shaped noteheads (triangle for *fa*, round for *sol*, square for *la*, diamond-shape for *mi*) in a system which was transferable to any piece of music. Hymn tune collections published as late as the mid-nineteenth century employed this so-called "shape-note" hymnody as a means of teaching "sacred harmony"; the enjoyment of reading it extends to our own day.

The proponents of the "Better Music Movement," dissatisfied with the folk-style singing of the Singing Schools, took the European tune as the model of "correct" music. Preferred tunes were simple, accompaniment was chordal, text underlay was syllabic, and texts were direct and plain. The central figure in this reform was Lowell Mason[14] (1792-1872) of Boston.

The music leader at John Street Methodist Episcopal Church, New York, in the early 1800s was James Evans, who promoted "better" sacred music in the city. Although Evans did not succeed in obtaining approval of the church's General Conference[15] for a standard tunebook, other Methodists were receptive to the idea, and he proceeded to privately publish David's Companion[16] in 1808. The appearance of this volume signals concern at a congregational level for improvement in standards of singing and for an increase in uniformity of music in Methodist public worship.

Tunebooks from various editors followed, notably the *Methodist Harmonist.*[17] Edited by Nathan Bangs, it provided a melody, one stanza of the hymn text, and a hymn number corresponding with the official hymnal in order to find additional stanzas. Several semiofficial tunebooks followed: *The Methodist Harmonist*[18] (1833) and *The Harmonist*[19] (1837). *Sacred Harmony*[20] was published in both round-note and shape-note editions, again with one stanza underlaid. Even with its European tunes, and lush harmonies, it was not well received, however, and 1849 brought the publication of the *Devotional Harmonist*[21]; it was keyed to the revised official hymn book, and was clearly patterned after the 1837 tunebook.

In response to demands of the 1850s for a resource containing the complete text and appropriate tune on an adjacent page, *Hymns for the Use of the Methodist Episcopal Church with Tunes for Congregational Worship*[22] was published. Each page contained a tune underlaid with one verse, followed by all other stanzas of the text. Another innovation pertained to the format; whereas tunebooks to this point had been oblong in shape (opening on the short side) this volume opens on the long side, in the format familiar to hymn singers today.

By mid-century, over 600 tunes with matching texts were available to Methodist hymn singers. Church records do not reveal which were chosen more often than others. However, several researchers have assumed that frequency of publication can be related to regard for, as well as need and stature of a hymn in the singing community.[23] A survey of eleven of the tunebooks[24] and hymn collections of the period, with the intent of discovering the most frequently published tunes, yields the following results.

Of the seventy-six tunes which appear most frequently, three originate in the sixteenth century, one in the seventeenth century, forty-four in the eighteenth century, and twenty-four were composed in the nineteenth century. Four tunes lack dates of origin. Fifteen tunes are found in ten of the eleven sources.[25] Of these, the three below are found in all sources.

I

AMSTERDAM (Figure 1)[26]

This was one of Wesley's favorite tunes, and was published in the *Foundery Collection* (London, 1742) after John Wesley learned it during his encounters with the Moravians in Georgia. It is a Particular Meter tune. The multiplicity of note-values (quarters, eights, sixteenths) may indicate the influence of secular musical techniques on Methodist tune writing.[27] The Methodist Episcopal Church enjoyed the following three texts associated with *Amsterdam* in the nineteenth century:

> O Almighty God of Love
> Thy holy arm display;
> Send me succour from above
> In this my evil day;
> Arm my weakness with thy power,
> Woman's seed, appear within!

AMSTERDAM. 11TH P. M. (76, 76, 77, 76.)

Dr. Nares.

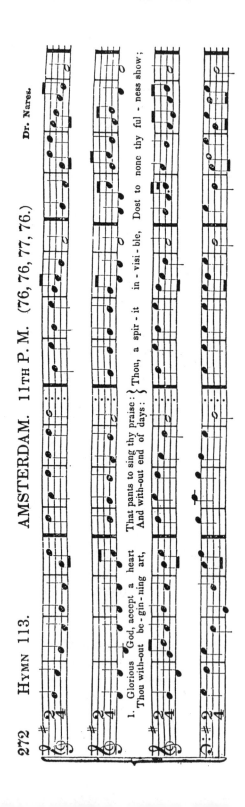

1. Glorious God, accept a heart   That pants to sing thy praise :   Thou, a spir - it in - visi - ble,   Dost to none thy ful - ness show;
2. Thou with-out be - gin - ning art,   And with-out end of days :

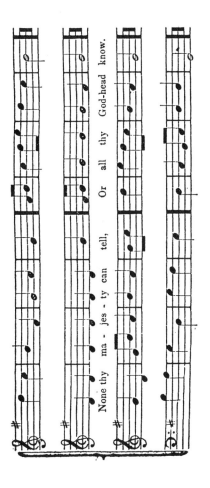

None thy ma - jes - ty can tell, Or all thy God-head know.

2. All thine attributes we own,
    Thy wisdom, power, and might :
  Happy in thyself alone,
    In goodness infinite ;
  Thou thy goodness hast displayed,
    On thine every work imprest ;
  Lov'st whate'er thy hands have made,
    But man thou lov'st the best.

3. Willing thou that all should know
    Thy saving truth and live ;
  Dost to each, or bliss or wo,
    With strictest justice give :
  Thou with perfect righteousness
    Renderest every man his due :
  Faithful in thy promises,
    And in thy threatenings too.

Figure 1

> Be my safeguard and my tower
> Against the face of sin.
>
> Glorious God, accept a heart
> that pants to sing thy praise:
> Thou without beginning art
> and without end of days;
>
> Thou a spirit invisible
> dost to none thy fulness show;
> none thy majesty can tell
> or all thy Godhead know.
>
> Rise, my soul, and stretch thy wings
> Thy better portion trace;
> Rise from all terrestrial things
> Towards heaven thy native place.
> Sun and moon and stars decay,
> Time shall soon this earth remove:
> Rise my soul and haste away
> to seats prepared above.

II

MEAR (Figure 2)

This tune was first published in *A Sett of Tunes in 3 Parts* ([London, ca. 1720]) and was issued 121 times prior to 1810. Its initial popularity was supported by the Isaac Watts text of Psalm 98: "Sing to the Lord, ye distant lands." Richard Crawford has noted that the tune was collected ca. 1980 from oral tradition singing of Primitive Baptists in the Blue Ridge region of Virginia and North Carolina.[28]

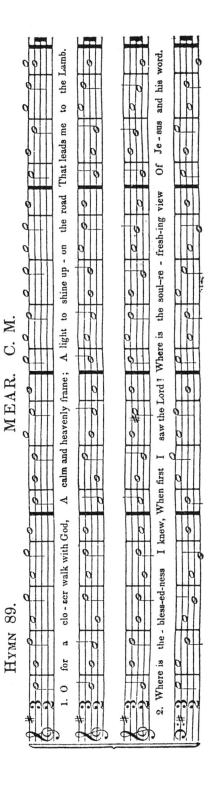

MEAR. C. M.

Hymn 89.

1. O for a clo - ser walk with God, A calm and heavenly frame; A light to shine up - on the road That leads me to the Lamb.

2. Where is the - bless-ed-ness I knew, When first I saw the Lord? Where is the soul-re - fresh-ing view Of Je - sus and his word.

Figure 2

Within the sphere of nineteenth-century Methodist use, *Mear* was cross-referenced with many texts of Common Meter, the following being the most frequent:

O for a closer walk with God,
A calm and heavenly frame;
A light to shine upon the road
That leads me to the Lamb.

O why did I my Savior leave?
So soon unfaithful prove:
How could I thy good spirit grieve,
And sin against thy love?

I would be thine: O take my heart
And fill it with thy love;
Thy sacred image, Lord, impart,
And seal it from above.

O 'twas a joyful sound to hear
Our tribes devoutly say,
"Up, Israel, to the temple haste,
And keep your festal day."

Lord, all I am is known to thee;
In vain my soul would try
To shun thy presence, or to flee
The notice of thine eye.

God moves in a mysterious way
His wonders to perform;
He plants his footsteps in the sea,
And rides upon the storm.

Vain man, thy fond pursuits forbear;
Repent, thine end is nigh;
Death, at the farthest, can't be far:
O think before thou die.

O God, our help in ages past,
Our hope for years to come,
Our shelter from the stormy blast,
And our eternal home!

III

OLD HUNDREDTH (Figure 3)

First published in North America in *The Psalms and Hymns, and Spiritual Songs of the Old and New Testament,* the ninth edition of the "Bay Psalm Book," (Boston, 1698)[29] the tune originates with the Psaumes de David, Geneva, 1551. Its harmonic setting is seldom altered, and throughout the period, only two texts are associated with it in the official and semiofficial sources.

Before Jehovah's awful throne,
Ye nations bow with sacred joy;
Know that the Lord is God alone,
He can create, and he destroy.

From all that dwell below the skies,
Let the Creator's praise arise;
Let the Creator's praise be sung
Through every land, by every tongue.

Of these tunes, only two survive in current United Methodist usage; *Amsterdam* has been reclaimed for use with the Charles Wesley text, "Praise the Lord who reigns above" (no. 96, The United Methodist Hymnal).

Today's Methodist singer will find the *Old Hundredth* three times, accompanying the texts "All people that on earth do dwell" (a paraphrase of Psalm 100), "Praise

Figure 3

God from whom all blessings flow," and "Be present at our table, Lord."

Only *Mear* has fallen into disuse, possibly due to a bland rhythm, its limited range, or its restricted harmonic possibilities. In the mid-nineteenth century, however, it held a favored position in the devotions of Methodists. In that era, tunes in the styles of *Amsterdam*, *Old Hundredth*, and *Mear* seemed to provide

> music of an elevated and devotional character ...
> producing a oneness of taste and practice ...[to]
> accomplish the prophetic desire: "Let the people
> praise thee, O God; let *all* the people praise thee!"[30]

Endnotes

1. The tunes and hymns cited here pertain to repertoire found in tunebooks in use in the United States, 1808-1878. This theme is developed more fully in the author's forthcoming book, *With One Heart and One Voice: A Core Repertory of Hymn Tunes in Use in the Methodist Episcopal Church, 1808-1878* (Scarecrow Press.) For comments on hymns and tunes which accompanied the loyalists who settled in eastern Canada, see the author's essay "Methodist Hymn Tunes in Atlantic Canada" in *John Webster Grant, and Charles H. H. Scobie, The Contribution of Methodism to Atlantic Canada* (Montreal: McGill-Queen's Press, 1992).

2. "Directions for Singing" from John Wesley's *Select Hymns,* 1761, cited in *The United Methodist Hymnal* (Nashville: The United Methodist Publishing House, 1989), vii.

3. For a detailed analysis of the role of fuging tunes in this era, see Nicholas Temperley and Charles G. Manns, *Fuging Tunes in the Eighteenth Century,* Detroit Studies in Music Bibliography, no. 49 (Detroit: Information Coordinators), 1983.

4. *The United Methodist Hymnal*, vii.

5. Erastus Wentworth, "Methodists and Music" in *Methodist Quarterly Review*, Vol. 47, (New York, July 1865), 375-78.

6. See F. Hildebrandt and O. A. Beckerlegge, eds., *The Works of John Wesley*, Vol. 7 (Oxford: Clarendon Press, 1983), 3, 75.

7. "His equipment...was his sound musical feeling, a very limited technical knowledge and an unusual practical sense." ... "His cardinal principle was that the tunes should invite the participation of all the people..." Louis F. Benson in *The English Hymn, Its Development and Use* (Richmond, VA: John Knox Press, 1962); cited in Carlton R. Young, "John Wesley's 1737 Charlestown Collection of Psalms and Hymns," *The Hymn*, Vol. 41, no. 4 (October, 1990), 19-27.

8. For a comprehensive account of Wesley's hymn and tunebooks, see *The Works of John Wesley*, Vol. 7, Appendices E-J, 738-787.

9. *Hymnal of the Methodist Episcopal Church with Tunes* (New York: Nelson and Phillips, 1878). For analysis of the impact of this publication, see Carlton R. Young, *Companion to the United Methodist Hymnal* (Nashville: Abingdon Press, 1993).

10. Henry Ainsworth, an English separatist minister residing in Amsterdam, compiled 39 tunes from English and Genevan sources; see the critical edition, Lorraine Inserra and H. Wiley Hitchcock, *The Music of Henry Ainsworth's Psalter* (Amsterdam, 1612) (Brooklyn, New York: Institute for Studies in American Music, 1981).

11. See Robin A. Leaver, *Goostly psalms and spirituall songes; English and Dutch Metrical Psalms from Coverdale to Utenhove (1535-1568)* (Oxford: Clarendon Press, 1991).

12. See Nicholas Temperley, "The Old Way of Singing," *Journal of the American Musicological Society*, Vol. 34, no. 3 (Fall, 1981), 524.

13. The result is described by Thomas Walter, *The Grounds and Rules of Music Explained or, An Introduction to the Art of Singing by Note* (Boston, 1721) as an "horrid Medley of confused and disorderly Noises"; cited in Gilbert Chase, *America's Music,* 2nd ed. rev. (New York: McGraw-Hill, 1966), 26.

14. Mason compiled over eighty volumes of music, wrote over 1,600 hymns and psalm tunes, and organized a system of music instruction in Boston schools. See Carol A. Pemberton, *Lowell Mason: His Life and Work* (Ann Arbor MI: UMI Research Press, 1985).

15. See *Journals of the General Conference of the Methodist Episcopal Church,* Vol. 1: 1796-1836 (New York: Carlton and Phillips, 1855), 74.

16. *David's Companion, being a choice selection of hymn and psalm tunes adapted to the words and measures of the Methodist Pocket Hymn Book, containing a variety of tunes to all the metres that are now in use in the different churches; with many new tunes, principally from Dr. Miller, Leach, and other composers* (New York: J. Evans, 1808). See also Thomas F. Bickley, "David's Harp (1813), a Methodist Tunebook from Baltimore: An Analysis and Facsimile" (MA dissertation, The American University, 1983) for discussion of the popular suspicion surrounding books recommended by church leadership.

17. *THE METHODIST HARMONIST, containing a great variety of tunes collected from the Best Authors, adapted to all the various metres in the Methodist Hymn-Book and Designed for the Use of the Methodist Episcopal Church in the United States. To which is added a choice selection of Anthems and Pieces* (New York: N. Bangs and T. Mason for the Methodist Episcopal Church, 1822).

18. *The METHODIST HARMONIST, containing A Collection of Tunes from the Best Authors, Embracing Every Variety of Metre and adapted to the Worship of the Methodist Episcopal Church, to which is added A Selection of Anthems, Pieces, and Sentences for Particular Occasions. New Edition, Revised and Greatly Enlarged* (New York: B. Waugh and T. Mason for the Methodist Episcopal Church at the Conference Office, 1833).

19. *The HARMONIST: being a Collection of Tunes from the Most Approved Authors; Adapted to Every Variety of Metre in the Methodist Hymn-Book. And, for particular occasions, a Selection of Anthems, Pieces and Sentences. New Edition in Patent Notes - Revised and Greatly Enlarged* (New York: G. Lane and P.P. Sandford [James Collord, Printer], 1837).

20. *SACRED HARMONY: A Collection of Music, adapted to the Greatest Variety of Metres Now in Use; And, for Special Occasions, A Choice Selection of Sentences, Anthems, Motets, and Chants, Harmonized, and Arranged with an Accompaniment for the Organ or Piano Forte, by S. Jackson, ed.* (New York: G. Lane and Charles B. Tippett, 1848).

21. *THE DEVOTIONAL HARMONIST: a Collection of Sacred Music, comprising a large variety of New and Original Tunes, Sentences, Anthems, etc., in addition to many of the most Popular Tunes in common use. Presenting a Greater Number of Metres than any Book Heretofore Published, to which is prefixed a Progressive System of Elementary Instruction for Schools and Private Tuition.* Charles Dingley, ed. (New York: George Lane and Levi Scott, 1849).

22. *Hymns for the Use of the Methodist Episcopal Church with Tunes for Congregational Worship* (New York: Carlton and Porter, 1857).

23. See Richard A. Crawford, *The Core Repertory of Early American Psalmody*, Recent Researches in American Music, Vol.11/12 (Madison WI: A-R Editions, 1984).

24. As described in Endnote 1 (above), the author's survey included *David's Companion*, 1808; *The Methodist Harmonist*, 1822; *The Methodist Harmonist*, 1833; *The Harmonist*, 1837; *Sacred Harmony*, 1848; *The Devotional Harmonist*, 1849; *The Lute of Zion*, 1853; *The New Lute of Zion*, 1856; *Hymns for the Use of the Methodist Episcopal Church with Tunes for Congregational Worship*, 1857; *New Hymn and Tune Book*, 1866; and *Hymnal of the Methodist Episcopal Church with Tunes*, 1878.

25. These are *Amsterdam, Aylesbury, Dundee, Eaton, Lenox, Luther's Hymn, Luton, Mear, Old Hundredth, Pleyel's Hymn, St. Thomas, Shirland, Thatcher, Truro, and Watchman.*

26. Tune settings in Figures 1, 2, and 3 are taken from *The Harmonist,* 1837. The melody occurs in the staff above the bass line.

27. See Crawford, *Core Repertory.*

28. *Ibid.*

29. For the modern critical edition see Richard G. Appel, *The Music of the Bay Psalm Book,* 9th ed. (New York: Institute for Studies in American Music, 1975). For historical commentary, see Barbara Owen, "The Bay Psalm Book and Its Era," *The Hymn,* Vol. 41, no. 4 (October 1990), 12-19.

30. Wentworth, "Methodists and Music." Italics added.

IS THE REFORMED CHURCH IN AMERICA
A LITURGICAL CHURCH?

Daniel James Meeter
Reformed Church in America

Overview

The Reformed Church in America (RCA) is the direct descendent of the Dutch Reformed Church of the Netherlands. It dates its founding to 1628, on the Island of Manhattan, in what was then the town of New Amsterdam and is now the City of New York. It claims to be the oldest Protestant denomination with a continuing ministry in North America. It is still popularly known as the "Dutch Reformed Church" and its pastors are often called "Dominie." It is a charter member of both the World Council and National Council of Churches. Of the "mainline" denominations, it is perhaps the smallest, numbering just under a thousand congregations in the United States and Canada. It is also perhaps the most theologically conservative.

The Reformed Church in America shares the Dutch Reformed tradition with a number of even more conservative split-off denominations. The Christian Reformed Church (CRC) seceded from the RCA in 1857, and is now about the same size as the RCA. There are four more groups which are still more conservative and much smaller. The Protestant Reformed Church seceded from the CRC in the 1920s. The Free Reformed Church, the Netherlands Reformed Congregations, and the Canadian Reformed Church represent North American transplants of secessions in the Netherlands. All six of these denominations are organized according to the presbyterian system of church government. They share identical "Calvinistic" doctrinal standards (the Belgic Confession, the Heidelberg Catechism, and the Canons of Dort). They differ in how closely they expect their officers and members to adhere to those standards, and they differ in the wideness of their ecumenical contacts.[1] All of them use the English language, although in each of them some congregations maintain worship in Dutch. The RCA is the least exclusively Dutch in background. From the very beginning it has included significant numbers of French and German people, and its members who claim Dutch ancestry are now only a minority. The RCA claims the difficult middle ground between ecumenical Christianity and the distinctive Dutch Reformed tradition. The other denominations keep much closer to the Dutch traditions, although the Christian Reformed Church has recently taken in a number of minority congregations.

By today's standards, none of the Dutch Reformed denominations would have the reputation of being "liturgical" churches. Their sober tradition emphasizes preaching and sets little store by ceremony. Even so, every one of them has a *Liturgy*.[2] Every one of them makes the use of its *Liturgy* obligatory, especially when the sacraments are celebrated, when ordinations are performed, and when church discipline is practiced. The RCA's *Liturgy* is wholly a part of that church's formal constitution, equal in status to its Doctrinal Standards and its Church Order, although, characteristically, the RCA is the loosest in enforcing adherence to it.

Every one of these respective Liturgies is derived from a common source, the *Netherlands Liturgy* of the ancestral church in Europe. The Netherlands Liturgy first appeared in 1566. It was basically a Dutch translation of the liturgical sections of the Palatinate *Church Order* of 1563, which included the Heidelberg Catechism. The Netherlands Liturgy was subsequently modified and expanded by the Dutch Reformed Church until it reached its definitive shape under the 1619 Synod of Dort. Less than a decade later, in 1628, the Netherlands Liturgy came into regular use by the Dutch Reformed congregation on Manhattan Island. Even in 1992 the Dutch version was still being used by a number of congregations in the United States and Canada.

The Dutch Reformed Liturgy has a place within the wider history of worship. Howard Hageman has described it as "the oldest Reformation liturgy continually in use."[3] He continues:

> May I summarize its pedigree? The liturgy of the Dutch church was German in origin, composed of elements drawn from the liturgies of the French church in Strassburg, the Dutch church in London, the Lutheran church in Würtemberg, woven together by a compiler whose theological cast was overwhelmingly Zwinglian. But the story does not end there. Soon after its official adoption by the Dutch church, it was translated into English, and that started it on an entirely new career.

The English translation which Hageman refers to appeared in 1767. It was published by the Consistory of the Dutch Reformed Church in the City of New York for the use of its own congregation, which had just begun to hold divine service in the English language. Twenty-five years later, in 1792, the General Synod of the Reformed Dutch Church in North America, as the RCA was known then, adopted the New York Consistory's translation for the whole denomination, and published it in 1793 as part of the Church's *Constitution*. This is the North American Liturgy of the Dutch Reformed Church.[4] During the last century this North American translation was adopted by all the other Dutch Reformed groups when they each, in turn, introduced the use of the English language. Over the years all these groups have made their own revisions of the North American Liturgy.[5] It has also been further translated into at least four other languages.[6] The result is that, since 1793, the North American Liturgy of the Reformed Church has served the various Dutch Reformed denominations not only in North America, but also in Africa, Asia, and Australia as their standard English language liturgical text.

Unfortunately, already by 1814 a number of unauthorized changes had corrupted the received text of the Liturgy. These found their way into all subsequent versions, so that none of the currently available editions of the Liturgy truly represent the original, constitutional version of 1793. By 1885 the RCA Classis of New Brunswick saw the need for a critical edition of the Liturgy, and petitioned the General Synod to prepare one. The Synod agreed to go even further and prepare a critical edition of the whole Constitution—Doctrine, Liturgy, and Church Order.[7] An initial report was made the Synod of 1886, but then, unaccountably, the project abruptly died, and nothing came of it.

This is an example of the general truth that the Reformed Church in America and the other denominations in its tradition have had only a poor understanding of their liturgical history. The fact that most of that history is in what is now a foreign language has no doubt contributed to this state of affairs, but probably more significant is the general declension in the liturgical character of the tradition. An anti-liturgical spirit which rejects the authority of written liturgies and prayers has simmered within the Dutch Reformed churches for 250 years. This spirit is shared by both conservatives and liberals. The conservatives reject the use of such forms, while the liberals, who may actually use many "liturgies" for this and that, ignore the authority of the forms; both sides, in common, refuse to submit to the discipline that the forms enjoin.

The survival and strengthening of this spirit in the RCA has recently resulted in the move to replace the Liturgy in the Constitution with a Directory of Worship, the kind of document that is characteristic of the Presbyterian denominations. The effect of the Directory is to make all the forms in the Liturgy only specimens to be used at the option of the Pastor. The goal is to allow the free use of liturgies taken from other traditions. It would be up to the Pastor, on the spot, to determine whether a particular liturgical form conflicts with Reformed doctrine and the procedures recommended by the Directory. The result would be, for example, enormous license in the practice of celebrating the Sacraments.

The Nineteenth Century

This anti-liturgical spirit was not always the dominant one in the RCA. In the middle of the nineteenth century, the Dutch Reformed Church was unique among North American Calvinistic bodies in its liturgical practice. This practice was described by Charles Baird in 1855, an outside observer who noted that of all the Calvinistic Churches represented in these United States, the Reformed Dutch denomination alone has faithfully retained her ancient forms of worship. . . . The earliest member of the Presbyterian family transplanted to these western shores, she exhibits to us in this respect more perfectly than any other the natural outgrowth of the system from which she sprung. . . .

. . . Notwithstanding the abandonment of the use of written prayers in the [ordinary] Sabbath services, there has not been a total relinquishment of the liturgical character of worship. The main elements of the Calvinistic service are there retained, viz.: the Lord's Prayer, Ten Commandments and Creed, besides the features of a "Salutation" at the commencement of the service, and a Doxology at the close. In Holland universally, and in America to some extent, the clergy wear an official dress during the performance of their public functions.

But while it is true that the forms of common prayer have thus fallen into disuse, what is perhaps more important, the administration of the sacraments and ordinances remains unimpaired, according to the original model of the Reformation. The Constitution of the Dutch Church enjoins upon ministers the use of the forms of Baptism, Communion, and Ordination; which, accordingly, are celebrated to this day in the order and manner of their liturgical prescription.[8]

In the same year a similar observation was made by the German Reformed historian Philip Schaff, as follows:

In worship, the Dutch Reformed denomination has not given itself up to the exclusive dominion of extemporaneous prayer, which rules in the Puritan and Presbyterian bodies of America, but still holds fast to a part, at least, of the old Palatinate liturgy, though it is now engaged in revising and modernizing it.[9]

Schaff attributed this, however, not so much to a positive liturgical spirit as to what he called the "theological stagnation" of the Dutch Reformed Church, and its "aversion to anything new."[10]   In Schaff's words:

> They are generally considered . . . the stiffest and most immovable of all the most respectable Protestant churches in America, and would fain be regarded as the very Gibraltar of old-fashioned Protestantism, in the happy dream that the venerable Synod of Dort settled all theological questions in 1618. . . .[11]

In other words, it was only the denomination's deeper concern for orthodox doctrine and Calvinistic discipline, symbolized by the Synod of Dort, which caused its liturgical fidelity.

This is certainly true.   For the Reformed Church there was an obvious connection to be made between the doctrine that was confessed and the doctrine that was celebrated.   Later, in 1901, a liturgical revision committee reported the following to the General Synod:

> . . . to change the Forms in any essential statement or feature would be to change the doctrines of the Church, the Church everywhere being regarded as a Teacher not only in her faith-confessions but in her Liturgy as well.   This was the principle pursued by Peter Dathenus in the first draft of the Forms for Church Service, published in 1566, and confirmed by the Synod of Wesel two years later, in the formal declaration "that it is necessary to arrange a perfect correspondence between all parts of doctrine, ceremonies, and discipline"—dat van noden was een eenparige voet te beramen, ente onderhouden in Leer, Ceremonien, en Discipline.[12]

Indeed, when compared with other liturgical traditions, the chief virtues of the Dutch Reformed *Liturgy* were sober self-discipline and, above all, catechetical clarity.

Another factor that undoubtedly informed the RCA's liturgical practice was the denomination's strong sense of historical rootedness. This pertained to both doctrine and worship. An earlier revision committee had reported to the General Synod of 1885 as follows:

> The past is valuable; our Constitution and history, as they have come down to us, have the savor of wisdom. Let them stand. Our Doctrinal Standards and older Liturgy (as we have said) connect us, as being their work, with that great general assembly of original churches, whose delegates assembled at Dort. They represent this oneness and unity down at the bottom. And whilst Catholic and Episcopal churches are making such use of antiquity; whilst pedigree and ancestry are becoming so valuable in other directions, why should we, who have it as a Church, spoil our "coat of arms," our Standards and Liturgy? We are not a Church of yesterday, but of centuries.[13]

But this historicism was regarded as a negative and stifling factor by the critics of the Dutch Reformed Church.

As Schaff had pointed out, attempts at revising and modernizing the Liturgy were being made already in the 1850s, but the denomination, "stiff" and "immovable" as it was, kept refusing to give these changes official approval. The synodical committee of 1901 concluded from all this "that the Church has never found it an easy or safe thing to tamper with her ancient and time-honored Forms."[14] Yet it would be inaccurate to see this as a purely negative loyalty. Mancius Hutton, for example, who was the leader in the move for liturgical reform, and who certainly had his eye open to what other traditions were doing, articulated a liturgical spirit that was both loyal and positive within his report to the General Synod of 1871:

> Our historical position is without doubt that of a *Reformed* Presbyterian and *Liturgical* church; neither falling into the formality of the episcopacy nor into the baldness of Puritanism. So have we stood for two centuries, and so stand we to-day. *The Evangelical Presbyterian Liturgical Church.*[15]

Hutton's idea of holding to a middle way between the extremes of ceremonialism on one hand and Puritanism on the other has been, in fact, typical of the practice of worship in the Reformed Church throughout its history.

The Twentieth Century

In the century since Hutton's statement, Protestant churches have been pushing liturgical practice to its extremes on both sides. The middle way is getting increasingly wider as a consequence. The characteristic loyalty of the Dutch Reformed churches to their ancient Liturgy has become very much weaker. In 1977, one RCA leader made the following pessimistic comment:

> In fact, there have been Reformed Church congregations with hardly a hair of the historic liturgy on their heads, while others have been more formal by far than the Archbishop of Canterbury, and still others neither more or less reformed or liturgical than the local fire hall.[16]

This is an overstatement, of course, but it points to the current liturgical diversity within the denomination. What happened?

The first step was that the denomination was finally able to revise its Liturgy in 1906. There was a new Order of Morning Worship, based on Anglican Morning Prayer. There were wholly new forms for Weddings and Funerals. The offices for the Ordination of Pastors and of Elders and Deacons were significantly abridged. There were new forms for the two sacraments. These were also abridgments of the older forms, with a good deal of what was most pungent removed. However, unlike the case with the Ordination forms, the original two sacramental forms were kept in the book, and the new abridgements were included as alternates. The rubrics stated, "Either Form may be used, at the discretion of the Minister." This was new to the Reformed Church, which heretofore had located all liturgical authority within the whole Consistory. Undoubtedly, this rubric only reflected the license that many ministers had long been taking, and which had forced Abraham Kuyper's comments, that the Reformed Liturgy protects the congregation from its minister.[17]

The major effect of the 1906 Liturgy was to introduce the idea of multiple forms. This was further compounded by the next published revision, the 1968 *Liturgy and Psalms* (which may yet prove to have been the high water mark of RCA worship). There was a new and quite admirable Order of Sunday Service, a new Order for Holy Communion, the very best thing in the book, and a new Order for Baptism, which was the weakest. In order to gain acceptance for these new forms, the same strategy was used: the old ones would be kept as alternates. The result was that there were now three alternative forms for each sacrament and two alternative forms for Sunday morning, and the most recent form for each of these differed significantly from the earlier ones. The 1901 General Synod's ideal of a "perfect correspondence between all parts of doctrine, ceremonies, and discipline" was out of the question.

The publication of new forms has accelerated so much in the Reformed Church that the Liturgy of this once "stiff and immovable" denomination is now published only as a loose-leaf book. There are now four forms for Baptism, for example, and the fourth is a radical departure from the other three. Doubtless, each new liturgical form has value, but the multiplicity and variety of them indicate that the denomination has lost its liturgical convictions. The liturgies of the loose-leaf have become "resources" rather than the living constitution which gives shape to the denomination.

The result is that, whereas in 1871, Hutton called the RCA a "liturgical church," by 1953 even Howard Hageman had to be content with calling it a "semi-liturgical church."[18] This term had already been current in the RCA for some time, and Hageman gave it the best possible interpretation. Yet, from a rigorously Reformed point of view, "semi-liturgical" is a contradiction in terms. A Liturgy either has authority or it doesn't. Liturgy implies Discipline, and the truly Reformed liturgical spirit places a high value on self-discipline and doctrinal integrity. Therefore, in spite of its many new liturgies (or perhaps just because of them) the Reformed Church is probably less "liturgical" than it ever has been.

Signs of Hope

The anti-liturgical spirit has not yet totally won. The last generation has also seen a revival of interest in the liturgical heritage of the Reformed Church. This revival has been a by-product, not of provincialism or chauvinism, but of responsible scholarship. There has been a general renewal of scholarly interest in Reformation history and theology. Martin Bucer and John Calvin have come to be understood in a new light, and they are better appreciated for their liturgical contributions. This could not help but reflect well on the Dutch Reformed Liturgy, which is, after all, North America's "only sixteenth-century Reformed liturgy still in even partial use."[19]

A second impetus to the liturgical revival in the Reformed Church has been scholarly contacts with the Liturgical Movement. This kind of thing was described by the Swedish Lutheran theologian Yngve Brilioth when he wrote, "The experience of the fuller sacramental life of the English Church has helped more than anything to open my eyes to the hidden, half-forgotten riches of my own Church."[20] The responsible ecumenical appreciation that comes from a more catholic knowledge of liturgy in general has awakened some members of the Reformed Church to "the hidden, half-forgotten riches" of their own tradition in particular.

No one has this been more true of in the Reformed Church than Howard Hageman. He has made his contributions as both a Reformation scholar and a leading participant in the ecumenical liturgical movement. His reputation outside of the Reformed Church has been equalled by his singular and universal esteem within it. A member of the denomination by choice, rather than by birth, he has been alive to its treasures without being confined to its habits. He has been a warm advocate of its historic doctrines as expressed in the Heidelberg Catechism and the Belgic Confession (often as a lonely voice) as well as setting an example of open ecumenical involvement. He is the "Evangelical Catholic" par excellence, and if the Reformed Church has any future as a liturgical church, it will have to thank him.

Perhaps his greatest achievement has been to bring the Reformed Church's practice of the Eucharist into the Catholic mainstream. His 1968 revision of the Order for Holy Communion, done under the auspices of a synodical committee, has been enormously successful. It has been warmly accepted by all parties within the denomination and it continues as the standard form for the rite. In the Communion Form, Hageman was able to pour the distinctive theology of the old Dutch-Palatinate Supper Form into a recognizably Catholic eucharistic liturgy. His short Instruction and Invitation, which is always an important part of Dutch Reformed sacramental practice, just may be the best short piece on the Eucharist written this century, and is a model of great liturgical rhetoric:

> Beloved in the Lord Jesus Christ, the holy Supper which we are about to celebrate is a feast of remembrance, of communion, and of hope.
>
> We come in remembrance that our Lord Jesus Christ was sent of the Father into the world to assume our flesh and blood and to fulfill for us all obedience to the divine law, even to the bitter and shameful death of the cross. By his death, resurrection, and ascension he established a new and eternal covenant of grace and reconciliation that we might be accepted of God and never be forsaken by him.
>
> We come to have communion with this same Christ who has promised to be with us always, even to the end of the world. In the breaking of the bread he makes himself known to us as the true heavenly Bread that strengthens us unto life eternal. In the cup of blessing he comes to us as the Vine in whom we must abide if we are to bear fruit.
>
> We come in hope, believing that this bread and this cup are a pledge and foretaste of the feast of

love of which we shall partake when his kingdom has fully come, when with unveiled face we shall behold him, made like unto him in his glory.

Since by his death, resurrection, and ascension he has obtained for us the life-giving Spirit who unites us all in one body, so are we to receive this Supper in true brotherly love, mindful of the communion of saints. Come, for all things are now ready.

Endnotes

1. Each one of the four small denominations rallies around one or two specific doctrinal issues which are virtually impossible to explain to those outside the tradition.

2. Remarkably, of all Protestant traditions, only the Dutch Reformed have consistently used "Liturgy" as the accepted title of their whole form of worship in their common service books, anticipating the modern use of the word already in 1566.

3. Howard Hageman, "The Liturgical Origins of the Reformed Churches," *The Heritage of John Calvin*: Heritage Hall Lectures 1960-1970, John H. Bratt, ed. (Grand Rapids, MI: Eerdmans, 1973), 135-6.

4. Cf. Daniel Meeter, The "North American Liturgy": A critical edition of the Reformed Dutch Church in North America, 1793, Ph.D. dissertation, Drew University, 1989; Ann Arbor: University Microfilms, #8921810. This edition provides an amended English text alongside the received Dutch text, plus historical notes and commentary. A forthcoming revision of this will be published by Eerdmans as part of the Historical Series of the Reformed Church.

5. The two editions which keep closest to the Dutch original are the "Liturgical Forms" in the *Book of Praise: Anglo-Genevan Psalter* (Winnipeg, Manitoba: Premier Printing, 1984) of the Canadian Reformed Church and the "Liturgy" in *The Psalter* (Grand Rapids, MI, 1987) of the Netherlands Reformed Congregations.

6. Tamil, Telugu, Japanese, and German.

7. "Since there has been as yet no correctly prepared edition of the Constitution, and especially its Liturgy, let a suitable committee be appointed to prepare an accurate one as to translation, arrangement, etc., for future publication, as proposed by the Classis of New Brunswick." *The Acts and Proceedings of the Seventy-Ninth Regular Session of the General Synod of the Reformed Church in America, 1885* (New York: Board of Publication of the Reformed Church in America, 1885), 706.

8. Charles W. Baird, *[Eutaxia,] The Presbyterian Liturgies: Historical Sketches* (New York, 1855; reprint ed., Grand Rapids, MI, 1957), 207-10.

9. Philip Schaff, *America: A Sketch of the Political, Social, and Religious Character of the United States of North America, in Two Lectures* (New York: C. Scribner, 1855), 152.

10. Schaff, *America*, 151-52.

11. Schaff, *America*, 150.

12. Edward Tanjore Corwin, *A Digest of Constitutional and Synodical Legislation of the Reformed Church in America.* (New York, 1906), 77.

13. *The Acts and Proceedings of the General Synod of the Reformed Church in America, 1885*, 706.

14. Corwin, *Digest*, 79.

15. *The Acts and Proceedings of the General Synod of the Reformed Church in America, 1871*, 282.

16. Arie R. Brouwer, *Reformed Church Roots: Thirty-five Formative Events* (New York, 1977), 20.

17. Abraham Kuyper, *Onze Eeredienst* (Kampen, 1911), 9-11.

18. Howard Hageman, *Lily Among the Thorns* (New York: Reformed Church Press, 1953), 113.

19. James Hastings Nichols, *Corporate Worship in the Reformed Tradition* (Philadelphia: The Westminster Press, 1968), 155.

20. Yngve Brilioth, *Eucharistic Faith & Practice: Evangelical & Catholic* (London: SPCK, 1939), viii.

LOCATING CHRIST:
A STRUCTURAL ANALYSIS OF THE
SACRED SPACE AT ST. MARY'S ABBEY

Edward C. Zaragoza
Phillips Theological Seminary

Religion, Clifford Geertz tells us, is a social institution made up of "systems of signification," that is, symbols or patterns of meanings which are available to us. These systems of signification, however, are also open to change and alteration. When they do change, the social institution changes with them. Thus, alterations in social institutions can be charted by the changes in how their sacred symbols are appropriated.[1] One such sacred symbol is Christ. For centuries Christians have struggled to live like Christ, not only because it is a scriptural imperative, but also because Christ, as a sacred symbol, synthesizes Christianity's worldview (its most basic ideas about the nature of reality) and its ethos (how Christians are supposed to live their lives). Moreover, the worldview and the ethos reiterate and reinforce the other's authority and power.[2] The worldview makes sense, is intellectually satisfying, and the ethos feels right, is emotionally gratifying.

One answer to the struggle of how to live like Christ can be found in the monastic movement and its notion of place. Place meant that Christ, symbolized in the institution of the church, could be located and, therefore, be available to Christians in this life. The monastic institution gradually, as we shall see, moved out of the open spaces of the desert into the enclosed places of the monastery, redefining the way of Christ and, with it, the monastic movement. The wide-open spaces became enfolded by architectural forms, and the newly defined places unfolded their meaning through symbols.

This movement from an autonomous way of life to an institutionally regulated community with its architectural and symbolic representations provides the background for our discussion of place. In particular, the Benedictine monastery, St. Mary's Abbey in Morristown, New Jersey, will serve as our example. Preliminary to looking at this abbey church, an excursus in Benedictine history is necessary to situate St. Mary's. It is possible to see in a general way how perceptions of place, when institutionalized in different epochs, in turn generate different physical expressions pertinent to the time out of which they emerge.

In examining the shifts of consciousness from the desert fathers to the ideal medieval Benedictine monastery to a modern embodiment of the Benedictine ideal, one can trace changes in institutional self-awareness through modifications in architectural expression. No claims are made for completeness in this general study. What is at stake is the concretization of a vision, a vision which in the abstract wants meaning. Without being experienced, the vision remains ephemeral and unfounded. Without being embodied, the vision has no meaning.

Deeply engraved in the history of monasticism is an essential dualism between good and evil, heaven and hell, Christ and the devil. The ideal was to be like Christ, to share his sufferings, and to renounce Satan and all his works. An *imitatio Christi* was the road to perfection. *The Life of St. Anthony* depicts the early life of the desert fathers as one of spiritual combat, a never-ending battle against the onslaughts of the demons who are often portrayed as wild beasts which buffet the monk's entire body.[3] In the tradition of St. Anthony, Evagrius Ponticus describes the divine predicament of the eremetic:

> The devil so passionately envies the man who prays that he employs every device to frustrate that purpose. Thus he does not cease to stir up thoughts of various affairs by means of the memory. He stirs up all the passions by means of the flesh. In this way he hopes to offer some obstacle to that excellent course pursued in prayer on the journey toward God.[4]

This *imitatio Christi* was a solitary life of prayer and mortification. There were no assemblies of believers, no formal liturgy, no institutional monastic structure, no architectural expression beyond caves, huts or the open spaces. A shift began to occur when due to their holiness of life, the eremetics gained renown, and with it, followers. It was just this kind of situation that developed around St. Benedict of Nursia. It is here, in the sixth century, that signs of institutionalization begin to be seen, evolving into a situation that remains with us today. The Benedictine monastery grows out of the desire of ordinary men and women to follow the life exemplified by their forebears in the desert. To accommodate this, Benedict, borrowing from earlier outlines, wrote his *Rule for Monasteries* which prescribed how a person should live in cenobitic or communal houses. Its distinguishing marks are moderate asceticism as practiced in the four virtues of poverty, chastity, obedience, and stability, and a life of unceasing prayer. The foundation of the monastic life continues to rest on the dualistic structure of a life centered on Christ to the exclusion of the world. Benedict, in his "school for the

Lord's service" has devised a training program for soldiers of Christ to continue battle against the devil. The militant tone of his *Rule* is evident:

> But it, for some good reason, for the amendment of evil habit or the preservation of charity, there be some strictness of discipline, do not be dismayed and run away from the way of salvation, of which the entrance needs be narrow. But, as we progress in our monastic life and in faith, our hearts shall be enlarged, and we shall run with unspeakable sweetness of love in the way of God's commandments; so that, never abandoning his rule but persevering in his teaching in the monastery until death, we shall share by patience in the sufferings of Christ, that we may deserve to be partakers also of his kingdom.[5]

This strictness of discipline and narrowness of entrance took shape in the regimentation of duties, works, and prayers that characterizes the *Rule*. The heroic life of the desert now had a handbook, a house, and a hierarchical social structure. The singular devotion to Christ in the desert has been mediated by another Father, the Abbot. But it is not until the later Middle Ages that the Benedictine system reached its zenith.

The dramatic dualism of "this world" over against "the other-worldly" became fully institutionalized in the social fabric of the medieval period in the form of the Benedictine understanding of the outside and the inside: the walled enclosure. While built to keep wild beasts and barbarians out, the monastic enclosure served equally to keep the monks in. Outside the walls was "this world," a world inhabited by the demons of politics, sexuality, decadence. Inside the monastic enclosure Benedictine monasticism, now very elitist in character, built the "other world:" the City of God, the New Jerusalem. Unlike the outside, the inside of Jerusalem's walls became the center of the world, a place inhabited by angelic-like monks, who, while denying their bodies in favor of their souls, nonetheless erected walls around their bodies proclaiming the arrival of the celestial city. The basis for these boundaries was the understanding that medieval monastic culture could not live in a marginal state. Monastic culture had to live inside a boundary. Another expression of this divine realm was the image of the *via regia*.[6] As Christ was "the Way," monastic living, after the model of Christ, was the unobstructed road by which the pilgrim as royalty traveled to the heavenly city. No pothole or detour could slow or divert the monk's movement upward, through asceticism and prayer, to God.

Thus monastic communities took on the appearance of miniature cities. Monastic culture had condensed in its monasteries all that was necessary for the sustaining of life, both physical and spiritual. In fact, many monasteries were so effective in their example that actual cities began to grow up around them, often forcing the monastic community to depart to a more secluded spot. An excellent example of the breadth of monastic culture and its striving for permanence in a temporal world is the plan of St. Gall. Though never built, this monastic edifice reflects the medieval monastic ideal *par excellence*. It went far beyond the requirements laid out in the *Rule for Monasteries*. Benedict required the following to be enclosed: a mill and stream; a garden; a church or oratory; a sacristy; a chapter house; a cemetery; a common dormitory for monks; a library and scriptorium; a novitiate; a bakery; a winery; a tool shed; a tailor shop; an infirmary; a guest house for men and women; a refectory for novices, monks, and guests; an almonry; a large gate; craft shops; a kitchen; and a place for study. In addition the ideal plan of St. Gall included: a calefactory; the abbot's house; a school for lay students; a school for monks; stables for various kinds of animals; a barn and a threshing floor; latrines for monks, guests, and visitors; a pharmacy; a physician's house; and baths.[7]

Salvation soon became associated not so much with faith, virtuous living, or martyrdom but with *place*. This shift in social consciousness from the primitive hermit's life of virtue to the cenobite's monastic *Rule* and enclosure brought about a corresponding shift in the self-understanding of monasticism as an institution. No longer content to be in the wilderness, Benedictine monasticism aimed at what Vernon Kroening has called "the institutionalization of heaven," and created architectural forms to assure heaven's permanence on earth. St. Gall is the logical result of the young Benedict who began his holy life in a cave at Subiaco and ended it on top of a mountain at the monastery at Monte Cassino. No longer did men and women aspire to be holy by means of the solitary life of the desert. They entered the otherworldly regimen of the monastery. Heaven could be reconstructed in miniature on earth. The monk was exhorted, in the words of Evagrius,

> to banish the things of this world. Have heaven for your homeland and live there constantly--not in mere word but in actions that imitate the angels...[8]

Therefore, salvation became indissolubly linked with the concept of place. Like the psalms they sang, the monks could call their home a place where God dwells—a kingdom, a tent, a mountain, a land, a temple, and most of all—an enclosure. The Benedictine monastery was all of this and more. It became more than any ordinary *place*. Men experience and communicate with God there. The world and the earth, on the other hand are perishable, profane, uninterrupted temporal spaces in which vice flourishes, power destroys, selfish desires abound, and devils wait to do combat with the soul. The world outside the monastic walls—outside the enclosed stability of the monastic community—was dangerous for the individual whose life was committed to the vision and union with God.[9]

Since the outside world was dangerous in that it threatened stability, the monk vowed to remain in one place. Italian society, at the time of Benedict, was in a state of upheaval, a sure sign of the devil's domain. Social disorder took the form of barbarian invasions, institutional disintegration, agricultural and economic collapse, and moral corruption. But what the monastic culture realized was that the devil could not be entirely walled out. The devil came into the monastery in the person of the monk himself. The disorder and pollution that the monk carried with him came to be known in monastic spirituality as the eight passionate thoughts or cardinal sins: gluttony, covetousness, anger, melancholy, accidie, vanity, and pride. To correct these disorders of the soul Benedict, and monks to follow, established a ritual frame by which perceptions of reality were changed and thereby their concomitant experiences were altered.[10] This ritual frame was the *opus dei*, the divine office of prayer. It served as an apprenticeship for eternity. Disorder was abolished by centering on Christ, the victor. The rigorous spiritual exercise of daily rounds of unceasing prayer minimized opportunities for the invasion of the passions. Along with a moderate asceticism which mortified the flesh, perpetual prayer served to mortify the will. Ritual, then, served to concentrate the monks' mind on higher states in an attempt to leave this world and its distractions behind.[11]

As with the ideal plan of St. Gall, the institutionalization of the kingdom of God demanded concrete symbols and architectural forms to express in physical terms its reality. Though this is not the place to discuss the development of western monastic architecture, it is important to recall that monasteries were built not for laypeople but for citizens of heaven. These monasteries were earthly reflections of a heavenly reality. Precedent for this belief is readily found in the Book of Revelation:

> I also saw a new Jerusalem, a holy city, coming down out of heaven from God, beautiful as a bride prepared to meet her husband. I heard a loud voice from the throne cry: this is God's dwelling among people. (ch. 21)

Thus the architectural plan of the monastery has a divine counterpart designed by God. Through God's grace humankind attains a vision of this world, and then seeks to reproduce it on earth.[12] There is in monastic architecture a belief that there is a connection between the heavenly reality and the physical, earth-bound model—the monastic enclosure is an extension of reality itself. Clifford Geertz expresses it this way:

> ...it is the conviction that the values one holds are grounded in the inherent structure of reality, that between the way we ought to live and the way things really are there is an unbreakable inner connection. What sacred symbols do for those to whom they are sacred is to formulate an image of the world's construction and a program for human conduct that are mere reflexes of one another.[13]

The monastic experience is a particular way of looking at the world. Although we no longer live in the Middle Ages, we do have access to Benedictine monasteries today. Today's monastery is no longer the *civitas dei* of centuries ago; the monastic ethos of the twentieth century is different from that of the sixth or the twelfth. The worldview has also changed. And yet traces of earlier days remain in a modern monastery's spirit and expression. However, Vatican II reform has opened up the liturgical space of monasteries in order to claim all of the faithful as "the household of God." This shift in monastic consciousness, following the lead of the Roman Catholic Church, has led to a corresponding shift in monastic social structures, which, in turn, is reflected in modern monastic architectural forms. Though architecturally speaking American monastic architecture may not be essentially different in its design from that of the parish, it is still significant that abbey churches are now public places where the divine office is no longer seen as a private privilege only for monks. Living spaces are still off-limits to nonresidents, but their sacred spaces are now open to all.

One example of a modern monastic church is St. Mary's Abbey. Constructed in the late 1960s, this Benedictine monastic community itself can trace its ties back to Monte Cassino. It is not surprising, therefore, that there still remains, in continuity with the past, an essential dualism in modern Benedictine monasticism. The monks have not renounced their vows or given up living in community. But they have given up the cloister and live life as apostles. Before discussing the architecture and symbols of the abbey church's articulation of space, it is useful to see what we mean by the word symbol.

Anthropologist Victor Turner has done impressive work on the nature of symbols, which is helpful to us here.[14] Symbols, first and foremost, carry meaning, and they are best understood in relation to other symbols. For

Turner there are two basic kinds of symbols: dominant and instrumental. Dominant symbols are central in that they embody a given religious ritual activity without differentiating that activity into parts. This function accounts for the three characteristics of dominant symbols. First, dominant symbols are multivalent because they have multiple referents. Second, these symbols connect these multiple referents. Third, dominant symbols sum up the system of social and moral orders in the form of everyday objects such as bread and wine. This summing up is powerful because the individual can relate to a whole range of meanings in a single object.

Instrumental symbols are symbols which elaborate on dominant symbols by differentiating them into their multiple referents. While the individual relates to a whole range of meanings held in dominant symbols, that same individual can communicate these meanings by referring to the instrumental symbols. This is why Turner says that instrumental symbols help fulfill the purpose of a given ritual. Instrumental symbols make the articulation of meaning and the ordering of experience possible because they break the ritual up into parts.

Thus, while dominant symbols hold in themselves multiple referents, these referents are only identifiable, and therefore more meaningful, when instrumental symbols cluster around dominant symbols as keys to their identity. Moreover, it is only through these multiple symbolic relationships that a grasp of the meaning of dominant symbols and rituals in which they are found can occur.

In this study, the dominant symbol is the life of Christ. The instrumental symbols are where the model for that life is located, namely, the monastery, its worship space, and the eucharist.

The abbey church at St. Mary's fulfills ancient ideas about sacred places. It is constructed in a forest, on a hill, and near a spring. The building itself is basically an imposing cube that sits in stark contrast to the lush, rolling green hills upon which is was built. This is the outside of the building. Of great interest is the inside.

The floor plan of the abbey church shows that its design is basically that of a circle in a square. This view of place is very profound; for it symbolizes not only the *mandala*, the person in community, the relationship of the human being to the world, but it is primarily a maternal symbol as well. It is the primordial womb, the loving mother's face, the nourishing breast. The location of the altar-table in the very center of the circle intensifies the last description. The altar-table can be seen as the nipple of the breast, the center of nourishment in a person's life. The floor plan not only suggests this, but eucharistic theology also supports it. One instance is given in a second century psalm book, *The Odes of Solomon*. A hymn praises the eucharist as the milk of God.

> A cup of milk was offered to me: and I drank it in the sweetness of the delight of the Lord. The Son is the cup, and He who was milked is the Father: and the Holy Spirit milked Him: because His breasts were full, and it was necessary for Him that His milk should be sufficiently released; and the Holy Spirit opened His bosom and mingled the milk from the two breasts of the Father; and gave them mixture to the world without their knowing: and they who receive in its fulness are the ones on the right hand.[15]

Christ, the giver of life, is made manifest in the eucharist. The communicant eats his body and drinks his blood for nourishment. In this feeding and in this drinking, the

participant is united to Christ.   The eucharist points
symbolically to the image of double birth: as the child
comes from the mother's womb, so the communicant
continues to live and grow in his or her new mother, in
God. Like a mother, the eucharist is the giver and sustainer
of abundant life itself. Hugh of St. Victor expresses the
intimacy of the relationship between Christ and the
communicant:

> Thus then in His sacrament now He comes
> temporarily to you and He is by means of it
> corporeally with you, that you through His corporeal
> presence may be raised to seek the spiritual and be
> assisted in finding it....But after the corporeal feeling
> in receiving fails, then the corporeal presence is not
> to be sought but the spiritual is to be retained ...
> [Christ says] I am the food of the great, increase and
> you will eat me, not that you may change me into
> you as the food of your flesh but you will be changed
> into me.[16]

The circle in the square is bathed in a white light, a light
that radiates out from the center, the altar-table, beckoning,
motioning, calling the person back from his or her
peregrinations to the very stuff of life. The light is all-
encompassing in its embrace and inviting in its greeting,
delighting in illuminating the place where one is held in the
"unspeakable sweetness of love."

Other characteristics of the circle in the square
include very smooth, white walls and floors. Nothing
detracts from the center image; everything enhances it.
There is no large crucifix over the altar-table. Nor are the
Scriptures or the ambo given the power that comes with
centrality. Both are off to the side. The circle itself is

enclosed by walls high enough that one cannot see over them easily.

The walls are, however, interrupted or broken by several narrow archways through which one can enter and exit. When one crosses the threshold from the lighted side, one is immediately engulfed in shadow. One has left the security of the womb for the ambiguity of the world. This shadowy area is chaos symbolized. Home and its attendant closeness has been exchanged for distraction and distance. When one has separated oneself from the source of light and life and passes through the liminal point, that person, in the symbolic design of the abbey church, becomes lost in shadow. The circular walls have heretofore served to keep out the darkness and its chaos of unseen demons. This area between the white walls of the circle and the external boundaries of the abbey church is called the circumambulatory. Some light enters this space from the slit-like windows in the exterior walls. Other light comes from the center of the circle. But it is the ragged exterior wall construction which really adds to the symbolic impact intended by chaos. This space is confusing and disorienting. When one tries to walk around the circle, the jagged walls give one the feeling of dizziness, of being afloat on rough seas. Clear direction is difficult unless one returns by the light to the center. In addition, the floor of the circumambulatory is rough like the ocean floor. Its texture is created by a collage of sand, stones, and shells. They are symbols of the primordial sea of chaos, of the dangerous sea that must be crossed to get to God.

The outside of the monastery gives one the impression of a fortress, almost castle-like in its narrow slit-like windows. There is just enough room for an archer to stand, poised to shoot. The hulking monastery appears unapproachable, a strange figure rising up out of the earth, strangely out of place. Yet, it is an expression of place. As an otherworldly symbol, the abbey church succeeds in distinguishing itself from the land. What is apparent in the church is its subtle new orientation. Symbols of the outside chaos that monks of the Middle Ages strove so earnestly to put off are, in St. Mary's, enclosed within the church structure itself. Chaos has found a home within the stable, reposed square. It is held in tension with the creation and re-creation as symbolized by the circle. Place at St. Mary's is no longer an attempt absolutely to separate chaos from creation. Rather, an acceptance of ambiguity emerges in the dialectic of inside and outside that is represented by the many thresholds which open the sacred circular space to the circumambulatory. Out through these archways, light radiates into the darkness, making what was once truly dark now only darkling.[17] The only absolute remaining is the light. The demons are now seen in their true light; darkness is dispersed by the light; the light being, in monastic consciousness, Christ. At last, the monastic enclosure begins to mirror the Incarnation. As in Christ, human frailty and divine glory live side by side in the same form, as the circle resides in the square.

For the light of the altar-table now also serves in its several radii as spokes of a wheel. With the eucharist at the wheel's center, the shadowy circumference is held in balance with the lighted center. This kind of place has the power to rescue, to heal, to save. This kind of place is where the desert fathers and mothers sought to overcome the demons in their own souls. In the medieval monastic institution this kind of place closed its doors to the world in hope of finding a better one. But the monastic tradition has turned another curve in the modern period. The abbey church in Morristown, New Jersey, displays a willingness to hold to its bosom the ambiguity of this world while proclaiming the reality of the other world. This is the significance and power of place to give meaning. It shows how human beings see themselves and their world. At last, the monastic enclosure begins to mirror the Incarnation. As with Christ, human frailty lives side by side with divine glory in the same place.

Endnotes

1. Clifford Geertz, *Islam Observed* (Chicago: University Press, 1968), 19.

2. Clifford Geertz, "Religion as a Cultural System," chap. in *The Interpretation of Cultures* (New York: Basic Books, 1973), 89-90.

3. Evagrius Ponticus, *Chapters on Prayer* (Spencer, MA: Cistercian Publications, 1970), #91.

4. *Ibid.*, #46.

5. Benedict of Nursia, *The Rule of Saint Benedict* (Westminster, MD: Newman Press, 1952), 13.

6. Vernon Kroening, "Structures of Consciousness and Urban Designs: The Early Medieval Monastery", (unpublished manuscript, New School of Social Research, 1980), 10. I am indebted to Mr. Kroening for his insights.

7. *Ibid.*, 20.

8. Evagrius, *Ibid.*, #142.

9. Kroening, *Ibid.*, 6-7. His emphasis.

10. Mary Douglas, *Purity and Danger* (London: Routledge and Kegan Paul, 1966), 64.

11. *Ibid.*, 63.

12. Kroening, *Ibid.*, 22.

13. Geertz, *Islam Observed*, 97.

14. For a discussion of Turner's ideas about symbols, see: Victor and Edith Turner, *Image and Pilgrimage in Christian Culture* (New York: Columbia University Press, 1978), 243-248. See also Jacob Pandian, *Culture, Religion, and the Sacred Self: A Critical Introduction to the Anthropological Study of Religion* (Englewood Cliffs, NJ: Prentice Hall, 1991), 88, for Sherry B. Ortner's helpful language about "key"symbols.

15. *The Odes of Solomon* (Cambridge, MA: Harvard University Press, 1909), 114.

16. Hugh of St. Victor, *On the Sacraments of the Christian Church* (Cambridge, MA: The Medieval Academy of America, 1951), 314.

17. Light is very important to the thought of Athanasius. See Jaroslav Pelikan, *The Light of the World* (New York: Harper and Brothers Publishers, 1962), 39ff.

ON THE ALTAR OF THE GOSPEL:
REFORMING PREACHING AND WORSHIP

Heather Murray Elkins
Drew University

prae, before + *texere*, to weave

In any text there are pre-texts, strands of experience that are intimately connected to the context from which a text emerges. The challenge of a festschrift is to weave these strands of text and context into a recognizable image of the man named Howard G. Hageman. The framing of this essay, its *praetextum*, began on a Fall day in 1981 as I presented myself for academic direction to Dean Bard Thompson as a new doctoral candidate in Liturgical Studies.

> "Courses?" I asked.
> "Mercersburg Theology, for one," was the answer.

Mercersburg Theology. It didn't sound Methodist. It didn't appear liturgical. It didn't fit the description of a comprehensively historical period.

> "Because. . ?" I ventured.
> "First, it produced a nineteenth-century Reformed liturgy with a reunion of Word and Sacrament. That should interest a Methodist."

218

It did. The United Methodist Section on Worship had recently published *Word and Table: A Basic Pattern of Sunday Worship for United Methodists.*[1] A pre-Vatican II Reformed service which linked the pulpit to the table stirred up visions of thesis designs.

> "And second?" I prompted.
> "Howard G. Hageman."

That one name response meant I had a lot to learn. I covered my nonrecognition with a respectful, "Ah," and hoped for more information. What I expected was a listing of credentials, publications, and contributions made by this unknown expert of the Reformed tradition. What I received was:

> "You know, I've watched him walk into countless rooms of clergy, laity and scholars. They always rise when he walks in."

I find myself now in the same position, seeking to rise to the occasion of Howard G. Hageman. The *praetextum* of this text took longer than expected. What was begun *in honor* is completed *in memory.* It is a simple gesture of respect for a great reformer whose life was laid "on the altar of the Gospel."

On the Altar of the Gospel: Reforming Word and Table

In October 1857, a *Provisional Liturgy* joined the list of liturgies of the Western Church, an American contribution to the historic forms of Protestant worship. Published in Philadelphia by directive of the German Reformed Church; it was, however, a *foster* text, a liturgy without formal church sanction. It carried "with it no authority. . . nothing to make the use of it of binding obligation, in any direction."[2] Placed within reach of the Reformed households of faith, its presence was a matter of choice. "No wish whatever is felt to have it brought into use, in any quarter soever, or farther, than the use of it may be really called for and desired."[3] Thus, this *Provisional Liturgy* made its cautious public entrance into a ecclesial context which was, in an understatement, *semi*-liturgical.

Provisional: For a Temporary Need[4]

Satisfaction was the liturgy's stated goal; its designers wanted to provide for an unacknowledged hunger for sacramental life within the American experience of Reformed worship. In 1849, the Synod and Committee had begun a book of forms for the pulpit. By 1857 a liturgy had emerged which was "an order of worship for the altar"[5] designed to meet "what is believed to be a growing want of the Reformed Church." The reunion of Word and Altar was carefully presented as a matter of choice. No church would be liturgically force-fed. The temporizing tone of the closing sentence of the liturgy's "Advertisement" underlines its *provisional* identity.

> Years may be required to settle the question of its ultimate adoption, as an authoritative standard of worship; and the interest involved in this question is so great, that none should object to have years allowed, if necessary, for its proper determination.[6]

It is now 135 years since this cautious, yet controversial liturgy proposed standards for "authoritative" worship. Its process of adoption is largely a matter for historians. It went from ignored, to igniting two decades of controversy before it settled into a *Revised Liturgy* whose influence continues to outstrip its use.

How can Mercersburg's persistent influence on those liturgical traditions which claim the Reformation as their ecclesiastical inheritance be explained? Was Mercersburg's service of the altar an anomaly or a prophetic form? Did this liturgy prove its designers' "provisional" claims to be too modest? Is there an enduring hunger in Protestantism for sacramental forms which a Word-dominated service cannot satisfy? Howard G. Hageman's description of the Mercersburg Festival of 1979 reinforces that conclusion.

I cannot believe that that large crowd assembled for an exact form of words, but I am sure they gathered in the expectation that the worship of that evening would be fully in accord with the spirit and tradition of Mercersburg. That congregation was not made up of ministers and students of Mercersburg theology; it was made up of farmers, teachers, lawyers, accountants, and housewives—men and women whose spiritual formation had been in the Mercersburg mold.[7]

Provisional: Demonstrating Foresight

Hindsight of almost a century-and-a-half restores a certain semantic depth to the term, "provisional." The choice of the term "provisional" did provide the German Reformed Committee[8] with an escape clause definition, "for a temporary need." But our twentieth-century vision reveals that this liturgy demonstrated the second definition of *provisional*, that of "demonstrating foresight, (esp. with trace of sense) carefully exercised."[9]

John Nevin and Philip Schaff, the Mercersburg men who led the committee, *were* provisional, looking ahead by engaging the Reformed Church in the action of providing a reforming form for worship. Their "seeing to things beforehand"[10] provided insightful directions for liturgical reformation in the next century.

Examples of their liturgical foresight included congregational responses, creeds, absolution, and an emphasis on baptismal grace as distinguished from baptismal regeneration. But central to the all the services contained in the *Provisional Liturgy* and in the theology known as Mercersburg was the altar. The communion service "was made to rule and control the movement of all its other services."[11]

How did an altar come to such paradoxical prominence within American Protestantism? What theological reconstruction lay behind its central place in an American context of campmeetings and revivals? Since "liturgy is one of the most experienced forms of theology,"[12] we will look to the liturgy itself for its interpretative key, "on the altar of the gospel."[13] Contained in one phrase are the essential components of Mercersburg's faith and order.

First, what is the nature of the gospel which undergirds this "altered" service of communion? In his *Vindication of The Revised Liturgy*, John Nevin writes:

> Where the Gospel is not apprehended as the historical, enduring, objective Manifestation of God in the flesh, there can be no steady apprehension of that which constitutes the proper mystery of it in this view, namely, the union there is in it of the supernatural with the natural in an abiding, historical (not magical) form. This precisely is the true object of all evangelical faith, in the New Testament sense; the objective power of salvation, through the apprehension of which only, faith becomes justifying and saving faith.[14]

Historical, enduring, objective is the gospel of the Incarnation, constituted by a unity of the Holy and the human and experienced in Word and Sacrament. Evangelical faith does not come by mere hearing, but through an apprehension of the objective power of salvation. Altar and Gospel are the two natures of this one abiding, historical mystery.

Second, the theological structure of this altar of the gospel is located within the primacy of scripture. The phrase is original to Philip Schaff who drafted the communion of the *Provisional Liturgy*. The phrase is first used in the Exhortation.

> Christ our Passover is sacrificed for us; therefore let us keep the feast, not with old leaven, neither with the leaven of malice and wickedness, but with the unleavened bread of sincerity and truth. [1 Cor. 5:7b-8] Present *yourselves on the altar of the Gospel, in union with His glorious merits. . .* [15]

The second use of the phrase occurs in the Anamnesis where it is woven between the language of scripture and *The Book of Common Prayer*. One additional original phrase by Schaff makes specific reference to "property and life." It suggests his recognition of the challenge that capitalism posed to American religious identity. Most importantly, the prayer reveals the biblical, historical, and theological integration of Altar and Gospel, which Mercersburg sought to reclaim in the name of Reformed worship. As such, it deserves to have a place among the post-Vatican II liturgies of American Protestantism.

> Have respect unto this glorious sacrifice, we beseech Thee, in union with which we here offer and present

> unto Thee, at the same time, O Lord, the reasonable
> sacrifice of our own persons; consecrating ourselves,
> on the altar of the gospel, in soul and body, property
> and life, to Thy most blessed service and praise.[16]

Provisional: To Prepare for Eventualities

A liturgy, however skillfully designed and politically positioned, remains a text. What factors are necessary to transform a historic liturgy's provisional claims into prophetic forms? Can this, or any liturgical text, effect reformation without the interpreting presence of a reformer who connects text to a worshipping community?

The publication date, 1962, of the now classic *Pulpit and Table*[17] highlights Dr. Howard G. Hageman's prophetic and provisory role as a twentieth-century liturgical reformer. Altar and Gospel, an objective unity of the form and spirit of the Incarnate Christ, were connected and reconnected throughout his ministry and scholarship. Not only did Hageman provide an interpretative reading of the tradition of Word and Sacrament, drawing on the history of the Reformation and the liturgical theology of Mercersburg, but his scholarly anamnesis then became a way of remembering into the future. The historic reunion of pulpit and table accomplished at Mercersburg became his interpretative tool which he used to prepare his Reformed tradition for the eventualities which came to mark the post-Vatican II liturgical world.

> The Christ who comes to us through the preaching of
> the Word is the same Christ who comes in the
> Eucharist. His presence in the Word is no less real
> than in the Sacrament. Obviously it is not possible to
> speak of degrees of Christ's presence.[18]

In his chapter, "Toward A Reformed Liturgy," this theological *unity* of Word and Sacrament becomes the prescription for the disease of American Protestant worship. Hageman prescribes the reunion of pulpit and table as a healing remedy for the Word/Sacrament fracture in the Body of Christ.

> In the act of Christian worship, Word and Sacrament belong together. Any attempt to set up an antithesis between them is completely false to the Biblical witness. They belong together not as successive or even complementary acts. They are aspects of a single whole. Word and Sacrament are only different media for the same reality, Christ's coming into the midst of his people.[19]

Hageman defends the Reformation's recovery of the primacy of scripture with the zeal of a great preacher. He understands the identity of his tradition as being "a church under the Word. We are the church which boasts that Scripture and Scripture alone determines its life."[20] Yet he challenges that church to bring its liturgical life "under the scrutiny of that Word."[21] His critique correctly names the brittle identity and sectarian vulnerability of a Word only pattern of worship.

> And there are further questions to be asked. Would the preaching in the Reformed churches have become so loosely connected with the gospel, as it has in some places at least, if every Sunday it had been followed by the proclamation of the Lord's death till he come? Or could the Reformed churches have proved such fertile soil for the growth of sectarianism, producing one schism after another in their history, if every week they had reminded themselves that "we being many are one bread, and one body: for we are all partakers of that one bread"? [22]

How to balance pulpit and table is a different question than how to discern the "one life-giving Word of God that is present in both the sermon and the Supper."[23] Hageman understands the Word of God as more than merely an act of human speech. For him, the sermon was a "direct mediation of the presence of Christ with his own, a living Word spoken by him through the lips of his servant the preacher."[24]   The Word of God was *ministered* by that holy/human mystery, "one could almost say *sacrament,*"[25] of preaching.

[The text of the last paragraph summons its own context.   The keepers of the flame of Mercersburg had gathered in an anniversary celebration of this long-lived provisional liturgy. The gospel was read from the back of a great bronze eagle which served as a lectern. Unlike the more demure of the species which reside in sanctuaries, this eagle held the Word aloft with defiantly outstretched wings, and its straining beak defied any hearer to risk a casual hearing.   What human speech could match this fierce vitality of Word? Hageman rose to preach, and in the end the Word was well-served by man and eagle alike.]

Does the unity of pulpit and table, word and sacrament, supernatural and natural require a *particular* historical form? Is the objective power of salvation to be indissolvably linked to a certain liturgy? For Hageman, the ongoing work of the Reformation is a search for a *liturgic,* not a liturgy.[26]   Liturgical uniformity will not meet the "eventuality" needs of reformation communions. Word and Sacrament belong together.   Pulpit and table are to be placed side by side.   It is in the response of the community to the gracious act of God who has provided us life and hope in Jesus Christ that authoritative worship is found.

Provisions for the Journey

In providing provisional/prophetic liturgies which hold to the centrality of Word and Sacrament, the lessons of Mercersburg can be combined with the ecumenical liturgical movements of the twentieth century. The Liturgical Movement now seems to have come to rest as traditions settle into orders of worship which affirm this liturgic of Christ's presence in preaching and the sacraments. But it began as a movement which became a journey filled with unusual traveling companions.

One example of odd coupling are Mercersburg and Methodism. Despite Dean Thompson's assurance that Mercersburg was a proper topic for a Methodist, there were historic quarrels between the two parties. Simply placing copies of Nevin's *Anxious Bench*,[27] *Liturgy of The Reformed Church*, and the provisional "Report of the United Methodist Section on Worship[28] on a single shelf forces a curious companionship between these traditions.

Nevin and Schaff[29] denounced American Protestantism in general and the Methodists in particular for their rejection of historical forms of worship, the liturgical apostasies of the campmeeting, and revivalism with its New Measures.[30] Methodism was pronounced the enemy of authentic worship and denounced in print and pulpit by the Mercersburg men.

> In worship, Methodism is not satisfied with the usual divinely ordained means of grace. It really little understands the use of the Sacraments, though it adheres traditionally to infant baptism, and four times a year celebrates the Lord's Supper as a simple commemoration. It has far more confidence in subjective means and exciting impressions, than in the

more quiet and unobserved but surer work of the old
church system of educational religion.[31]

A certain historical irony is obvious in seeking to
compare the work of Mercersburg's nineteenth-century
provisional liturgy with the late-twentieth-century liturgical
revision of United Methodism. Surely neither Nevin or
Schaff expected the "religious fanaticism" of Methodism[32]
to produce an order for Sunday worship of Word *and*
Table. The Methodists were guilty of the sacrilege of
defacing the altar of the gospel with their minimalist
"remembrances" of the Table, and preaching with its
excessive reliance on human techniques rather than the
sacramental presence of the Resurrected Christ.

> The Liturgy stands as a protest and defence against
> this sacrilege. It gives us the true Reformed view of
> Christ's presence in the Lord's Supper, in a form
> answering at the same time to the faith and worship
> of the Primitive Church. It teaches, that the Lord's
> Supper is more than an outward sign, and more than
> a mere calling to mind of our Savior's death as
> something past and gone. It teaches, that the value of
> Christ's sacrifice never dies, but is perennially
> continued in the power of His life. It teaches, that the
> outward side of the sacrament is mystically bound by
> the Holy Ghost to its inward invisible side; not
> fancifully, but really and truly; so that the undying
> power of Christ's life and sacrifice are there, in the
> transaction, for all who take part in it with faith. It
> teaches, that it is our duty to appropriate this grace,
> and to bring it before God (the 'memorial of the
> blessed sacrifice of His Son'), and the only ground of
> our trust and confidence in His presence. All this the
> Liturgy teaches.[33]

Odd companions for the journey, indeed. But John Wesley would delight in the fact that the American church's return to the apostolic union of Word and Table and Mercersburg's understanding of history as the revelation of Christ, who is the ultimate harmonizer of churches and sects, seem to have come of age. The "papists" and "apostates" have come to a common table. The long-awaited opportunity to break a single loaf remains beyond reach for all of the members of the divided body of Christ. We are continually invited to our own reconciliation by the Spirit and through the work of reformers such as Howard G. Hageman.

The liturgical leaders of United Methodism may have to practice the patience of Mercersburg until the actual practice of its liturgical revision can be seen. Indeed, "years may be required to settle the question of its ultimate adoption, as an authoritative standard of worship."[34] There may be future re-formations as the search for provisional *liturgic* continues. But the preparation for eventualities by members of the Committee on the Liturgy[35] and the Section on Worship,[36] demonstrate a vital union of profound learning and piety highly valued by liturgical reformers of the sixteenth, nineteenth, and twentieth centuries.

This vital union of learning and piety was opened to congregational life by the inclusion of the Service of Word and Table in the traditional book of Methodist theology, *The United Methodist Hymnal.*[37] In the introductory material to "The Basic Pattern of Worship"[38] is the following:

> This order for proclaiming God's Word and celebrating the Lord's Supper expresses the biblical, historical, and theological integrity of Christian

worship.   The several formats demonstrate its
flexibility for different situations, but in its essentials
it is one order.

This oneness of Word, this centering action of the
Incarnated Christ, is the source of United Methodism's
Word and Table and the Reformed Church's Pulpit and
Table. It is the Risen One who greets and teaches and is
recognized in the breaking of the bread.   This is the
undeniably "real presence" that bestows a biblical, historical
and theological integrity to our worship forms and reforms.

Endnotes

1. Supplemental Worship Resources #3. *Word and Table: A Basic
Pattern of Sunday Worship for United Methodists,* rev. ed. (Nashville:
Abingdon Press, 1980).

2. *A Liturgy : or, Order of Christian Worship Prepared and
Published by the Direction and for the Use of The German Reformed
Church in the United States of America* (Philadelphia: Lindsay &
Blakiston, 1857), iii.

3. *Ibid.*

4. *Oxford English Dictionary* (Oxford: Oxford University Press,
1971), 1525.

5. John W. Nevin, *Vindication of the Revised Liturgy: Historical and
Theological* (Philadelphia: Jas. B. Rodgers, Printer, 1867), 31.

6. *Ibid.*

7. Howard G. Hageman, "John W. Nevin: Reformed Theologian of Easter," *Perspectives, A Journal of Reformed Thought*, (April, 1987): 4.

8. Active members included: Philip Schaff, John Williamson Nevin, Bernard C. Wolff, John H.A.Bomberger, Henry Harbaugh, Elias Heiner, Daniel Zacharias, Thomas C. Porter, Emanual V. Gerhart, Samuel R. Fisher, Thomas G. Apple, John Rodenmayer, and Lewis Steiner.

9. *Oxford English Dictionary*, 1525.

10. *Ibid.*

11. John W. Nevin, *Vindication*, 31.

12. Howard G. Hageman, *Pulpit and Table: Some Chapters in the History of Worship in the Reformed Churches* (London: SCM Press; Richmond, VA: John Knox Press, 1962), 33.

13. *A Liturgy*, 193.

14. Nevin, *Vindication*, 78.

15. Jack Martin Maxwell, *Worship and Reformed Theology: The Liturgical Lessons of Mercersburg* (Pittsburgh: The Pickwick Press, 1976), 444.

16. *Ibid.*, 449.

17. Hageman, *Pulpit and Table*.

18. *Ibid.*, 114.

19. *Ibid.*, 112.

20. Hageman, *Pulpit and Table*, 115.

21. *Ibid.*

22. *Ibid.*, 114-115.

23. Dietrich Ritschl, *A Theology of Proclamation* (Richmond, VA: John Knox Press, 1960), 115.

24. Hageman, *Pulpit and Table*, 113.

25. *Ibid.*

26. *Ibid.*, 109.

27. See especially the second edition (Chambersburg, PA: Publication Office of the German Reformed Church, 1844).

28. The Report of the Section on Worship has subsequently been approved and published as *The United Methodist Book of Worship* (Nashville: The United Methodist Publishing House, 1992).

29. Philip Schaff, *America: A Sketch of the Political, Social, and Religious Character to the United States of North America* (New York: Scribner's, 1855).

30. Charles Yrigoyen, Jr., "Mercersburg's Quarrel With Methodism," *Methodist History* (19??): 3-18.

31. Philip Schaff, *America: A Sketch*, 173.

32. *Ibid.*, 175.

33. Nevin, *Vindication*, 92-93.

34. *A Liturgy*, iii.

35. For the history of *The United Methodist Book of Worship*, see Hoyt Hickman, *Companion to the United Methodist Book of Worship* (Nashville: Abingdon Press, 1990).

36. Chairs and editors included: Susan M. Morrison, chair, J. Lavon Wilson, Thomas A. Langford, III, Hoyt L. Hickman, Diana Sanchez, Ted G. Colescott, Lois Glory Neal, and Ann B. Sherer.

37. *The United Methodist Hymnal* (Nashville: The United Methodist Publishing House, 1989).

38. *Ibid.*, 2.

THE PASTORAL HYMNOLOGIST: THE CONTRIBUTION OF HOWARD G. HAGEMAN TO THE HYMNOLOGY OF THE REFORMED CHURCH IN AMERICA

Norman J. Kansfield
New Brunswick Seminary

Introduction: The Interplay of Folksong and Precept

Hymns are complex tools for worship. The texts and tunes of hymns are expected to be almost instantly accessible to ordinary persons. At the same time, each hymn is asked to educate the congregation by singing some new and truthful insight into the God we serve. The provision of hymns which meet these criteria is a tricky business. Authors and composers are asked to shape their work to reflect, with precision, where the church is in its present moment. At the same time (and in the same hymn) author and composer are asked to lead the church into some new truth -- to where the church has never been before. The good hymn, then, is that hymn which is: 1) quickly accessible to the ordinary persons of the Church and 2) truthful about God.

Erik Routley explored the issues of accessibility by envisioning hymns as "Christian folksongs." In his *Christian Hymns Observed* he reminded us that:

234

> Hymns are a kind of song: but they differ from a
> professional song or an art-song, in being songs for
> unmusical people to sing together. They are a kind of
> poetry, but they are such poetry as unliterary people
> can utter together.[1]

These, he felt, were some of the factors which brought
hymns into close relationship with folk songs, which are,
after all, the "kind of song which people sing without any
concern with who its composer was, or of the age from
which it came."[2]   Perhaps even more important is the
perception that a folk song typically is:

> concerned with the things that mean most to a
> community: basically these are love, work and death.
> . . . Folk song universalizes these experiences; it
> objectifies them, and by so doing detaches the singer
> from the anxieties which all three inevitably carry; the
> music and the verse smooth the asperities of the basic
> experiences of life, make them friendly and
> tractable.[3]

If hymns, then, are Christian folk songs, there must
be, within a good hymn, something which is able to make
our understanding of God "friendly and tractable." Routley
is very quick to spell out the dangers of this capacity of
hymns. Hymns can be so very busy being "friendly and
tractable" that they sacrifice their truthfulness for easy
acceptance and assimilation.

On the other hand, hymns can be so busy being
theologically accurate that they sacrifice their friendliness
and tractability. This has been the particular preoccupation
of most of the history of Reformed hymnody. When the
Protestant Reformation returned the sung praise of God to
the voices of the congregation, our part of that Reformation

—Calvinism—placed such a premium upon biblical and theological faithfulness that for almost two centuries the sung praise of God in Reformed worship was limited to the metrical psalter.   Finally, in eighteenth-century England, Isaac Watts (1674–1748) committed himself to revolutionize the apparently stodgy psalm-singing which was common to his time. He sought to keep faith with his forebears' concern for biblical truth and, at the same time, to provide the church with a hymnody which persons would enjoy singing. In 1707, when Watts published his *Hymns and Spiritual Songs*,[4] he included an essay entitled: "Towards the Improvement of Christian Psalmody, by Use of Evangelical Hymns in Worship, as well as the Psalms of David." This essay clearly prepared the way for his 1719 *The Psalms of David Imitated in the Language of the New Testament and Applied to the Christian State and Worship*[5] and suggests just how sensitive Watts was to the issues of accessibility and truth.

Charles Wesley (1707–1788) made English hymnody still more friendly and tractable by adding the warmth of Methodist piety and the fervor of revival to the elegant simplicity of Watts' kind of hymn text.[6] The complete prototype for an accessible English hymnody was created as soon as the Wesley texts were set to the tunes of John Frederic Lampe (1703–1751). In 1746, Lampe published *Hymns on the Great Festivals*, a collection of tunes for texts by Charles Wesley.[7] The impact of Lampe's style upon English church music has been compared to the way in which Handel transformed the English music of performance.[8]

Shaped by History: The Tradition of Hymnody in the Reformed Church in America

The Dutch Reformed folk who found themselves living in English-speaking eighteenth-century America did not allow this transformation of English hymnody to pass unnoticed. By the 1760s, English had become so pervasive among the Dutch immigrants that the Reformed Protestant Dutch Church of the City of New York (The Collegiate Churches or Collegiate Consistory) added the Rev. Archibald Laidlie (1727–1770) to its collegial clergy, a minister who was trained to carry on pastoral and liturgical responsibilities in the English language. At the same time they hired Francis Hopkinson (1737–1791), Organist of Christ Church, Philadelphia, and member of the Second Continental Congress, to prepare a psalm book which would allow congregations to sing the Lord's praise in English.[9] James L. H. Brumm has done a careful analysis of Hopkinson's work and has shown that most of the texts were taken directly from Tate and Brady[10] or were altered from those texts. Only about forty texts remain otherwise unidentified and may be the original work of Mr. Hopkinson. Brumm's research indicates that fewer than 12 of the Genevan psalm tunes were employed throughout the book—being used over and over again, "modified here and there, most likely at Hopkinson's hand."[11] In arranging for this publication, the Collegiate Consistory was walking a narrow path between two powerful demands: the need to provide an accessible hymnody for its English-speaking worshippers, on the one hand, and the need to remain submissive to the decrees of the Church Order of the Synod of Dort (1619), on the other. Dort understood truth to require that "the 150 *psalms* of David; the ten commandments; the Lord's prayer; the 12 articles of the

Christian faith; the *songs* of Mary, Zacharias, and Simeon, versified, only, shall be sung in public worship."[12]

After the conclusion of the War for Independence, as the Reformed Dutch congregations began to function together as a national organization, a "denominational" English-language psalter and hymnal was requested by the Synod of 1785.[13]   The Synod of 1787 appointed a committee to oversee the preparation of this book and named the Rev. Dr. John H. Livingston as its chairman. The committee was directed to select their materials from the psalm book of the Collegiate Church, the psalms of Tate and Brady, and the works of Isaac Watts. The Synod also explicitly instructed the Committee to "add some well-composed spiritual hymns" to the book of Psalms.   The resultant volume was published in 1789 as *The Psalms and Hymns of the Reformed Protestant Dutch Church in North America*.   Officially it was said that the book contained all 150 psalms plus 100.   In actuality, a single psalm or hymn might be made up of several independent texts placed together as "Part I," "Part II," etc.   When this is taken into consideration, the total of individual texts equals 272 psalm texts and 128 hymn texts within the book.

Of these 128, it has been possible to identify the authorship of 101. The identified hymns are the work of 21 different authors.   Those authors are identified in the following table:

Distribution of Authorship; *Psalms and Hymns, 1789*

Hymns

1.	Isaac Watts (1674–1748) Diss.	38
	(one shared with Fawcett)	
2.	Philip Doddridge (1702–1751) Diss.	10

3. John Newton (1725–1807) C. of E.   8
4. Anne Steele (1716–1778) Baptist   8
5. Joseph Hart (1712–1768) Independent   7
6. Charles Wesley (1707–1788) Methodist   5
7. Benjamin Beddome (1717–1795) Baptist   4
    (one shared with Gibbons)
8. Simon Browne (1680–1732) Independent   3
9. John Fawcett (1740–1817) Methodist to Baptist 3
    (one shared with Watts)
10. Joseph Stennett (1663–1713) Baptist   3
11. Samuel Davies (1723–1761) Presbyterian   2
12. Thomas Gibbons (1720–1785) Dissenter Congregational   2
    (one shared with Beddome)
13. John Needham (d. ca. 1786) Baptist   2
14. S. Collett (?) Unitarian (?)   1
15. William Cowper (1731–1800) C. of E.   1
16. Maurice Greene (1696–1755) C. of E.   1
17. Moravian Hymn Book (1754) Moravian   1
18. New Version, Tate & Brady, (1702) C. of E.   1
19. Sarah Slinn (fl. 1787) Baptist   1
20. Augustus Montague Toplady (1740–78) C. of E. 1
21. Nicholaus von Zinzendorf (1700–60) Moravian   1
    TOTAL IDENTIFIED   101
    TOTAL UNIDENTIFIED   27
    TOTAL HYMNS   128

It is no easy task to teach a church to sing hymns (in English!), when that church's worship has known only the singing of metrical psalms for as long as anyone can remember. And yet, somehow, *Psalms and Hymns* of 1789 managed to do just that. By selecting from so broad a range of authors—Baptist and Methodist, Dissenter and Church of England, Moravian and Unitarian—*Psalms and*

Hymns certainly risked being regarded as willing to sacrifice truth for accessibility, and orthodoxy for friendliness. The texts, however, were carefully selected and appear quickly to have gained the approbation of the congregations who made use of the book—congregations much used to exacting theological debate.[14]   It probably helped that the hymns numbered 1 through 52 (a total of 79 separate texts) were matched to the Lord's Days of the Heidelberg Catechism. In addition to assisting pastors with their preparation for Sunday worship, this order had the second benefit of suggesting that these hymns, even if a departure from the "psalms only" worship of the past, were still quite in harmony with the Church's favorite doctrinal statement.

The hymns numbered 53 through 73 "are adapted to the Holy Ordinance of the Lord's Supper."   The Dutch Church in America was quite used to singing psalms during the serving of the Lord's Supper. The presence of these hymns, expressing the meaning of the sacrament in new ways, certainly should have made the transition from psalm singing to hymn singing a little bit easier.   Hymns numbered 74 through 100 are described as "on various subjects and for special days."   These texts provided worship material for the celebration of holidays. Here also are prayer texts for special situations, and, of course, the New Testament hymns—*Magnificat, Benedictus*, and *Nunc Dimittis*.

Psalms and Hymns, 1789, was an auspicious beginning to the denomination's history of hymnbooks. It was ecumenical. It took the educational role of hymnody very seriously.   And, yet, it introduced hymns to the Reformed Protestant Dutch Congregations in America in a gentle and easy manner. At least nine psalms and eight hymns from *Psalms and Hymns*, 1789 are still in common usage and appear in the Church's current hymnal *Rejoice in the Lord*.[15]

Psalms and Hymns, 1789, also proved to be successful. The original format continued to shape the hymnody of the Reformed Church in America until 1860. A fully revised edition appeared in 1814, which was enlarged by "Additional Hymns" at several points between 1830 and 1859. By 1860, when this entire body of hymns was rearranged into a new outline, the total number of hymns had grown to 788. The *Psalms and Hymns* was once more issued, in 1866, as *The Book of Praise: The Psalms and Hymns of the Reformed Protestant Dutch Church in North America*.[16] This split-page volume, with "musical page independent of the poetic page," provided 373 hymn tunes and almost 70 chants—the first Reformed Dutch hymnal to provide tunes for the texts since the Collegiate Church's *Psalms of David* in 1767.

The General Synod of 1868 appointed a committee to develop a new hymnal for the Reformed Church. The Chairman of the Committee was John Bodine Thompson (1830–1907), pastor of the First Reformed Church, Tarrytown, New York. Dr. Thompson had a profound grasp of the history of hymnody in the Reformed Church, becoming, in every sense, the church's first hymnologist. The other two members of the committee were Ashbel Vermilye (1822–1899) and Alexander Ramsey Thompson (1822–1895). At the time of his work on the Committee, Vermilye was pastor of the Reformed Church in Utica, New York. He later worked as co-editor of *Hymns of Prayer and Praise*, with Alexander R. Thompson (1871), and of *Hymns and Songs of Praise* (1874) with Roswell D. Hitchcock (1817–1887) and Philip Schaff (1819–1893). Alexander Ramsey Thompson, apparently no relative of the other Thompson on the Committee, was pastor of the St.

Paul's Reformed Church in New York City from 1862-1873, where he was the successor to George Washington Bethune (1805–1862)—at the time of his death, the Reformed Church's most prolific writer of hymns. Thompson contributed two original hymns and several translations from the Latin to this and to later hymnals.

The committee enlisted Zachary Eddy (1815–1891), as principal editor. Eddy was ordained in the Cumberland Presbytery in 1835, and served several Presbyterian congregations before becoming the pastor of the Church on the Heights, Brooklyn, New York, from 1867-1871 (the only RCA parish he ever served). Uzziah C. Burnap (1834-1900) served as Music Editor. Burnap may have made his money as a dry-goods merchant, but he had received the degree of Doctor of Music from the University of Paris. For 37 years Burnap was the organist of the Church on the Heights, Brooklyn.

This very talented group—in a sense, the church's first hymnological professionals—put together a charming, ecumenical, and articulate hymnal, published in 1869 and called *Hymns of the Church.* Hymns from the early and medieval church were included for the first time (mostly in fresh translations prepared for this book). And, for the first time, a full set of indexes was provided: Subject Index, Scripture Index, First-Line Index, Alphabetic Index of Tunes, Metrical Index of Tunes, and Index of Chants.

Some of the tunes provided in the first edition proved to be slightly in advance of the Church. In 1874, the committee revised the book, leaving the texts as they had originally been issued, but changing many of the tunes.[17] Many of the tunes which were replaced by more traditional music actually remained present in the 1874 edition in a "Musical Appendix." The largest number of these tunes had been written by Burnap. But he was in good company. Three tunes by Mendelssohn were also replaced.

The ecumenical commitment of the committee and of the church in 1869 is really quite impressive. As things turned out, this ecumenicity was a two-directional activity. The committee included texts within the book from virtually every era and every denomination of the whole Church's experience. This welcomed the whole Church into the life and worship of the Reformed Church.

But the committee took ecumenicity in the other direction as well. This hymnal was reduced in size to include 321 hymns and chants and 158 tunes, reshaped slightly and marketed to congregations beyond as well as within the Reformed Church in America as *Hymns of Prayer and Praise*.[18] At the same time, John B. Thompson was working with William H. Platt (1822-1898) to rework about half of the original material into yet another hymnal: *Christian Praise: Hymns and Tunes for Public Worship*.[19] By altering three baptismal texts and making some other very minor alterations (the page format stayed the same), Thompson, a Reformed Church minister, and Platt, an Anglican priest, issued yet another version of this body of hymns: *Christian Praise: Hymns and Tunes for Baptist Worship*.[20] This particular piece of the Reformed Church's heritage of hymnody was, in this way, shared with Christians in other denominations.

In 1888, the General Synod again appointed a committee to review the current status of hymnody and nature of hymnbook needs felt within the congregations. This time the committee was faced with the need for a hymnody which could enable the Dutch immigrants, who had flocked to the United States in 1847 and thereafter, to make the transition from worship in the Dutch language to worship in English.[21] This committee reported to the

General Synod of 1890, submitting a long and detailed history of hymnody within the denomination, and endorsing a hymnal entitled: *The Church Hymnary.*[22]

The manuscript for this book had been prepared by Mr. Edwin A. Bedell (1853-1908), a member of the Reformed Church, an 1873 graduate of Hope College,[23] and a court reporter for the New York State Court of Appeals, Albany. Mr. Bedell also served as the organist of the Madison Avenue Reformed Church in Albany. Mr. William H. Clark, Chairman of the Committee, reported:

> This work has been a labor of love, and it was [Mr. Bedell's] ambition to prepare for the Church in which he was reared, and of which he is a member, a Hymnal of the highest excellence as a manual of Praise in the House of the Lord.
>
> The Rev. Dr. Collier and your Chairman have given to its examination many weeks of the most careful study. They each have gone over the entire manuscript several times, and every hymn and tune has passed under repeated review. Mr. Bedell requested them to make any suggestions they might deem proper, and has cheerfully assented to their recommendations with regard to both hymns and tunes.
>
> As a result, your Committee believed that "The Church Hymnary" is superior in the character of its hymns and tunes, and in its adaptation for practical use in the worship of the Sanctuary, to any collection now extant.[24]

The General Synod endorsed the book, and every evidence is that the book served the church very well. In taking this action, endorsing a hymnal which it had not commissioned, the General Synod of 1890 followed the example of several previous synods. However, the previous synods had made their endorsements in an environment where the hymnals so endorsed were basically functioning as supplemental to a vital and "official" denominational hymnal. In 1890 this was not the situation. *Hymns of the Church* had functioned for 20 years and was at the end of its tenure by the time that *Church Hymnary* came along. This placed the Synod's action in a very different context and set a synodical precedent which would often be followed during the next half century. So, the Synod of 1910 empowered a committee to examine *Hymns of Worship and Service* (New York: Century Co., 1905) and if it was found acceptable, to authorize its introduction. The Synod of 1912 took a similar action regarding *Hymns of the Christian Life* (New York: A. S. Barnes, 1910). The Synod of 1938 approved a total of four hymnals: 1) *The Hymnal* (Philadelphia: Presbyterian Board of Christian Education, 1933); 2) *Hymns for the Living Age* (New York: Century Co., 1923); 3) The *Interchurch Hymnal* (Chicago: Biglow & Main Publishing Co, 1930); and 4) The *New Church Hymnal* (New York: Appleton-Century, 1937).

Two times in the twentieth century, the Reformed Church in America has participated in the preparation of hymnbooks with other Reformed denominational bodies. Work began in 1913 on a hymnbook jointly developed by the Reformed Church in the United States and the Reformed Church in America and called *The Hymnal of the Reformed Church*. An Editorial Committee of 14 persons, seven from each denomination, was appointed to select the hymns and see the book through the press.[25] By 1920, the book was ready to be sold to the congregations at the price of $1.30 per copy, and by 1927 it was reported that a total of 29,000 copies were in use in 212 RCA congregations (There were 151,000 communicant members in 741 congregations in that year).

The *Hymnal* included 660 hymns, 46 chants, 20 doxologies, and was thoroughly indexed. The great body of the hymns came from the nineteenth century, but the eighteenth century was also well represented (40 hymns by Isaac Watts, for example). A very few hymns from the twentieth century were tried (one from 1919!). Ten hymn texts by members of the Reformed Church in America were included. Very little material representing the German chorale tradition of the RCUS and even less of the Genevan/Dutch tradition of the RCA was present. Only two Genevan tunes were used. The most often used composers were Lowell Mason (1792-1872), John Bacchus Dykes (1823-1876), Joseph Barnby (1838-1896), Arthur Sullivan (1842-1900), and William Bratchelder Bradbury (1816-1868), further emphasizing the Victorian character of the book.

The format selected for the presentation of hymns placed only the first stanza of each hymn between the musical staves. This elicited a considerable amount of negative response, culminating in a resolution, approved by the Synod of 1927, asking for a printing "in which all of the words are printed between the musical scores." In 1938, a special committee on hymnals distributed 675 questionnaires to pastors serving congregations. Of this total, 248 responded. Eighty-four congregations reported that they were using *The Reformed Church Hymnal*, and, of these, 57 indicated that they were dissatisfied with the book. These returns also showed that 14 different hymnbooks were in use within RCA congregations.

In 1944, work began with the United Presbyterian Church toward the development of two hymnals: A hymnal for young people called *Songs for Christian Worship*,[26] and the "primary" hymnal, which came to be called the *Hymnbook* and which was published in 1955 by the

Presbyterian Church in the United States, the United Presbyterian Church in the U.S.A., and the Reformed Church in America. David Hugh Jones (1900-1983) served as the Editor, working with an editorial committee of 23 members.[27]

This collection of 537 hymns and 73 elements of "service music" made a serious effort to reintroduce the psalm tradition of Geneva, both words and music. Six different Genevan tunes are employed with ten texts. The majestic hymn, often ascribed to Calvin, "I Greet Thee, Who My Sure Redeemer Art" (which was first introduced to Reformed folk in the *Hymnal* of 1920) was here appropriately set to a Genevan tune—the equally majestic *Toulon*.

The "Preface" suggests that the *Hymnbook* Committee paid considerable attention to the matter of the accessibility of the hymns it selected. By the "interweaving of the strands of worship from five denominations, each with its peculiar and precious heritage," it was possible to add "immeasurable richness to the book" and to include within the book many treasured hymns "which might have been missed by a committee representing a narrower tradition."[28] In addition to attempting to make folks comfortable by including the "favored few" hymns of each tradition, the *Hymnbook* included among its hymns some which in 1955 were new experiences. The enormously favored "Morning Has Broken," set to the Hebridian folk melody *Buneson*; the ancient Irish classic "Be Thou My Vision"; and Harry Emerson Fosdick's triumphant "God of Grace and God of Glory," serve as easy examples of the level of "tractability and friendliness" which the Committee sought. In addition, it introduced Reformed folk to Georgia Harkness' "Hope of the World," written in 1953 for the

1954 Evanston Assembly of the World Council of Churches.

In a way, the most unusual chapter in the history of Reformed Church hymnology is one which occurred between the *Hymnal of the Reformed Church* (1920) and the *Hymnbook* (1955). In 1939, the committedly ecumenical hymnal *Christian Worship and Praise* was published under the general editorship of Henry Hallam Tweedy (1868-1953). Fifteen men served with him as the editorial board, called "The Commission for Christian Worship and Praise." Five of the 15 persons who made up the Commission were Reformed Church pastors: John A. Ingham, (the Stated Clerk—the highest permanent office in the denomination); Arthur F. Mabon, (Fort Washington Collegiate Church, New York City); John H. Powell (Reformed Church, Bronxville, New York); Joseph R. Sizoo (St. Nicholas Collegiate Church, New York City); and John H. Warnshuis (Brighton Reformed Church, Staten Island). This kind of representation on the Commission was far out of proportion to the size of the Reformed Church and larger than any other denomination's representation.[29] Those five men, however, could hardly have been described as representative of the mainstream of the Reformed Church in America in 1939.

The "Preface" said of their work together:

> The volume is compiled by ministers belonging to various denominations and service congregations which share the social and intellectual outlook of the present day. In its aim the Commission has had in mind the various communions in the household of faith, with their different training, temperament and experience, seeking to hasten the unity of the Church by this contribution to the common medium of communion with God in the universal language of worship.[30]

In light of this purpose no one would have expected that this book would be a committedly Reformed hymnal. It is still surprising, however, to discover that with five Reformed pastors, four Presbyterian pastors, and two Congregational pastors on the Commission, there is so little material within the book which represents the Reformed contribution to hymnody. Three Genevan tunes are used with four hymns. Explicit psalm texts are even rarer. Of hymns by Reformed Church authors, only Denis Wortman"s "God of the Prophets" is present.

This hymnal is, however, filled with the bright hope of American Liberalism and with continued trust in "the brotherhood of man" and the long-cherished dream of a reunified church. In the midst of the Depression, with Hitler and Mussolini already assaulting Europe, here was a hymnal which rehearsed a profound belief in the goodness of humankind, and in the capacity of believers to correct the injustices and oppressions of this life. The General Synod of 1938 had appointed a committee called the "Permanent Committee on the Ministry of Music." This Committee reported to the Synod of 1939 that it had understood its task to be:

> to explore the possibility and means by which a permanent commission on music could be created which should not only exercise supervision of the kind of hymns and hymn books used in the churches, but should endeavor to focus and utilize the musical resources within our churches and seek preservation and expression of our Reformed Church heritages of psalmody, hymnology and worship traditions.[31]

The Committee then told the Synod: "We regret to report that we can find no practical way of accomplishing this."[32]

The Committee report went on to recommend that Synod continue to exercise its oversight of hymnals in use within Reformed congregations and suggested that the Board of Education create a standing committee whose task it would be to evaluate hymnals for such synodical approval. The Committee then immediately made its second recommendation: that the Synod approve the hymnal *Christian Worship and Praise*. The General Synod of 1939 went ahead and did just that. It bravely and forthrightly endorsed a hymnal that moved congregational singing in the Reformed Church in America well beyond its "heritages of psalmody, hymnology and worship traditions." And then, as if aware that this action was a radical departure, the Synod "rose and sang a Dutch Psalm."[33]

The book had a rocky and brief official history within the Reformed Church. By 1944, multiple official complaints against the theology of the book were being raised.[34] In 1945, the General Synod solemnly voted to withdraw its endorsement of *Christian Worship and Praise*. After this vote no Dutch Psalm was sung.

"Focus on the World": Howard Hageman's Hymnology

This hymnological history, in which the General Synod took so many and varied ways of providing the denomination with hymns for its worship, had a profound effect upon the members of the Church. Synod provided its members and congregations with very little definition of what a hymn should be. Therefore, the people in the pews came to think very little about the hymns or the hymnbooks which they used. This situation forms the context within which Howard Hageman has ministered. Throughout his career, hymns and their function in worship have continued to be a major focus of his personal interest and of his influence within the Reformed Church and the church at large.

One principal vehicle for Hageman's hymnological influence was the column which he wrote for the *Church Herald* from April 28, 1961 through December 16, 1988. The column was called "Focus on the World," and Hageman used it as a means of keeping the readers of the *Church Herald*[35] aware of items in the news the theological significance of which we otherwise might not have noticed. This purpose allowed him to choose his subjects from virtually any field and to vary the "focus" from column to column.

At least 38 times, during those years that he wrote the column, Hageman turn his attention, his insight, and his pen to matters of hymnology. These columns can be grouped into seven categories: 1) Some columns sought to make the RCA aware of its hymnological history; 2) Some attempted to help us understand what other Christian bodies were doing about hymns or hymnbooks; 3) Some explored the ways that congregations use hymns and church music; 4) Others asked why some hymns last while others pass out of usefulness; 5) A number attempted to suggest what makes a hymn "good"; 6) More than one explored the issues involved in textual alteration; and 7) After 1978, a number of columns dealt with the processes and progress of *Rejoice in the Lord*. Within the limits of this present research, the first, the fifth, and the seventh categories will be examined.

Toward an Awareness of Our Heritage

If the analysis is correct, that the General Synod of the Reformed Church in America provided the church with very little guidance regarding hymns and hymnology, then it is hardly surprising the someone as perceptive as Dr. Hageman should choose to provide some conception of what Reformed hymnody had been historically.

In his column of October 18, 1974 (p. 30), Hageman suggested that the hymns that we sing are really measures of the *pietas* of a congregation or denomination. "I use the Latin word," he wrote, "because I don't think its English derivative really gets at what I have in mind, the whole style with which a group of Christians thinks about and celebrates the Gospel." Then Hageman asserted:

> The hymns we like to sing are obvious outward signs of this *pietas*. Think, for example, of the number of congregations in which the hymns most often used are activist . . . or the number in which they are personal pietist . . . . I am not saying that anything is basically wrong with either. What I am saying is that our *pietas* may be in dire need of enlargement, and our preference in hymns can be one important sign of that need.

In this spirit Hageman explored the psalm-singing tradition of the church. On November 10, 1972, a column appeared in which he reminded us that John Calvin "insisted that psalms (and so, by extension, hymns) must be regarded as sung prayers" (p. 22). He picked up this theme again in his column for July 11, 1980. On that date he wrote:

> When our ancestors first came to these shores in the 17th century, and again in the 19th, they brought with them that great musical treasure called the Genevan Psalter, which had been adapted for use in the Netherlands as early as 1568. I wonder whether there need not be a reassessment of the place of Psalms in

our worship. Not only do I think that many of us are
weary of the elegant (and not so elegant)
subjectivities through which so many hymnbooks drag
us, but we have to face the question of whether John
Calvin was a complete booby when he insisted on the
centrality of the Psalms in worship. No one, I am
sure, wants to go back to their exclusive use, but if,
as we are discovering, the basis of Christian worship
is doxology and not spiritual massage, then the
Psalms deserve better than the role of antique
curiosities to be used only at historical gatherings (p.
30).

Howard Hageman, for all of this praise of the
psalms, well understood that the tradition of psalmody had
its problems. In 1968 he had written:

Personally, I am enough of a Calvinist to prefer
singing the psalter to almost any English hymn I
know. But I have to admit that for the most part our
English metrical psalms are doggerel.

    The old Dutch version of the Psalms (the one
on which some of my readers were raised) dates not
from the Reformation but from the year 1773.
According to those who should know, it was not
always faithful to the biblical text and strongly
reflected the age of the Enlightenment in which it was
produced. Not only was the vocabulary antique but
the theology reflected many Hellenic rather than
Hebrew ideas.

    For my dream psalter we should need not
only poets but musicians to create some new and
more flexible tunes for us unless, of course, by some
miracle we could revise the tunes of the Genevan
Psalter. Our Christian Reformed [colleagues] have
tried to do some of this, and I congratulate them for
it. . . . Have we so lost our sense of our own tradition

that it is of no concern to us? Have we no poets to volunteer their help? (December 6, 1968:9)

Regarding the origin of the hymn tradition in the American Reformed experience, Hageman interpreted the data this way:

As much as I love the Genevan (or Dutch) Psalter, I have to admit that the Reformed tradition of worship suffered because for something like 250 years it tried to limit the praises of God to those 150 [Psalm] selections and to permit nothing else. When that dam burst with a mighty flood in the early years of the 19th century, it carried everything of our tradition away with it, probably because of the resentment which had been built up over the years. (January 23, 1981:30)

At the very time at which we began to sing in English (about 1765 in the East and 1865 in the Midwest), American Christianity was dominated by the revival movement. All around us our neighbors were singing hymns which magnified personal Christian experience. The Psalms, when compared with these hymns, seemed somewhat objective and impersonal. The result was a half-hearted attempt to get the Psalms into English in the East in the 18th century and no attempt at all in the Midwest in the 19th.[36] We simply started to sing what our Presbyterian, Congregational, and (later) Methodist neighbors were singing since we shared their point of view. Needless to say, that uncritical adaptation led to many strange theological contradictions. (July 11, 1980:30)

Howard Hageman, in 1984, attempted to shape this inheritance into an authentic direction for the future. In a column entitled "Those Good Old Methodist Hymns," he reported: "From time to time while speaking on our new hymnal, *Rejoice in the Lord*, people say to me "I hope you're going to have a lot of those good old Methodist hymns in it!" After revealing that he was never sure what people actually understood by a "Methodist" hymn, Hageman said:

> I should have thought it was more important to have some "good old Reformed hymns" in *Rejoice in the Lord*. We have certainly tried for that. There is a splendid collection of the metrical psalms, both Scottish and Dutch, which is our peculiar musical heritage. Beyond that, there is a generous sampling of those masters of Calvinist hymnody, Isaac Watts and Philip Doddridge. We have a number of hymns by authors and composers from the Reformed Church in America. We have wanted to be especially loyal to our own tradition.
>
> In this day and age, however, it is most important of all to have a collection of hymns that is soundly Christian, regardless of the denominational affiliation. . . . The question really is not who wrote a particular hymn, but how faithful a witness is it to the Christian faith as we understand it.
>
> Maybe *Rejoice in the Lord* will give some folk the chance to discover what the "old Methodist hymns" really are. I hope it will give all of us opportunity to look at the authenticity of the Christian witness in whatever the hymn we may be singing. (July 13, 1984:30)

Toward an Understanding of What Makes a Good Hymn

After he had heard a radio lecture on opera in which the lecturer observed, "In opera the text must always be subordinate to the musical line," Dr. Hageman wrote:

> As soon as he had finished his sentences, I said to myself, "With hymns it is just the reverse; the music must always be subordinate to the text." Then I began to reflect: Isn't this really the problem we have with much of our hymnsinging? The purpose of the music is to enhance and make memorable the text, not to provide a catchy melody which we can whistle on the way home. For how many church members today has opera replaced hymnology? The words that they sing are ignored; so long as the tune is one which they like, they could just as well be singing from the yellow pages of the phone book! (November 15, 1985:30)

If the definition of a good hymn begins with the assertion that text has priority over tune, then the definition is obliged to suggest with what kinds of things a text ought to concern itself. Hageman had actually covered that point earlier. In 1981 he wrote about the tremendous popularity of the hymn "How Great Thou Art":

> In trying to analyze just what its virtues may be, I suddenly realized that it is one of the few items in the evangelical collection that fulfills one of the basic requirements of a hymn; it is addressed in praise to God. Look through any list of favorite evangelical songs and you will soon discover of how few of them that can be said.

When we have been singing about nothing but ourselves and our needs for a long time, it can get pretty boring. It really is a relief to sing about a good and gracious Father. Perhaps I should say more accurately, to sing *to* a good and gracious Father. For that is basically what a hymn is.

And that is what a Sunday service is—not an exercise directed to our inspiration or even to our enlightenment, but one which is directed to our Creator and Redeemer for all that he has done, is doing, and has promised to do for his people. "How Great Thou Art" strikes exactly the right note. (July 10, 1981:30)

In 1974, Hageman committed a very long column to what he called the "Unfinished Business" of liturgical renewal, which he feared had "pretty well spent itself" by then. In this article he defined four components which liturgical renewal up to 1974 had left unfinished and on which the church needed to continue to work if worship was to remain vital: 1) Worship is the joyful celebration of the people of God; 2) Worship is participation—the real ministers in worship are the people of God; 3) Worship is to be done with excellence—the best that we have to offer; 4) Worship recognizes the transcendence of God. (December 13, 1974:30) These four elements, which Hageman in this case applied to the whole of worship, succinctly summarize the characteristics which he often used to give definition to good hymns. A good hymn allows the people of God to celebrate God's relationship with us by taking part together in an expression of praise that is comprised of the best music and the most carefully crafted text that we can bring together, reminding us that God is both Emmanuel—God with us—*and* the High and Lofty One.

Toward *Rejoice in the Lord*

As early as 1970, Howard Hageman had envisioned a new hymnal for the Reformed Church in America. He wrote then:

> I must confess that I have never been a great admirer of *The Hymnbook*, if for no other reason than that it seems to me to reflect almost totally the traditions and tastes of its Presbyterian compilers rather than our own. I have no idea how matters stand with the *Psalter Hymnal* of our Christian Reformed [colleagues], but I have heard rumors that it too is in need of revising. I do know that the Christian Reformed Church by and large has a better sense of our tradition than we seem to. Well, what is there to hinder us from at least a joint exploration of the question, especially in this day and age when so much is happening in the world of church music? Instead of the torturous negotiations for union at top levels, we need first to start doing together what can be done. And what better thing could be done than singing together in praise of our common Redeemer and Lord? (October 2, 1970: 9, 21)

On April 7, 1978, Howard Hageman proposed that the Reformed Church in America should commemorate the 350 years of its life and witness in America by giving itself a birthday present. And he thought that he knew what that present should be. It ought to be a new hymnal. He reasoned this way:

> The last time that the Reformed Church in America produced its own hymnbook was in 1869. Ever since that time we have either cooperated with another denomination or endorsed someone else's production

as our official hymnal, the last time being in 1955. As a result, the situation in the Reformed Church hymnological world is pure chaos with just about every congregation (including my former one) selecting what it thinks it likes.

The excuse offered and usually accepted for such a condition is that we are too small a denomination to do anything else. In view of 1869, I find that hard to believe. When we last published our own hymnal, our total membership numbered 58,796, a little more than a quarter of what it does today. How did they finance it? Good Dutchmen that they were, they persuaded the firm of A. S. Barnes and Co. to undertake all of the risks of publication and pay the General Synod a royalty of 15c per copy to boot! In their report to the Synod of 1869, the Committee stated that "several congregations of the Presbyterian, Congregational, and other denominational bodies are preparing to introduce (our hymnal) at once." Given the hymnbook situation in some of those same denominations today, I think the same thing could happen if we did our homework.

The other excuse offered for our chaotic situation is the wide diversity of tastes within even so small a denomination as ours. No one can deny the truth of such an assertion, but I think it might be worth trying to work it through. For one thing, such an effort might have a unifying effect on some of the divisions which we so much deplore. For another, such an effort might surprise us into realizing that our tastes are not really as different as we had supposed.

I would like to see us celebrate our heritage, not as a museum of Dutch antiquities, but as a people who believes that it has something significant to offer in meaningful worship and significant theology. (April 7, 1978:30)

The General Synod of 1978 cautiously responded to Hageman's suggestion. It appointed a committee "to study the various possibilities for future hymnals for the Reformed Church in America and to report to the next General Synod."[37] When the committee reported to the General Synod of 1979 it did not directly recommend that the denomination proceed to develop its own hymnal. Rather, it recommended that a seven-person committee be asked "to develop a plan whereby such a hymnbook could be produced" with such a detailed plan to be reported to the General Synod of 1980.[38] The committee insisted that it could only endorse the development of a "*Reformed hymnal of excellence.*" Such a book was defined as a hymnal that:

a.   recognizes our Calvinist heritage of psalmody as a central element in the praise of God;

b.   uses Biblical and theological integrity as a primary criterion in its selections; and

c.   while accepting the best of contemporary hymn-writing, strives to avoid the ephemeral and the *trendy.*[39]

The General Synod adopted the proposal and undertook the preparation of its own hymnal for the first time in 110 years. This commitment, along with the recruitment of Dr. Erik Routley (1917-1982) to serve as the Editor, and the resultant hymnbook itself, all bear eloquent witness to the effectiveness of Howard G. Hageman as a hymnologist. The future of our hymnody will be forever in his debt.

Endnotes

1. Routley, Erik, *Christian Hymns Observed* (Princeton: Prestige Publications, Inc., 1982), 1.

2. *Ibid.*

3. *Ibid.*

4. Isaac Watts, *Hymns and Spiritual Songs* (London: Printed by J. Humphreys for John Lawrence, at the Angel in the Poultry, 1707).

5. Isaac Watts, *Psalms of David*, (London: Printed for J. Clark, R, Ford, and R. Cruttenden, 1719).

6. The hymnody of Watts and the character of what he sought to accomplish have been often explored. Among the more outstanding studies are: Arthur Paul Davis, *Isaac Watts: His Life and Works* (New York: Dryden Press, 1943), and Harry Escott, *Isaac Watts, Hymnographer: A Study of the Beginnings, Development, and Philosophy of the English Hymn* (London: Independent Press Ltd., 1962). Many scholars have carefully analyzed the impact of both John and Charles Wesley upon English hymnody. My personal favorite is Erik Routley's, *The Musical Wesleys*, (New York: Oxford University Press, 1968).

7. *Hymns on the Great Festivals, And Other Occasions* (London: Printed for M. Cooper and sold by T. Tyre, 1746).

8. Erik Routley did not hesitate to state that Lampe "brought to Wesleyan hymnody the florid, Continental style of melody, which it soon developed so fully that the style is more often referred to as Methodist than Continental. His tunes all show, however, the free melodic style of his native country, and he can be said to have done for hymnody what Handel did for English music in general." K. L. Parry, ed., *Companion to Congregational Praise* (London: Independent Press, Ltd., 1953), pp. 443-444. In spite of this high praise, only one of

Lampe's tunes—KENT—remains in common usage in the United States
See, for example, *Rejoice in the Lord*, (Hereinafter, *RIL*) (Grand Rapids,
MI: Eerdmans, 1985), #56 and #476.

9. *Psalms of David . . . For the Use of the Reformed Protestant Dutch
Church of the City of New York*, (New York: James Parker, 1767).

10. Nahum Tate and Nicholas Brady, *New Version of the Psalms*,
(London: 1696, withdrawn and reissued in 1698).

11. James L. H. Brumm, *Singing the Lord's Song: A History of the
English Language Hymnals of the Reformed Church in America* (New
Brunswick, NJ: Historical Society of the Reformed Church in America,
1990), 9.

12. Article 69. See Edwin Tanjore Corwin, *A Digest of Constitutional
and Synodical Legislation of the Reformed Church in America* (New
York: The Board of Publication of the Reformed Church in America,
1906), p. lxx.

13. Reformed Protestant Dutch Church (Reformed Church in America),
Minutes of the General Synod, vol 1 (New York: Board of Publication
of the Reformed Church in America, 1859), 142. Hereinafter, *MGS*.

14. The American Church's first Constitution, usually referred to as the
Explanatory Articles, requires that "No psalms or hymns may be
publicly sung in the Reformed Dutch Churches, but such as are
approved and recommended by the General Synod." Article LXV. *The
Constitution of the Reformed Dutch Church in the United States of
America* (New York: Printed and Sold by William Durell, 1793).
Please note that the *Explanatory Articles* were published in 1793. In
advance of the articulation of this requirement, it appears that the
General Synod was asked neither to approve the texts nor to
recommend the *Psalms and Hymns* of 1789 to the churches.

15. The psalm texts include: Psalm 19 (Watts), *RIL* #87; Psalm 34 (Tate
and Brady), *RIL* #98; Psalm 90 (Watts), *RIL* #1; Psalm 98 (Watts), *RIL*
#198; Psalm 117 (Watts), *RIL* #126; Psalm 118 (Watts), *RIL* #127/28;
Psalm 119 (Watts), *RIL* #129; Psalm 132 (Watts), *RIL* #135; Psalm 145

(Watts), *RIL* #139. The hymn texts, in the order of 1789, include: #10—"God Moves in a Mysterious Way," (Cowper), *RIL* #36; #14/I—"Hark, the Glad Sound!" (Doddridge), *RIL* #251; #21/II—"Blest Be the Tie that Binds," (Fawcett), *RIL* #407/408; #22/II—"Amazing Grace," (Newton), *RIL* #456; #29—"Jesus Invites His Saints," (Watts), *RIL* #540; #78—"Hark, the Herald Angels Sing," (Wesley), *RIL* #196; #79—"Christ the Lord is Risen Today," (Wesley), *RIL* #325; #80—"Rejoice, the Lord is King," (Wesley), *RIL* #596/597.

16. *Book of Praise* (New York: Board of Publication of the Reformed Church in America, 1866). Sylvanus Billings Pond (1792-1871) was the musical editor.

17. *Hymns of the Church, With Tunes* (New York: A. S. Barnes, 1969, 1874). For the revision of the tunes, see: *MGS*, 1874: 111-112.

18. *Hymns of Prayer and Praise* (New York: A. S. Barnes, 1871).

19. *Christian Praise: Hymns and Tunes for Public Worship* (New York: F. J. Huntington and Co., 1870).

20. *Christian Praise: Hymns and Tunes for Baptist Worship* (New York: F. J. Huntington and Co., 1871).

21. *MGS*, 1888: 599, 600, 602.

22. Edwin A. Bedell, *The Church Hymnary: A Collection of Hymns and Tunes for Public Worship* (New York: Board of Publication of the Reformed Church in America, 1890; Charles E. Merrill, 1892). Bedell revised this hymnal with John B. Calvert and reissued it in 1900, when, because of Calvert's connections, it sold very well to Baptist congregations.

23. Wynand Wichers, in his history of Hope College, indicates that Hope awarded the degree of Mus.D. to Bedell in 1894—the first time in its history that Hope awarded honorary degrees. Wichers then offers this assessment: "He was a nephew of Dr. Phelps [the first President of Hope College], and was a collector of hymns. In 1891, he published *The Church Hymnary*, which was said to contain the best of Christian

hymns of all nations. The General Synod of the Reformed Church adopted it and recommended its use in all churches. It was never used at Hope. There was a noticeable omission of some of the beautiful old hymns." Wynand Wichers, *A Century of Hope: 1866-1966* (Grand Rapids, MI: Eerdmans, 1968), 128.

24. *MGS*, 1890: 101.

25. From the Reformed Church in the United States: James I. Good, Co-chair; Ambrose Schmidt, Secretary; Henry Nott, E. P. Skyles, J. H. Rettig, Joseph Apple, and E. L Coblentz. From the Reformed Church in America: Edward Johnson, Co-chair; William Bruce, Arthur Mabon, Edward Collier (who had served on every synodical committee regarding hymnals since 1884), Ame Vennema, Matthew Kolyn, and George Schnucker.

26. *Songs for Christian Worship* (Philadelphia: Board of Christian Education of the United Presbyterian Church in the U.S.A., 1950).

27. When the work was first undertaken, the Associate Reformed Presbyterian Church was represented by Arthur J. Ranson; the United Presbyterian Church was represented by Richard W. Graves, William T. Lytle, and Sanuel W. Shane; the Presbyterian Church (U.S.A.) by Eugene Carson Blake, Leonard V. Buschman, Joseph J. Copeland, Walter L. Jenkins, George Litch Knight, and Harold R. Martin; the Presbyterian Church (U.S.) by Cameron D. Deans, William H. Foster, Jr., Edward D. Grant, Austin C. Lovelace, Stuart R. Oglesby, Harmon B. Ramsey, James R. Sydnor, Hubert V. Taylor, W. Talliaferro Thompson, and Albert K. Kissling, who served as Chair. The Reformed Church in America was represented by Gerard R. Gnade, Bernard J. Mulder, and William A. Weber.

28. *Hymnbook*, 5-6.

29. Allen Knight Chalmers and Frederick Keller Stamm were Congregationalists; Finis Schuyler Idleman and Lewis Ward McCrear y were in the Christian Church/Disciples of Christ; John Newton Davies and Dorr Frank Diefendorfer were Methodists; and Robert Warren

Anthony, Paul Robinson Hickok, Archibald Gordon Sinclair and Edmund Melville Wylie were Presbyterians.

30. *Christian Worship and Praise* (New York: A. S. Barnes, 1939), viii.

31. *MGS*, 1939: 168.

32. *Ibid.*

33. *Ibid.*, 169.

34. Echoes of this theological dissatisfaction can still be heard in Howard Hageman's "Focus on the World" column in the *Church Herald*, April 9, 1965:22.

35. From this point, unless otherwise noted, all references are to the *Church Herald*, an official publication of the Reformed Church in America. All references will be by date of issue, with the page number indicated within parentheses within the text.

36. For additional development of this social analysis, see: Eugene P. Heideman, "The Descendants of VanRaalte," *Reformed Review* 12 (March 1959): 33-42; and Sietze Buning, "That Stone on Five Easters," in *Purpaleanie and Other Permutations* (Orange City, IA: Middleburg Press, 1978), 93-100. Hageman's conclusion that no effort was made in the Midwest toward the development of an English psalmody for the Dutch immigrant Reformed Churches is probably correct as stated. Note should be taken, however, of an alternate approach toward the provision of an accessible vocabulary of praise. Three pastors in Grand Rapids—Henry Uttewick (1841-1928), Peter dePree (1839-1915) and Adrian Kriekard (1839-1925), all of whom attended Rutgers College and New Brunswick Theological Seminary together—sensitively attempted to lead the Dutch congregations into responsible psalmody and hymnody by publishing a new Dutch-language hymnal: *Lofzangen en Geestlijke Liederen* (Cincinnati: C. J. Krehbiel, Aldine Printing Works, 1885). Of this book it was said: "One of its chief objects is to lead the Holland people to the use of hymn-books in the English language."

37. *MGS*, 1978:241.

38. *MGS*, 1979:164

39. *Ibid.*

AND AS THIS GRAIN HAS BEEN GATHERED

Words and Music by David M. Tripold
Westminster Choir College of Rider University

Introduction by Heather Murray Elkins
Drew University

And as This Grain has been Gathered, the communion hymn dedicated to Howard G. Hageman by David M. Tripold, strikes the concluding note of this festschrift. Protestantism's liturgical tradition of scripture, preaching, sacrament, and congregational song may be best expressed as a prophetic act of praise: "Let the people praise thee, O God; let all the people praise thee."

This text for the Table was Tripold's response to reading Hageman's *Pulpit and Table*. The Reformed understanding of the living and mystical presence of Christ, communed and communicated to the Body of Christ, is expressed in "the food that gives us life," and "God's life-spirit and eternal grace."

Here one can find the bread that gives strength for the work of justice and the cup that gives rest, the same bread and cup that sustained Hageman's work as a pastor in the city of Newark during the struggle for civil rights. Here is John Williamson Nevin's insistence on the objective, historical, sacrificial, and sacramental presence of the Incarnated Christ, an insistence that Hageman shared. Here is a sung response of faith to the one life-giving Word of God in the theo-poetic tradition of historian Philip Schaff who wrote and translated hymn texts for congregational use. *Rejoice in the Lord* (1985), the hymnal of the Reformed Church in America, bears the textual marks of Hageman's continuing presence, but it is in the eschatological sounds of saints, singing before "the altar of the Gospel" that the voice of Howard G. Hageman can now be heard.

*Permission to use hymn is granted. Copyright 1992 David M. Tripold.

And as this Grain has been Gathered

Words by
Dr. Howard G. Hageman

Music by
David M. Tripold

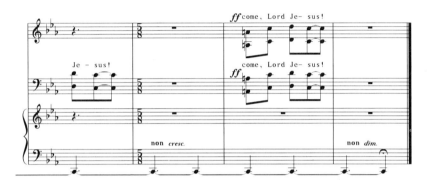

A CHRONOLOGICAL BIBLIOGRAPHY
OF THE WORKS OF HOWARD G. HAGEMAN

Rochelle A. Stackhouse
United Church of Christ

"A Catholic and Reformed Liturgy." In *Scholarship, Sacraments and Service: Historical Studies in Protestant Tradition: Essays in Honor of Bard Thompson*, ed. Daniel Clendenin and W. David Buschart, 147-158. Lewiston, NY: Edwin Mellen Press, 1990.

"The Eucharistic Prayer in the Reformed Tradition." In *Eucharistic Prayer for Reformed Churches. Reformed Liturgy and Music*, ed. Peter C. Bower, 22 (Fall 1988): 190-193.

"Needed: A Liberal Dialogue." *Unitarian Universalist Christian* 42 (1987): 20-22.

"Rioting in Switzerland." *Reformed Journal* 37 (Oct 1987): 7.

"The First Boston (Lincolnshire, Great Britain)." *Reformed Journal* 37 (March 1987): 6.

"Reformed Spirituality." In *Protestant Spriritual Traditions*, ed. Frank C. Senn, 55-79. New York: Paulist Press, 1986.

"The Lasting Significance of Ursinus." In *Controversy and Conciliation: The Reformation and the Palatinate, 1559*-ed. *1583*, ed. Derk Visser, 227-239. Pittsburgh: Pickwick Publications, 1986.

"The Mystical Presence: A Sermon." New *Mercersburg Review* 2 (Autumn 1986): 47-49.

"The Synod of Dort and American Beginnings." *Reformed Review* 38 (Winter 1985): 99-108.

Two Centuries Plus: The Story of New Brunswick Seminary. Grand Rapids, MI: Eerdmans, 1984.

Worship in the Reformed Tradition. 3 Cassettes. Omaha Presbyterian Seminary Foundation, 1984.

"Some Notes on the Use of the Lectionary in the Reformed Tradition." In *The Divine Drama in History and Liturgy: Essays Presented to Horton Davies on his Retirement from Princeton University.* ed. John E. Booty, 163-178. Pittsburgh: Pickwick, 1984.

"Changing Understandings of Reformed Corporate Worship." *Reformed Liturgy and Music* 18 (Fall 1984): 155-158.

"A Brief Study of the British Lectionary." *Worship* 56 (July 1982): 356-364.

Reformed Theology in Practice. 6 Cassettes. Northwestern College, 1981.

"Preaching is Alive and Well." (Review Article) *Theology Today* 37 (January 1981): 493-497.

"The Reformed Churches: Enlarging their Witness." *The Christian Century* 96 (Feb. 21, 1979): 177-181.

"New York's First Domine." *Reformed Review* 37 (Spring 1978): 119-126.

Questions About Church Growth. 1 Cassette. Thesis Theological Cassettes, 1977.

"Conducting the Liturgy of the Word." In *Celebrating the Word: The Third Symposium of the Canadian Liturgical Society.* ed. James Schmeiser, 54-74. Toronto: Anglican Book Centre, 1977.

"Die Reformierte Kirche in Amerika." In *Die Reformierte Kirchen.* ed. Karl Halaski, 270-293. Stuttgart: Evangelisches Verlagswerk, 1977.

"Eucharistic Prayer in the Reformed Church in America." *Reformed Review* 30 (Spring 1977): 166-179.

"William Bertholf: Pioneer Domine of New Jersey." *Reformed Review* 29 (1976): 73-80.

"Response to 'The Supper as Eucharistic Sacrifice' by Joseph Tylenda." In *Renaissance, Reformation, Resurgence: Papers, Calvin and Calvin Studies held at Calvin Theological Seminary April 22-23, 1976,* ed. Peter De Klerk. Grand Rapids, MI: Calvin Theological Seminary, 1976.

(Co-author) with J.C. Beker. *Easter*. Proclamation, Series C. Philadelphia: Fortress Press, 1975.

"The Law in the Liturgy." In *God and the Good: Essays in Honor of Henry Stob*, ed. Clifton Orlebeke, 35-45. Grand Rapids, MI: Eerdmans, 1975.

"Need and Promise of Reformed Preaching." *Reformed Review* 28 (Winter 1975): 75-84.

"In No Strange Land (John 21:3-4)." *Princeton Seminary Bulletin* 68 (Autumn 1975): 48-52.

"A Funny Thing Happened on the Way to New Brunswick." (Inauguration Address) *Reformed Review* 27 (Winter 1974): 83-88.

"Old and New in the Worshipbook." *Theology Today* 31 (October 1974): 207-213.

"What's the Big Idea?" *Theology Today* 30 (January 1974): 331-338.

"The Liturgical Origins of the Reformed Churches." In *The Heritage of John Calvin: Heritage Hall Lectures 1960-1970*, ed. John H. Bratt, 110-136. Grand Rapids, MI: Eerdmans, 1973.

A Twentieth-Century God: Six Sermons. 6 Cassettes. Blackstone Conference Center, 1969.

"Liturgical Developments in the Reformed Church of America, 1868-1947." *Journal of Presbyterian History* 47 (September 1969): 262-289.

New Days, New Ways. 1 Cassette. Address recorded at a National Minister's Conference, Montreat, North Carolina, 1968.

Out of the Shackles of Traditionalism. 1 Cassette. Address recorded at the National Ministries Conference, Montreat, North Carolina, 1967.

(Co-author) with Ruth Douglas. *That the World May Know.* Richmond, VA: Covenant Life Curriculum Press, 1965.

Bible Studies. 1 Cassette. Four Bible Studies recorded at the 19th General Council of the World Alliance of Reformed Churches, Frankfurt-on-the-Main, Germany, 1964.

"The Catechism in Christian Nurture." In *Essays on the Heidelberg Catechism*, ed. Bard Thompson, 158-179. Philadelphia: United Church Press, 1963.

Predestination. Philadelphia: Fortress Press, 1963.

"Coming-of-age of the Liturgical Movement: Report on Section IV of the Montreal Conference." *Studia Liturgica* 2 (December 1963): 256-265.

"Heidelberg Catechism as a Means of Christian Nurture." *Theology and Life* 6 (Autumn 1963): 239-254.

"Liturgical Place." *Princeton Seminary Bulletin* 56 (Fall 1963): 29-39.

"Tribute to the Heidelberg Catechism." *Reformed and Presbyterian World* 27 (September 1963): 201-206.

Pulpit and Table: Some Chapters in the History of Worship in the Reformed Churches. Richmond, VA: John Knox Press, 1962. (Also London: SCM Press, 1962.)

"Liturgy and Mission." *Theology Today* 19 (July 1962): 169-170.

We Call This Friday Good. Philadelphia: Fortress Press, 1961.

"Focus on the World," column in the *Church Herald,* April 28, 1961 through December 16, 1988.

"Reformed Worship: Yesterday and Today." *Theology Today* 18 (April 1961): 30-40.

"Religious Boom and Moral Bust." *Christianity Today* 5 (Feb. 13, 1961): 16-18.

"Three Reformed Liturgies." *Theology Today* 15 (January 1959): 507-520.

Lily Among the Thorns. New York: Half Moon Press, 1953; reprint, New York: Reformed Church Press, 1975.

"Liturgical Revival." *Theology Today* 6 (January 1950): 490-505.

Our Reformed Church. New York: Half Moon Press, 1948.

"The Other Sacrament." In *Baptism, Confirmation: Implications for the Younger Generation.* 22-46. New York: Department of Youth Ministry, National Council of Churches USA, date unknown.

CONTRIBUTORS

RANDALL BALMER, Professor of Religion, Barnard College, Columbia University, received masters' degrees from Trinity College, Trinity Evangelical Divinity School, and Princeton University. He was awarded his Ph.D. at Princeton. In addition to his teaching responsibilities, Dr. Palmer writes a weekly commentary, "By the Way," for the Religious News Service. His major publications include *A Perfect Babel of Confusion: Dutch Religion and English Culture in the Middle Colonies* (Oxford University Press, 1989), *Mine Eyes Have Seen the Glory: A Journey into the Evangelical Sub-Culture in America* (Oxford University Press, 1989), and *The Presbyterians*, co-authored with John R. Fitzmier (Greenwood Press, 1993). His text, *Mine Eyes Have Seen the Glory*, became the three-part documentary series featured on PBS.

MARTIN L. COX, JR., minister of the Hawley United Methodist Church, received a master of theology from the Lutheran School of Theology in Chicago, a master of divinity at Gordon-Conwell, and a master of arts at Drew University. Rev. Cox chairs the United Methodist Worship Commission of the Wyoming conference, and teaches at Lackawanna Jr. College. His recent article, "To Be the Church: Nevin's Critique of Sectarianism" appeared in the *New Mercersburg Review*.

HORTON DAVIES, emeritus, Princeton University, adjunct professor of liturgics, Drew University. A native of

280

South Wales, Dr. Davies received his B.D. and M.A. from the University of Edinburgh, and was awarded a D.Phil., and a D.Litt. from Oxford. While at Princeton, he held the Henry W. Putman chair of the History of Christianity, as well as serving as a Fellow at the Center of Theological Inquiry. Dr. Davies has been the recipient of Berakah award from the National Academy of Liturgy, and serves as an contributing editor to *Studia Liturgica*. Among his numerous publications are *Worship and Theology in England, Vols. 1-5* (Princeton University Press, 1961-75); *Like Angels On a Cloud: The English Metaphysical Preachers 1588-1646* (Huntington Library, 1986); *The Worship of the American Puritans* (P. Lang, 1990); and *The Bread of Life and Cup of Joy* (Eerdmans; Gracewing, 1993).

HEATHER MURRAY ELKINS, Associate Professor of Worship and Liturgical Studies, Drew University, studied anthropology and received an M.A. in Fine Arts from the University of Arizona. Her divinity degree is from Duke University, and her doctorate from Drew University. As an ordained minister in the United Methodist Church, Dr. Elkins often serves as conference preacher and lecturer for the denomination. Among her publications are *Worshiping Women: Re-forming God's People for Praise* (Abingdon, 1994), *Abingdon's Preacher's Annual* (vols. 1991-95), *Testimony* (1989), and *Forked Tongues: Methods in Bilingual Drama* (1972).

FRED KIMBALL GRAHAM is Consultant for Congregational Worship (Liturgy, Church Music, Architecture), The United Church of Canada. A church musician, Dr. Graham has performed in Canada, the United States, and Europe. He holds a MusBac from the University of Toronto, a M.M. from Eastman School of Music, Rochester, Ph.D. from Drew University, FRCO (Fellowship of the Royal College of Organists, London), and ARCT (Associateship in the Royal Conservatory, Toronto). As a member of the Consultation on Common Texts, he served on the Revision Task Force for the Revised Common Lectionary. His forthcoming publication is entitled *With One Heart and One Voice: a Core Repertory of Methodist Hymn Tunes, 1808-1876.*

A. CASPER HONDERS, emeritus Professor of Liturgiology, Rijksuniversiteit Groningen, the Netherlands, studied in theology in Leiden, Zurich, and Basle (with Karl Barth), and completed his doctorate at the University of Amsterdam. Dr. Honders, an ordained minister of the Dutch Reformed Church, was the first Director of the Liturgical Institute of Groningen University from 1963 until his retirement in 1984. His publications include *Valerandus Pollanus Liturgia Sacra 1551-1555* (E. J. Brill, 1970), *Over Bachs schouder... Een bundel opstellen* (1985), *Liturgie: Barsten en breuken* (1988), and *Mijn lief is mijn... Over het Hooglied in het werk van J.S. Bach* (1988).

NORMAN J. KANSFIELD is President of New Brunswick Theological Seminary, New Jersey and the John Henry Livingston Professor of Theology. An ordained minister in the Reformed Church, Dr. Kansfield received his B.D. from Western Theological Seminary, an S.T.M. at Union Theological Seminary in New York, and his M.A. and Ph.D. from the University of Chicago. Prior to his presidency at New Brunswick, Dr. Kansfield held the position of Director of Library Services and Professor of Church History at Colgate Rochester Divinity School/Bexley Hall/Crozer Theological Seminary. He served on the editorial board of the hymnal, *Rejoice in the Lord*, and has numerous articles in denominational journals. One forthcoming publication is "Envisioning a World Future for Theological Libraries," *ATLA Proceedings* 48 (1994).

ROBIN A. LEAVER is Professor of Church Music, Westminster Choir College of Rider University, and Visiting Professor of Liturgy, Drew University. British-born, Dr. Leaver studied theology at Clifton Theological (now Trinity) College, Bristol, and completed his doctorate at the Rijksuniversiteit Groningen, the Netherlands. An ordained minister in the Church of England, Dr. Leaver taught at Wycliffe Hall, Oxford, before coming to the United States in 1984. A select listing of his numerous publications include *Bachs theologische Bibliothek* (Hanssler-Verlag, 1983), *J.S. Bach and Scripture: Glosses from the Calov Bible Commentary* (1985), *The Theological Character of Music in Worship* (1989), and *"Goostly psalmes and spirituall songes": English and Dutch Metrical Psalters from Coverdale to Utenhove 1535-1566* (Oxford University Press; Clarendon Press, 1991).

GREGG A. MAST is the senior minister of the First Church in Albany, which was founded in 1642. He received his divinity degree from New Brunswick Theological Seminary, and his doctorate in liturgical studies at Drew University. Dr. Mast is a regular columnist for *The Church Herald*, a national magazine of the Reformed Church in America and has provided leadership as a pastor and national staff person. His publications include: *Living Free-Ten Guides to Service* (1989); *Christian Baptism - A Pastoral Letter to Families*; *Sign and Seal: A Reformed*

Understanding of Ritual in the Church; and a monthly column in *The Church Herald.*

DANIEL JAMES MEETER is pastor of the Community Church of Hoboken, a congregation of United Methodist and Reformed origins. Dr. Meeter studied at Calvin College and New Brunswick Theological Seminary, and received his doctorate in liturgical studies from Drew University. He has served Reformed churches in the U.S. and Canada and presently chairs the standing ecumenical committee of the Reformed Church in America. Recent publications include *Meeting Each Other in Doctrine, Liturgy, and Government: The Bicentennial of the Constitution of the Reformed Church in America* (Eerdmans, 1993), "The Puritan and Presbyterian Versions of the Netherlands Liturgy," in *Nederlands Archief voor Kerkgeschiedenis,* and "Genevan Jig-Saw: The Tunes of the New York Psalmbook of 1767," in *Ars et musica in liturgia: Celebratory volume presented to Casper Honders.*

DIRK W. RODGERS studied theology at Alliance Theological Seminary, and received his doctorate from Drew University in the field of Reformation studies. Dr. Rodgers has served on the faculties of Florida International University, Miami; Broward Community College, Florida; Canadian Theological Seminary, Saskatchewan; and Nyack College, New York. His book, *John à Lasco in England,* will be available in 1996.

KENNETH E. ROWE, Professor of Church History at Drew University, received his divinity degree at Yale, his M.L.S. at Rutgers, and was awarded his doctorate at Drew University. Dr. Rowe, an ordained minister in the United Methodist Church, and librarian of the Methodist Archives and History Center, is convener of the Liturgical Studies program at Drew. His major publications include *United Methodist Studies: Basic Bibliographies* (three editions since 1983, Abingdon Press); editor of *Rethinking Methodist History* (Kingswood Books, United Methodist Publishing House, 1985), and *Perspectives of American Methodism* (Kingswood Books, 1993); and *United Methodism in America,* with Frederick E. Maser and Charles Yrigoyen Jr. (Abingdon, 1992)

ROCHELLE ANN STACKHOUSE is senior pastor at the United Church of Christ, Congregational, of Norwell, Massachusetts. Dr. Stackhouse received her divinity degree from Princeton and her doctoral degree from Drew University. She is a contributing editor to the new United Church of Christ's lectionary series, *The Word Among Us.* Two of her recent articles have appeared in denominational publications, "Hymns of Love and Praise," in *Prism* and "Ordinary Miracles: Changing the Language of the Church's Song," in *Hymn.*

DAVID TRIPOLD is the organist and director of music at the Presbyterian Church on the Hill, Ocean Township, New Jersey. Mr. Tripold holds a B.M. degree from Westminster Choir College of Rider University, Princeton, New Jersey, and is currently completing a master's degree in church music at the same institution. His composition, "And as this grain has been gathered," was written in honor of Howard Hageman, in response to a passage in Dr. Hageman's text, *Pulpit and Table.*

EDWARD C. ZARAGOZA (B.A., Wheaton College; Th.M., Boston University School of Theology; Ph.D., Drew University) is Assistant Professor of Church History at

Phillips Theological Seminary in Enid, Oklahoma, where he teaches Medieval, Reformation, Modern, and American Christianity, as well as a course in the parish ministry track of the Doctor of Ministry Program. An ordained minister in The Presbyterian Church (U.S.A.), Dr. Zaragoza has served churches in New Jersey and Ohio. He is author of *St. James in the Streets: The Religious Processions of Loíza Aldea, Puerto Rico* (Scarecrow, 1995).